Supporting Families through Short-term Fostering

Studies in Evaluating the Children Act 1989

Series editors:
Dr Carolyn Davies, Prof. Jane Aldgate

Other titles in the series include
From Care to Accommodation
Parental Perspectives on Care Proceedings
The Last Resort
Leaving Care in Partnership
Safeguarding Children with the Children Act 1989
The Best-Laid Plans
Expert Evidence in Child Protection Litigation

STUDIES IN EVALUATING THE CHILDREN ACT 1989

Supporting Families through Short-term Fostering

Jane Aldgate
Marie Bradley

School of Health and Social Welfare, The Open University
and
Department of Social Policy and Social Work,
University of Oxford

First published 1999

ISBN 0 11 322271 8

Published by The Stationery Office and available from:

The Publications Centre
(mail, telephone and fax orders only)
PO Box 276, London SW8 5DT
Telephone orders/enquiries 00870 600 5522
Fax orders 0870 600 5533

The Stationery Office Bookshops
123 Kingsway, London WC2B 6PQ
020 7242 6393 Fax 020 7242 6394
68–69 Bull Street, Birmingham B4 6AD
0121 236 9696 Fax 0121 236 9699
33 Wine Street, Bristol BS1 2BQ
0117 926 4306 Fax 0117 929 4515
9–21 Princess Street, Manchester M60 8AS
0161 834 7201 Fax 0161 833 0634
16 Arthur Street, Belfast BT1 4GD
028 9023 8451 Fax 028 9023 5401
The Stationery Office Oriel Bookshop
18–19 High Street, Cardiff CF1 2BZ
029 2039 5548 Fax 029 2038 4347
71 Lothian Road, Edinburgh EH3 9AZ
0131 228 4181 Fax 0131 622 7017

The Stationery Office's Accredited Agents
(see Yellow Pages)

and through good booksellers

Printed in the United Kingdom by The Stationery Office
J0091736 9/99 450117 19585

For Tony and Hannah Aldgate,
Emily Goodman and Yasmina Goodman-Nazir

Contents

Figures and tables

Figures

Tables

Foreword

The Children Act 1989 was implemented on 14 October 1991. At its launch the then Lord Chancellor, Lord Mackay, described the Act as 'the most radical legislative reform to children's services this century'. Shortly after the launch the Department of Health put together a strategy to monitor and evaluate the initial impact of the Act. Taking a tripartite approach, this drew on evidence from statistical returns, inspections and research to develop a rounded appreciation of early implementation. The subsequent strategy plan was published and circulated to relevant bodies, including social services and the major voluntary agencies, in 1993. This plan formed the backcloth for a programme of research studies commissioned by the Department of Health to explore early evaluation in more depth. It is these studies, some 20 in all, which form this new series.

The programme studies investigate the implementation of key changes introduced by the Act and evaluate the facilitators and inhibitors to the meeting of key objectives. A longer-term goal of the programme is to review the aims of the Act in the light of implementation with a view to reconsideration or amendment should this be felt necessary. Finally, a more general and important scientific aim is to consider how far change could be achieved successfully by changing the law.

There are several principles underlying the Children Act 1989 that permeate the research studies. An important strand of the Act is to bring together private and public law so that the needs of all children whose welfare is at risk might be approached in the same way. This philosophy is underpinned by the principle of promoting children's welfare. There should be recognition of children's time-scales and, in court cases, children's welfare should be paramount. To aid this paramountcy principle there should be a welfare checklist and delays in court hearings should be avoided.

The promotion of children's welfare takes a child development focus, urging local authorities to take a holistic and corporate approach to providing services. Departments such as health, education, housing, police, social services and recreation should work together to respond to children's needs. Children, the Act argues, are best looked after within their families wherever possible and, where not, the continuing support of parents and wider kin should be facilitated by avoiding compulsory proceedings whenever possible. Parents should be partners in any intervention process, and children's views should be sought and listened to in any decision-making affecting their lives. To promote continuity for children looked after, contact with families should be encouraged and children's religion, culture, ethnicity and language should be preserved.

Local authorities have a duty to move from services to prevent care to a broader remit of providing family support, which could include planned periods away from home. However, family support services should not be universal but target those most in need. The introduction of Children's Services Plans in 1996 has made the idea of corporate responsibility a more tangible reality and seeks to help local authorities look at how they may use scarce resources cost-effectively.

The themes of the Children Act have relevance for the millennium. The concern with combating social exclusion is echoed through several of the studies, especially those on family support and young people looked after by local authorities. The value of early intervention is also a theme in the studies on family centres, day care and services for children defined as 'in need' under the Act. Further, the research on the implementation of the Looking After Children Schedules emphasises the importance to children in foster and residential care of attaining good outcomes in education. Lastly, attending to the health of parents and their children is another strand in both the family support and 'children looked after' studies.

To accompany the 20 individual studies in the research programme the Department of Health has commissioned an overview of the findings, to be published by The Stationery Office in the style of similar previous publications from HMSO: *Social Work Decisions in Child Care 1985*; *Patterns and Outcomes in Child Care 1991*; *Child Protection: Messages from Research 1996*; and *Focus on Teenagers 1997*.

The editors would like to express their appreciation to the members of the research community; professionals from different disciplines, and service users, among others, who have contributed so willingly and generously to the successful completion of the research studies and to the construction of the overview. Without their help, none of the research would have been written or disseminated.

Carolyn Davies
Jane Aldgate

Acknowledgements

There are many people we would like to thank who made the production of this book possible. We appreciate very much the participation of the social services departments, social workers, parents, children and foster carers who took part. We are indebted to David Hawley and Margaret Duggan, key members of the research team. Our thanks are due to St Hilda's College, Oxford and the Universities of Oxford and Leicester for supporting our efforts. There were many in or attached to these universities whose help, expertise and support was crucial: Jane Barlow, Malayne Bowler, Christina Cazalet, Hedy Cleaver, Daniel Cleaver, Dr Richard Colman, Susan Dyson, Pauline Hardiker, Geoff Hurd, Dr K. Owusu Bempah, Mary Perry, Prof. Stein Ringen, Janet Seden, Janet West. Special gratitude goes to Dr Carolyn Davies at the Department of Health and to Wendy Rose and Rupert Hughes. We also wish to express our thanks to our Advisory Group: Geoff James, Prof. Roy Parker, Jane Rowe, Peter Smith, Prof. June Thoburn and Dr Harriet Ward. Finally, we are forever in the debt of Emily Goodman, Tony Aldgate and Hannah Aldgate.

Jane Aldgate
Marie Bradley

1 The origins of short-term accommodation

This chapter first appeared in Marsh and Triseliotis (eds) *Prevention and Reunification in Child Care*, B T Batsford, London, 1993, and is included here by kind permission of the Free Association Press.

Short-term accommodation was introduced as a new provision for children 'looked after' by the local authority under the Children Act 1989 but has its origins in what has been for a long time called 'respite care'. Respite care has been part of normal family child care for generations worldwide. Informally, in many cultures, the network of grandparents, aunts, uncles and other extended family has provided primary carers, usually mothers, with short-term relief from the demands of young children. In some cultures, respite has a more formal educative function, such as among the Kikuyu people in Kenya, where children are expected to spend time with the grandparents from whom they inherit their lineage. In Britain, the informal network of respite carers within the family continues to provide a source of support to parents and, arguably, is becoming even more important in providing continuity for children at a time when divorce has brought an increase in family transitions and periods of discontinuity for children.

There have also been, since 1948, professionally organised short-term family or residential placements to relieve families under stress who are unable to find respite care without some help from social workers. In this form of voluntary arrangement between the family and the state, respite care has benefitted both the primary carers and the children. Its purposes have been manifold: from temporary relief for parents from the stress of caring for a child with severe and demanding disabilities to a planned 'package' of services where respite care is offered to a wide range of families in conjunction with a variety of social work interventions aimed at achieving some defined change in child or parent or both. More recently, respite care for established foster carers has been added to the equation. Although, prior to 1991 and the implementation of the Children Act 1989, it was generally accepted that one period of respite would last for days or weeks rather than months, its total duration in a child's life could be one weekend or several years. Such a breadth of purpose and duration has bedevilled a common definition in the literature of previous decades. At best, it can be said that professionally organised respite care has usually meant the provision of some short-term relief for child or parents from a stressful relationship.

Professionally recruited respite carers have traditionally been drawn both from members of a child's extended family, whose circumstances preclude them from taking on the task without financial remuneration, or from approved providers such as child-minders, foster carers or residential social workers. It follows that respite care may be offered in a variety of settings including family centres, foster homes, residential homes, preparation-for-independence units or even holiday accommodation at the seaside or in the country.

Respite care: an established service for children with disabilities

In recent years there has been a tendency to equate respite care with the range of well-developed services on offer to parents who have children with severe learning or physical disabilities. Oswin (1984), Robinson (1987) and Stalker (1989), among others, have provided excellent empirical data on the application in practice of this kind of care. Robinson (1987) believes there are clear benefits to parents for whom respite care may provide: a sense of relief and support; more time for other children and partners; the ability to go out like an ordinary family; the ability to go on holiday; the ability to get more sleep and catch up with housework.

Often these services have been offered in a spirit of partnership where parents themselves take the lead in defining both the duration and mode of delivery of respite services they need. Invariably, for some families, as children's disabilities take their toll on parents a point is reached at which families need to move from a structure for *coping* to a structure for *living* (Bayley 1987). Respite care may then become a permanent part of the ongoing services aimed at enhancing the quality of life for both child and parents. From the various research studies in this field, several indicators of a successful respite service can be identified. Respite care can be offered to a wide range of children with disabilities and is helpful when:

◆ it is a local service, where the child can continue to attend his/her own school;

◆ it provides good-quality child care, which treats the child not as a patient but as a child who happens to have a disability;

◆ it is available on demand. Research strongly indicates the importance of parental control and choice over facilities and length of time;

- it lasts for short periods. Often days, with the possibility of an overnight stop from time to time, seem to work better than longer all-week breaks;

- there is recognition of children's individual personalities in designing packages of care. Some children are very upset by frequent separations, others love it;

- it is age-appropriate care so adolescents and small children are stimulated and not bored;

- it is part of an integrated programme of family support, which includes other services; and

- it is planned in quantity, purpose and duration to avoid slippage into long-term arrangements.

Although parents of children with disabilities undoubtedly benefit from respite services, several researchers have found that it is not always without some costs to the children. Robinson (1987), for example, believes that while many children gain from mixing with another family, the quality of care has sometimes not been as good as it could have been and, further, stresses the need to place an emphasis on 'good child care principles' in arranging a placement and to pay attention to the supervision and support of homes (p. 280). In common with Robinson, both Oswin (1984) and Stalker (1989) urge recognition of the potential ill-effects of separation on children and the importance of good preparation and matching with carers to counteract this.

A wider definition of respite care

The idea of a wider use of respite care services for other children who are in need of social services is not new but has only resurfaced as a preferred social service in the last few years, after two decades of decline. In the early days of the post-war children's departments, respite care was a normal part of the services on offer. Sometimes short holidays were arranged separately for children and parents with the aim of bringing temporary relief from the drudgery of living in permanent poverty. Such paternalism sits uneasily in the context of the 1990s although poverty is still very much with us. Respite care, including holidays, does still exist, but now it is seen much more in the context of widening children's horizons, 'promoting their welfare', and giving parents the break from their responsibilities that many in more affluent circumstances would take for granted.

It is interesting to trace briefly the decline and restoration of respite care over the last three decades. The decline can probably be pinpointed from the implementation of the 1963 Children and Young Persons' Act during the late 1960s. In a brave attempt to prevent family breakdown, social workers were instructed to use services in the community to 'diminish the need to receive children into care'. The term 'prevention' came into being in a social rather than a medical context. Preventive intervention was, however, defined rather narrowly with the concomitant stigmatising of the 'in care' services. An inevitable watershed occurred between being 'in' or 'out' of care (pre-1989 English law usage).

The 1975 Children Act skewed the use of voluntary care even more by introducing sanctions on the immediate return of children after they had been away from home more than six months. The power balance between parents and social workers was thus altered. Going into care became even more stigmatised than it had been post-1963. Combined with the other parts of the Act which extended the potential for effecting permanent out-of-home placements, reception into care became an event to be used only as a last resort. Thus an important voluntary responsive service provision for families under stress was almost completely run down during the early part of the 1980s.

The continuing evidence for the usefulness of respite care

The need was, however, still there. In 1980 an independent working party chaired by Roy Parker had argued strongly for a wider definition of preventive social work which would necessitate a breaking down of barriers in service provision for children in and out of care (Parker 1980). Research findings from the mid-1980s confirmed the working party's view.

Firstly, there was the wealth of evidence to show that the longer children were in care, the more likely they were to remain there. There was also evidence of a clear association between parental contact and restoration (Aldgate 1980; Millham et al. 1986). In addition, there was growing evidence that those who enter the care system for the first time aged 10 or over were likely to find most chance of a long-lasting relationship with their own families when they left care (Stein and Carey 1986; Thoburn et al. 1986).

Secondly, there were research findings on the outcome of growing up in the care system: the sadness of young people who had lost links with their families and the findings that, even though a stable foster home may offer much, some young people leave care uncertain about their identity and unconfident about the future (Triseliotis 1980, 1989; Triseliotis and Russell 1984; Stein and Carey 1986). This evidence was further fuelled by studies on the poor educational outcome (Aldgate and Heath 1992) and the health of children 'looked after' (DoH 1991b).

Thirdly, the user studies of parents of children looked after by the local authority reported parents' wishes to fulfil their parental responsibility (Rowe et al. 1984; DoH 1985b; Fisher et al. 1986), and clearly identified circumstances in which shared parental responsibility might be achieved (Millham et al. 1986). The evidence-based work of the Family Rights Group (1982) added a substantial dossier of cases of responsible parents who had received a raw deal from social workers. These supported the arguments which had been put forward by Holman (1980) for changing attitudes from exclusion to inclusion of parents of children looked after.

Fourthly, the most compelling evidence for respite care in the 1980s came from parents of children within the care system who told several researchers that they would have appreciated some relief at an earlier stage but that their requests for placements were often turned down. They were only able to get their children admitted to care in extreme circumstances (see DHSS 1985b and especially Fisher et al. 1986).

Not surprisingly, therefore, the research from the early 1980s led to the unequivocal conclusion that there were:

> potentialities of using short-term care as a means of preventing the permanent break-up of families by offering temporary relief care. (DHSS, 1985b, p. 16)

A change in the law in England and Wales

This evidence was accepted by the government-led bodies reviewing the child care law in England and Wales in the mid-1980s. This resulted in a wider definition of preventive services (DHSS 1984), a case for the provision of respite and shared care (DHSS 1985a) and was subsequently incorporated into the White Paper preceding the Children Act 1989 (DHSS 1987). Although the distinction between respite and shared care was abandoned in the White Paper, using out-of-home placements was to be retained with:

> the positive aim of providing care away from the family home as a means of providing support to the family and reducing the risk of long-term family breakdown. (DHSS 1987, p. 5).

The widening of the context of preventive services to *promote the welfare of children* meant that all children in need would come under the umbrella of the Act. The need for specialist respite care for children with disabilities and more general respite for other children would be part of the same range of services, assessed on the same criteria and monitored under the same statutory regulations and guidance. Within this context, respite care would be unacceptable to families if it carried any suggestion of a hidden agenda of child rescue. There would be 'a new focus on the provision of services in voluntary partnership with parents' (DHSS 1987, p. 4).

To reinforce the point, the term 'care' would be confined to cases where children were compulsorily looked after away from home. Any voluntary placements would be called 'accommodation' to avoid stigma.

The Department of Health guide *The Care of Children: Principles and Practice in Regulations and Guidance* (DoH 1990) accompanying the new Children Act in England and Wales encapsulated these points, giving a clear mandate to widen the scope of what have traditionally been called 'preventive services' to include short-term out-of-home placements as a viable option for *any* family of a child in need, not just those with disabled children:

> A wide variety of services, including short-term out-of-home placements,
> may need to be employed in order to sustain some families through
> particularly difficult periods. The provision of services to maintain the family
> home is a requirement of the Children Act 1989 (Schedule 2, paras. 8, 9, 10).
> (p. 8)

Introducing a wider system of family support to include planned out-of-home placements values parents as resources to promote children's welfare and helps to lay the ghost of 'less eligibility', the distinction between the deserving and the undeserving which has been so deeply embedded in attitudes towards those seeking social help from the state for centuries. The principles underpinning the law demand that social workers recognise that:

> *Parents are individuals with needs of their own.* Even though services may
> be offered primarily on behalf of children, parents are entitled to help and
> consideration in their own right. Just as some young people are more
> vulnerable than others, so are some mothers and fathers. Their parenting
> capacity may be limited temporarily or permanently by poverty, racism,
> poor housing or unemployment or by personal or marital problems,
> sensory or physical disability, mental illness or past life experiences. Lack of

parenting skills or inability to provide adequate care should not be equated
with lack of affection or irresponsibility. (DoH 1990, p. 8)

Furthermore, the social services have to recognise a diversity of family life and
therefore a diversity of need: 'Although some basic needs are universal, there
can be a variety of ways of meeting them' (DoH 1990 p. 7).

Putting this rhetoric into practice is no easy matter. Apart from balancing
supply and demand, there remains the problem of defining just what short-
term accommodation ought to be. Holman (1988), for example, while
generally supporting the idea of short-term 'respite' care, argues that, after
a month or so, respite becomes shared care. Furthermore, the prolonging of
responsive services could create dependence if they draw families long-term
into the welfare net.

The Department of Health is also aware of the need for caution in separat-
ing children from their parents in any circumstances and urges that attention
should be paid to maximising continuities between home and accommodation in any out-of-home placement: 'Continuity of relationships is important,
and attachments should be respected, sustained and developed' (DoH 1990,
p. 9).

Mindful of the potential damage to children of being in badly planned out-
of-home placements, the new legislation places tight boundaries around
short-term placements. Regulation 13 of the *Guidance and Regulations* in
relation to family placements that accompany the Children Act 1989 allows
for a series of pre-planned placements to be treated as a single placement but
this series must all occur within one year, have no single placement longer
than four weeks and a total duration not exceeding 90 days. Most importantly, they must all be with the same carer (DoH 1991a, p. 5).

The Children Act definition of short-term accommodation offers clear guidance on service delivery and simplifies the fiscal organisation to the advantage
of families and those providing the service. The only disadvantage is that too
rigid an interpretation of this regulation could result in a new watershed
between short-term and full-term accommodation. However, the return to
the drifting of children into unplanned long-term arrangements reported in
the early 1970s (Rowe and Lambert 1973) would be as bad as the automatic
severing of attachments from carers as soon as a short-term placement
exceeded the limit. Implementing short-term accommodation arrangements
has to make sure that each child's individual needs take precedence over
administrative arrangements.

Accepting accommodation as part of family support services

Although short-term accommodation for children in need was greeted with some enthusiasm by the legislators of the Children Act 1989, research prior to the Act suggested that there might be several problems about expanding its application in practice. The research from the 1980s had indicated that social workers would need a substantial change in attitude if the legacy of child rescue strengthened during the 1980s were to be counteracted (DHSS 1985b).

However, the results of a small study in one English county immediately prior to the Act suggested that social workers might be more responsive to change than the 1980s research has suggested. This study surveyed practitioners at different levels in one shire county social services department during 1989 to elicit their views on the more widespread use of respite care (soon to be short-term accommodation) in their area. The findings suggested that, although some changes in social worker attitude towards a user-led process of decision-making would be necessary, the motivation to move from a crisis-driven service to a responsive user-led mode was very strong. Workers believed that the expansion of short-term accommodation services from children with disabilities to others who were receiving 'preventive' help would be very welcome (Webb and Aldgate 1990).

The second problem is that, prior to this study, there were few published examples of respite care on which practitioners could model their short-term accommodation services. Reviewing the literature, Webb (1990) did find one or two positive examples in the UK and several more in the USA. A Scottish experiment, for example, described a short-stay refuge facility to prevent family breakdown by providing a community-based support system for adolescents (Swanson 1988). Aldgate et al. (1989) reported on the use of planned respite care in Oxfordshire to empower single parents and widen children's experience of living in a two-parent family. Subramanian (1985) also described the use of emergency respite care as a means of reducing the risk of child abuse. There were more overtly therapeutic examples elsewhere, such as the weekend programme for children with emotional and psychiatric problems in the USA described by Astrachan and Harris (1983).

Thirdly, prior to the Children Act there had been no conceptual framework from within which to evaluate different modes of respite. However, just prior to implementation Webb (1990, p. 25) usefully distinguished three dimensions of respite care:

Crisis driven Respite is used here on an emergency basis. It is seen as a temporary, 'stop-gap' provision which provides a period of immediate relief for both parents and children. Its rationale is largely agency-orientated. By using respite in a crisis situation after family breakdown or disruption, practitioners would gain additional time and space for planned alternatives, and would be able to avoid an either/or decision about using Emergency Care Orders or permanently removing children. A respite provision for such crisis situations would also extend the options available to duty and emergency teams during weekends, which are often stressful for families.

Contingency driven Here, respite care is based on the idea of prevention and conceived as part of a planned package of care resources. It is based on partnership with families. Statutory powers need not be invoked as a vehicle for using respite and its rationale is largely consumer-orientated. It should be noted that respite as a contingency-driven option would enable practitioners to plan its use strategically within a range of services and over a specified period of time. The trust between clients and practitioners might be enhanced by using respite, and the stigma attached to the 'social work visit' might be reduced.

Fiscally driven Respite care in this case is a matter of reducing the cost of care. Respite care provision is seen as an economically viable alternative to both foster care and residential placements for children. This is the cost-effective approach. It becomes a more attractive option if parents are willing to pay for the use of respite. Some practitioners will object to a market-led respite provision, and means testing certainly would have to be considered as an option in this context. However, practitioners might find that families who are able to pay something towards respite care will have a positive view of participating in the definition of their needs, and defining the quality and range of preventative services.

The foundations for the current study

The current study was commissioned in two stages. The first phase of the study, in 1992–94, reviewed 13 examples of respite care that had made the transition from respite care to short-term accommodation immediately after the Act. From the review of these schemes was developed a guide for practitioners, which is currently being modified to take account of the findings from the current study. Some social workers were using respite care on an individual basis, drawing their carers either from family placement teams or from residential centres. In addition, there was a scattering of more organised schemes that provided respite care to a wide age range of children. These schemes were generally organised in two modes: as a discrete service or as part of a package of services, very much along the lines of Webb's contingency-driven model. There was little evidence of respite being used as a fiscally driven service.

Within both these modes, short-term accommodation was seen by families to fulfil one or more of the following purposes:

♦ to provide relief from the normal stresses of being a parent;

♦ to provide adolescents with relief from stressful family living;

♦ to help with children's behaviour problems;

♦ to provide relief where families live in social isolation;

♦ to help relieve the stress of living in continuing poverty;

♦ as an alternative to admission to full-time accommodation;

♦ to provide a safe place for a break for adolescents who are fostered; and

♦ to provide relief for sick parents.

Short-term accommodation was also seen by social workers as a contingency-driven mode of intervention, either alone or in association with other services, which could have the following aims:

♦ to prevent long-term family breakdown, both in birth and in foster families;

♦ to support families with under-fives as part of Social Services' normal activity to promote children's welfare;

♦ to relieve parental stress, caused by a variety of factors, which might lead to child neglect;

♦ to prevent possible physical child abuse caused by continuing parental strain;

♦ to enhance the effectiveness of other intervention;

♦ to empower parents by recognising their needs;

♦ to improve or widen the quality of life for children; and

♦ to improve the quality of parenting skills.

The first part of the study suggested that, in the early 1990s, all the respite accommodation studied had clearly defined gatekeeping mechanisms for deciding who should be given services. Often families had to resort to exaggerating their problems (see also Fisher et al. 1986) even to be considered for services. Similarly, social workers had to over-emphasise their clients' problems in order to gain them priority access to Section 17 services. There was a confusion about terminology. A needs-led service was often equated with an open-access service, with accompanying fears that demand would totally outstrip supply. Accordingly, there was strong gatekeeping of access to services.

Once short-term accommodation was on offer, a choice of placement similar to that offered to potential long-term foster carers or adopters proved viable in one or two of the schemes reviewed. One actually encouraged families to visit several potential carers before a placement was agreed (see Case study 1). Carers found this acceptable and believed it empowered parents and enhanced the commitment of parents and children to the placement.

In the early 1990s, at the point of transition to the Act, respite care was seen as part of family support services with considerable potential for extending its use under the umbrella of short-term accommodation. There were several ways in which the service might be organised. Short-term accommodation was sometimes an offshoot of family placement services. It was linked in one case to an extended child-minding service; in others it was residentially based. In some cases, one team of workers was responsible for child, family and placement. In others, responsibilities were shared between those working with families and those recruiting and supporting carers. Whatever the arrangements, workers were clear that in order to ensure that short-term accommodation was located within family support services, the budget attached to accommodation would have to be located within the new Section 17 budget for children in need. Otherwise there would be dangers that the old tariff system of in and out of care would resurface.

Three case studies from the first phase of the study, which exemplify some of the varieties of respite care that can be developed within the personal social services, follow. Two can be classified as short-term accommodation under the Children Act 1989; the third, while reflecting the ethos of a family support service offered in partnership with parents, comes under Scottish legislation. These models would fit happily within either local authority or voluntary agency arrangements anywhere in the UK and beyond.

CASE STUDY 1

This is a good example of how a locality-based service delivery model accessing a range of provisions, including a mix of residential and family-based respite care, can be used to advantage to meet the needs of a wide age range of children. Respite is organised by a family support team working from a children's resource centre in a large Midlands city social services department. The team, therefore, has access to family centres and family aides, and can offer counselling. The team also controls its own budget and is therefore able to have some flexibility over the use of financial resources. Respite is only one of a range of accommodation placements offered by the team to children of all ages, although caution is exercised in placing the under-fives. The comprehensiveness of their service delivery allows a flexibility whereby the transition from one type of accommodation to another can be co-ordinated easily.

The present centre was set up in the mid-1980s, as part of a strategy to provide community-based substitute care for all children in an area of high socio-economic deprivation, traditionally the source of frequent referrals for social work support. Initially, part of the centre was adapted as a 'crash pad' for young people who were having family problems. Now there is a comprehensive approach to each child referred with a corresponding wide range of resources. There is a 24-hour social work service, a range of substitute carers and access to seven residential units, which offer different types of care. Family carers are drawn from a pool of local child-minders rather than from foster carers. There is a strongly held view that child-minders are:

- preferred by families because they are local;
- can be more easily of the same race;
- used to 'doing business' with families; and
- less likely to see themselves as child rescuers.

Because there are also flexible residential resources, respite may be offered short term as a 'crash pad' for young people or for children and their families, or may be offered from the start with a community family as part of a package of intervention.

The aim of respite here is twofold: the prevention of full-time accommodation and the diversion of young people from custody. There are approximately ten referrals for respite a month out of a total of 150 referrals for a wide range of services. There is no typical user-family other than that they live in the area. Neither is there a typical pattern of use. Each period of respite is fully negotiated on terms to meet the needs of individuals and can be for weeks or months.

A common scenario might be for a parent to come to the centre requesting full-time accommodation for a child. After a full assessment respite may be offered as a less drastic alternative. Another frequent event is a young person threatening to leave home. Emergency respite is offered overnight but only on condition that a full planning meeting with the young person and family follows the next morning. Planned respite might then be offered as one option but on condition that the young person and the family work with the social workers to resolve the problems that have led to friction. It is unlikely that respite would be used where children are at risk of significant harm.

Inevitably, there is a strong element of gatekeeping, with the workers controlling the use of the resource. Once that initial stage has been passed, potential users, both children and parents, are given a choice about the most suitable family or residential unit for them. They may visit several before a placement is decided.

Apart from the initial overnight stay, respite is always offered as part of a package addressing family difficulties. A written agreement is incorporated into the planning meeting minutes. The content will depend on the issues to be addressed. There is no set format. This is part of the of centre's conscious philosophy to empower children and families. The system has been developed as a response to users' wishes for a more informal relationship with workers and their disenchantment with the formality of statutory services. There is a great effort to make users feel in control of the services offered. Negotiation is the most prominent social work skill on offer, but it is underpinned by frequent formal reviews of arrangements, firstly, after 72 hours and then generally fortnightly or weekly if necessary. Parental, child and carer attendance is obligatory. Once arrangements have stabilised reviews may be reduced to monthly, or six-monthly in long-term arrangements. Such an ethos is impressive but undoubtedly makes considerable demands on the workers' time. This is not a 9 to 5 service. The five workers and the team leader are fully stretched, even though they have an accommodation officer and a day care officer who recruit, prepare and make a provisional selection of carers for families to meet. Their commitment, charisma and professionalism are undoubtedly major factors in the success of the enterprise. Training is on offer both to workers and carers and is well used.

● ● ●

CASE STUDY 2

This is an extremely imaginative scheme developed by the social work department of a large city in Scotland to meet the needs of children and their parents where HIV is an issue. Because of differences in legislation, the terminology is 'respite care'. Nevertheless, the principles of a family support service are the same as those in England.

The project is funded by and developed out of the mainstream family placement services in response to requests from medical social workers for crisis care when parents were admitted to hospital in an emergency. Social workers were increasingly aware of the difficulties and needs of parents diagnosed HIV+ but also of their reluctance to approach statutory services, and their anger when their children were taken into care. The respite is offered to children of all ages.

The respite on offer is organised through a social work referral system and the facility is offered after assessment of need. The service aims to keep children within their families for as long as possible, supporting the primary carer while giving them time to plan for a permanent future for their children when they are too ill to look after their children any more. Because of the uncertainties of the time-scale for the development of AIDS, respite with a reliable, accepting and supportive carer offers children much-needed stability. The focus of the placement is, however, very much family centred. The needs of the parents are as important as those of the child. That parents are valued for themselves in spite of their stigmatising illness and their, sometimes, alternative lifestyle. This acceptance helps them, in turn, to accept respite for their children more readily. Many of the parents are single mothers, some are prostitutes or drug abusers.

The workers acknowledge that these are high-risk families and are mindful of child protection issues. Nevertheless, their experience has shown them that child protection can be achieved within a supportive framework of intervention. The greatest difficulty is overcoming parents' suspicion and fear about social work involvement but there are also issues of structuring intervention with families whose lifestyle tends to be somewhat chaotic or who deliberately set themselves apart from mainstream society. Respite is always offered within the context of planning for the future. It may sometimes exist alongside a range of other supportive services, such as family aides, home helps, day care for the under-fives and community nursing support. Children seem to view respite as something that happens because of their parent's illness. Older children find a degree of security in it as part of the plans for their care as their parent's health declines.

Normally carers come from the pool of mainstream foster carers but a few are specially recruited. Currently about 20 carers are available. Most are couple families from a wide range of socio-economic backgrounds. Carers who offer only respite will take one, or at most, two families at any one time. Financial remuneration takes into account the need to retain their services for specific families. Respite carers share the comprehensive training offered to all foster carers, including information on loss and attachment, HIV/AIDS, child abuse and direct work with children but are given additional input on the likely effects of the work on the carer family and the need for a strong support network. Carers have a support group, training event and consistent individual social work support. Their family network also seems to be an important source of nurture. Clearly, the carers are special individuals who can tolerate uncertainty and who have come to terms with the idea that children in their care may themselves be HIV+ as well as their parents.

An increasing problem for the workers is whether the respite carers should become the permanent family in the long term. The norm has been to reserve the pool of carers especially for respite and to try to find an alternative family for life, preferably within the child's extended family. If parents, carers or social workers see the status quo as the preferred permanent option there is a real dilemma: preserving continuity for one child has the danger of constantly draining a highly trained resource for others.

● ● ●

CASE STUDY 3

This scheme, started in an English county in 1985, was the prototype for the current study (see Aldgate et al. 1989). It was developed to relieve family stress without precipitating children who were on the margins of 'care' (pre-1989 usage) into the care system. But the intention was also rather broader than simply 'diminishing the need to receive children into care'. An important feature has always been that respite is seen as an integral part of community-based services to promote children's welfare. It is seen equally as a service for parents. Consequently it is only offered as part of an intervention strategy which has several components. These may include individual counselling for parents and children, self-help groups for parents within family centres, family aides to teach parenting skills, day care support for families with children under five and child psychiatry. The aim is always to give parents enough relief and support to enable them to care for their children permanently, to encourage parents to use the time away from their children creatively as part of a self-realisation process and to give children the experience of time spent with another family both complimentary to but different from their own. A secondary aim has always been to use respite care to address any problems of children's material needs by using financial support from boarding-out allowances to purchase clothes, toys and equipment for children which become the permanent property of children at the end of the placement. This is a controversial and delicate area of help. Material help is offered only where it is seen as being helpful by the birth parent and the child. It is in no way the intention to undermine the independence of families. In practice, most families living in enduring poverty welcome this practical support.

Families are drawn from the whole county. Most families are white, reflecting the racial distribution in this rural area and are from large council estates on the fringes of towns. Currently there are between 12 and 20 placements on offer. Siblings are usually accommodated together except in cases where respite is aimed specifically at addressing an individual's behaviour problems. It has also been found from experience that respite does not work well for children under five because of attachment issues. Nor has it been very successful for older adolescents who have their own agenda of working towards independence and find the structured approach too confining. To some extent, therefore, these constraints set natural limits on the children for whom respite is used. Recently, recruitment of families has been extended to include long-term foster families who are looking after children with severe behaviour or emotional difficulties. The same principles of planning, promotion of welfare and partnership obtain.

Respite care is always planned and of finite duration, over several months up to a maximum of one year. The normal pattern is for children to spend one weekend in four with carers. The initial choice of carer family is made by the social worker with the strengths of carers and parents, locality, ethnicity, age and sex of the child to be important factors in any matching process, as well as any special needs children and parents may have. It may be, for example, that a child has a behavioural problem or that there is special emphasis on enhancing the parent's child care skills. Users meet carers before the respite begins. There is an element of choice on both sides but users do not have the opportunity to select carers as in the Midlands scheme. Written agreements are integral to the process and have always reflected the partnership ethos which has underpinned the scheme.

Carers are normally specially recruited, although recently some have been diverted from mainstream short-term fostering. As in the Scottish scheme, no carer family is allowed to link with more than one family or two at a time but every attempt is made to place siblings together. Carers have a primary commitment to recognise and enhance the strengths of birth families. They are recruited for their acceptance of families' frailties, their willingness to work professionally in partnership with them and their understanding of the significance of parents in children's lives. This attitude is reinforced by carers reporting direct to parents after each weekend and consistently using parents as expert informants about children's progress. Sometimes carers will write to parents between placements reaffirming their interest in and commitment to the family. Carers are constantly urged to be vigilant about any action that might undermine child and parent's attachment to each other.

The success rate, in terms of helping to prevent family breakdown, is high, possibly due to the tremendous amount of planning and ongoing support put into each placement. Families are supported by the child's social worker who also liaises with the carers. Additionally, carers have support individually and through group support from the family placement team. Placements rarely break down but if they do no blame is attached to anyone. Rather a sensible analysis is attempted to prevent a similar occurrence.

Postscript: Ironically, soon after the current study began, as shown in Chapter 2, the example described in Case Study 3 was closed down and resources diverted elsewhere.

● ●

Context for the current study

This then was the context for the current study. It showed that there was the potential before the Children Act 1989 for using short-term accommodation as a viable family support service. The Act's intentions of breaking down the barriers between home and out-of-home placements had already been put into practice in a minority of places. Most importantly, the Act was not conceived in a vacuum but had been built on sound child care principles and good child care practice which transcended any legislative change.

2 *The research study: aims and methods*

Aims

The main aim of the study was to investigate the use of short-term accommodation for the express purposes of supporting families and helping to prevent family breakdown in the long term, within the rubric of the Children Act 1989 (Section 20) for children in need defined under (a) and (b) of Section 17, thus excluding children defined under Section 17(c) as disabled.

Section 17(10) states that a child is 'in need' if:

(a)   he is unlikely to achieve or maintain or to have the opportunity of achieving or maintaining, a reasonable standard of health or development without the provision for him of services by a local authority;

(b)   his health or development is likely to be significantly impaired, or further impaired, without the provision for him of such services; or

(c)   he is disabled.

Additionally, the *Guidance and Regulations* Volume 2 states:

> The definition of need . . . is deliberately wide to reinforce the emphasis on preventive support and service to families. It has three categories: a reasonable standard of health or development; significant impairment of health or development and disablement. It would not be acceptable for an authority to exclude any of these three – for example, by confining services to children at risk of significant harm which attracts the duty to investigate under Section 47. (DoH 1991b, p. 5)

Children in need may benefit from many services. Among them is the provision of accommodation. As suggested in Chapter 1, accommodation is a new provision outlined in Section 20 of the Children Act 1989. It is characterised by being offered without any sanctions, in voluntary agreement with both parents and children, all of whom must be consulted before arrangements are made. In particular, a child's wishes and feelings must be considered if accommodation is being planned.

The general conditions under which accommodation may be used are outlined in Section 20(1):

> (1)   Every local authority shall provide accommodation for any child in need within their area who appears to them to require accommodation as a result of
>
> (a)   there being no person who has parental responsibility for him;
>
> (b)   his being lost or being abandoned; or
>
> (c)   the person who has been caring for him being prevented (whether or not permanently, and for whatever reason) from providing him with suitable accommodation or care.

These conditions have some similarities in their first part to those in earlier legislation. The main difference is the inclusion of the concept of parental responsibility which, as Packman and Hall (1995) suggest, recasts the concept of parental rights. Parental responsibility is the cornerstone of the Children Act:

> The Act uses the phrase parental responsibility to sum up the collection of duties, rights and authority which a parent has in respect of his child. The choice of words emphasises that the duty to care for the child and to raise him to moral physical and emotional health is the fundamental task of parenthood and the only justification for the authority it confers. (DoH 1989, p .1)

The Act recognises that there are times when, although parents technically can exercise parental responsibility, they may not be able to do this as well as they should. At these times, accommodation can be offered as a source of positive family support.

Section 20(4) states:

> A local authority may provide accommodation for any child in their area (even though a person who has parental responsibility for him is able to provide him with accommodation) if they consider that to do so would safeguard or promote the child's welfare.

This clause suggests that out-of-home placements may be used as a preventive measure to support families in times of stress, where that stress has caused children to be 'in need'.

Short-term accommodation, the successor to the traditional out-of-home 'respite' placement used to support families is also defined carefully to avoid any confusion over its purpose or duration in two Statutory Instruments: *Arrangements for Placement of Children (General) Regulations 1991* under Regulation 13 and in the *Foster Placement (Children) Regulations 1991* under Regulation 9 (see DoH 1991a). The legal requirements for short-term accommodation have been used to define short-term accommodation in this study:

♦ the placement should be with the same carer;

♦ all the placements occur within a period which does not exceed one year;

♦ no single placement is for a duration of more than four weeks; and

♦ the total duration of the placements does not exceed 90 days.

Within the general scrutiny of short-term accommodation arrangements, more specifically, the study aimed to address the following issues:

1 to identify the characteristics of children and families to whom short-term accommodation had been offered in the study areas;

2 at the beginning of the intervention, to ask social workers, children, parents and carers to assess the purpose and likely outcome of short-term accommodation from their perspectives, and to explore the process of making arrangements with respect to consultation and partnership;

3 to explore the implementation of the Children Act *Guidance and Regulations* in relation to child care plans and written agreements for children in short-term accommodation;

4 to trace the use of accommodation over a minimum of nine months or until the point it terminated, if this was shorter, in order to monitor:
a) the experience of children and their families
b) the contribution of the carers to the service
c) the social work input; and

5 to identify the outcome of using short-term accommodation in terms of:
a) whether the family had remained intact
b) whether problems had been ameliorated
c) whether social work aims had been met
d) whether users felt the service had met their needs.

Developing the study design

There were two major influences which shaped the way the study was designed:

1   earlier research; and

2   the Children Act 1989.

Earlier research

The first influence derived from the findings from the earlier study already described in detail in Chapter 1. This explored the use of respite care for families under stress over the period the Children Act was introduced and implemented; it provided the context for the current study by identifying patterns of service provision and delivery. Information for the findings described in Chapter 1 was gathered by several methods:

- ♦   scrutiny of agency documentation on the service;

- ♦   interviews with social workers responsible for delivering the service in all agencies; and

- ♦   interviews with a small number of parents (eight) to give a user perspective.

The Children Act 1989

The implementation of the Children Act influenced the design of the study in several ways.

Meeting the primary aim of the study to investigate the use of short-term accommodation as part of family support services to prevent family breakdown could have been achieved in a number of ways. A file search of children newly accommodated full-time would have yielded some information on those who had previously received short-term accommodation. However, this would only have defined family breakdown in terms of children being looked after and would have failed to yield information about family perspectives on the service.

Alternatively, the study could have concentrated on the views of social workers, which would have shown the advantages and difficulties agencies encountered in the transition period of implementing the Children Act but would again have excluded users' perspectives.

Users' perspectives are important because of the emphasis in the Children Act on working in partnership with parents and children. The underlying philosophy of the Act emphasises the positive use of accommodation as part of family support services, when arrangements are made in partnership with parents and in consultation with children. It is required that these arrangements are voluntary in order to preserve parental responsibility. The accompanying *Guidance and Regulations* in Volume 3 says that in such arrangements:

> The parents contribute their experience and knowledge of the child to the decision. The local authority brings a capacity to provide services, to co-ordinate the contribution of other agencies and to plan for and review the child's needs. (DoH 1991a, p. 5)

Given the emphasis in the Act on the potential of developing a needs-led as opposed to an agency-led service, it was essential to include, alongside social work assessments of family breakdown, the perspectives of children and parents.

The study locations

The study was located in four local authority social services departments which show variations in demographic characteristics of their catchment areas, ranging from urban areas with 'inner city' characteristics, to moderately large shire towns which include some rural areas in their catchment area for short-term accommodation.

Within the study areas, there were two ways of organising short-term accommodation services. Interestingly, these could be divided between the area under scrutiny in Midcity, part of a large city with many inner city characteristics and the three other local authority schemes. These three areas, while having some key differences within each one, included city, shire town, rural and seaport areas.

The areas and the organisation of service provision

Originally, the study was to be conducted in three areas which had a well-developed service of respite care prior to the introduction of the Children Act 1989. However, although all gave formal undertakings to participate in the study, one was unable to provide cases for the study. This was the result of reorganisation and a reluctance to continue to participate in the study. In another area, a major policy change away from a broad provision of family support services towards a concentration on disabled children and a concomitant concentration on child protection enquiries led to a sudden and dramatic end to the provision of general short-term accommodation. As a result the research was extended to two further study areas – providing four authorities to be called Midcity, River Town, Ferryport and Spire City.

The areas differed in terms of their geography and demography. Although it cannot be claimed that the four local authorities were representative of all authorities, none the less between them they served very different geographical areas.

Midcity

The Midcity scheme covered part of a large city. The area the short-term accommodation scheme covered was one half of the city with a population of 273,000 with a wide range of ethnic and economic backgrounds. There are pockets of socio-economic deprivation located both in a number of outer city housing estates and in inner city terraces and high-rise flats.

River Town

River Town covered the central part of a county town, with a population of 134,300 in the area served by the scheme. The town is a mixture of affluence, moderate wealth and poverty. The families served by the scheme lived mainly on council estates located on the periphery of the well-to-do areas of the town.

Ferryport

Ferryport included one-third of a large and busy seaport, and the area served by the scheme has a population of 82,500 and represents a densely populated urban area, with a dominance of council housing. The area has a significant proportion of families of African-Caribbean and mixed heritage origin. There are pockets of socio-economic deprivation.

Spire City

Spire City represents one half of a large, industrial city. The population of the area served by the scheme is 194,000. In this area, there is a minority ethnic population of 10%, comprising both black and Asian families.

The timing of the research: special circumstances affecting the research locations

Since the study spanned the period leading up to and following on from the implementation of the Children Act 1989, the social services departments concerned were affected by this transition. There were understandable anxieties about the changes demanded by the new legislation and its philosophy. Social workers and their managers were anxious about implementing the changes. For the agencies involved in the study, the concerns about interpreting and using the Children Act properly were paramount.

Initially, the clear and stringent regulations presented worries to agencies about the legality of any ongoing respite care arrangements. Consequently, scheme managers sought the advice of their legal departments about whether they should change their procedures and practices. In the event, all four departments found flexible and creative ways of adapting to the new requirements so that their practices conformed with the relevant Children Act *Guidance and Regulations.*

Midcity initially made most of its arrangements under Section 17 as part of a decisive policy of reaching out to families of children in need. There was a clear belief that these families would be at risk of breakdown if early supportive measures were not offered. Their policy for developing short-term accommodation was also shaped by a decision to make use of a well-established 'extended child-minding' service. This had recruited extensively from the local community carers who were offering both day and overnight care. There was concern that these child-minders would balk at being assessed and registered as foster carers, which would be necessary if they were to continue to offer short-term 'breaks' to children in need. Despite the worries, all of the carers were retained, assessed and approved, and found advantages in their revised status. They told the research team in the earlier study that, as short-term foster carers, they had a clear professional identity and a greater sense of being part of a professional network.

River Town, Ferryport and Spire City mostly used carers who were already approved as foster carers, some of whom were 'mainstream carers' and some of whom were specialist 'respite carers' and were thus less affected by regulations relating to carers.

Variations between schemes

The evolution of the short-term accommodation schemes from child-minding or foster care was one factor among others which differentiated the schemes. For example, the Midcity scheme had originally been funded by an urban aid grant administered by social services. At the time of the study it was being funded by social services. Its financial resources were ring-fenced with a scheme leader who selected and trained carers and assessed and managed arrangements for children and families. Families were offered a fixed number of short-term breaks to be taken in a finite period of up to six months. Parents could choose within this period when the breaks should take place. Most parents took their breaks within a three-month period.

By contrast, in the three other authorities, River Town, Ferryport and Spire City, the short-term accommodation service was funded in two parts. Carers were funded under family placement services offered to all children accommodated or in care whereas workers who helped families access the service were part of the mainstream children and families provision. Therefore, rather than one worker co-ordinating all tasks, as in Midcity, the role was split. Carers were recruited and supported as foster carers through family placement services. Families accessed the service either through family centres (Ferryport) or through child and family social workers (River Town and Spire City). The length and type of arrangements were negotiated between the two workers and the families.

The sample

There were 60 children included in the study. There was only one index child in each family even if other children were accommodated along with the index child. In all cases when more than one child was accommodated the eldest child was identified as the index child in order to facilitate interviews with children.

A case was defined when short-term accommodation had been offered and accepted by child and parents. The child's main carer was the adult subject although views of the other parents or any significant others present (for example, grandparents) were noted qualitatively.

The sample was prospective, purposive and sequential. The families of all children offered short-term accommodation from a specified date were approached by the research team until 60 cases had been recruited between the four authorities. Due to the difficulties in recruiting families in River Town and Spire City, as already outlined, these authorities contributed fewer cases. However, it was clear from later analysis of family characteristics that very similar families were using the service in the four areas. The 60 cases were distributed as shown in Table 2.1.

Table 2.1 *Case distribution between the four study local authorities (n=60)*

Local authority	Number of cases	Percentage
Midcity	31	52
River Town	8	13
Spire City	9	15
Ferryport	12	20

Any difference between the organisation of the service in the four authorities was taken into account by exploring the delivery and outcome of the service from the social work perspective.

Normally with this kind of intensive study, the findings would be set within a wider context. However, there were several obstacles preventing the development of a wider context.

The short-term accommodation service was new and as a result there was no local or national statistical information available in which to set the findings. National statistics on short-term accommodation were not requested from social services departments by the Department of Health until three years after the start of the study.

Another problem related to the newness of the service was that this type of help had been treated previously as either 'preventive services' under Section 1 of the 1980 Child Care Act or 'voluntary care' under Section 2 of the 1980 Act. As a result of this split, the setting of the current study in retrospective data was impossible.

One way round this would have been to use locally held records. Unfortunately, only two local authorities kept consistent records of the numbers of children using the scheme in any one year.

Where short-term accommodation had been classed as a family support service, because there was no national requirement to make returns to the Department of Health on family support cases at this time, it would have been an impossible task to trawl through all family records in the areas to identify all who fell within our criteria.

The only national context available was that from the study of the first 18 months' implementation of Section 17 by Aldgate and Tunstill (1995) which suggested that 83% of the 82 social services departments in the study were offering some form of general short-term accommodation. This is clear in Figure 2.1.

Figure 2.1 *Modes of provision of general respite care by local authorities (n=82)*

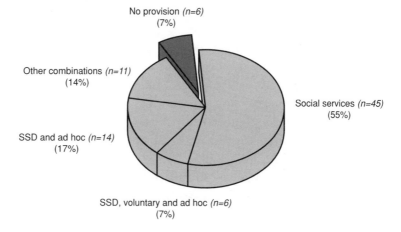

No provision *(n=6)*
(7%)

Other combinations *(n=11)*
(14%)

Social services *(n=45)*
(55%)

SSD and ad hoc *(n=14)*
(17%)

SSD, voluntary and ad hoc *(n=6)*
(7%)

Source: Aldgate and Tunstill 1995

However, the Aldgate and Tunstill study was concerned only to identify service provision and not service uptake and can therefore give no idea of the numbers using the service nationally in 1992–93. Nor was it clear from this study whether short-term accommodation was used explicitly for family support purposes as opposed to being part of the wider services for looked-after children.

Given all these problems, it was decided to abandon a quest for a context and reconcile the research team to the fact that the important part of the study was to explore the provision of a new service for some families in four areas, exploring how that service had been offered and received.

Recruiting families to the study

The process of recruiting families to the study had several stages. First, at the point where families had accepted the offer of short-term accommodation, social workers gave families a pre-printed letter from the research team inviting them to participate in the project. This informed them about the study, assured them about independence from social services and confidentiality and sought their participation. If families indicated to social workers that they were willing to participate, workers sent the name and address of the family to the research team on a prepared pro forma. Alternatively, families could write to the research team themselves if they did not wish to make an instant commitment to participate and were provided with a pre-paid envelope for this purpose. The procedure was set up with the full co-operation of social workers and their agreement not to put families under pressure in any way.

Secondly, if the parent agreed to participate, the research team sent a letter explaining the research and offering an appointment. Letters were sent with a pre-printed opt-out reply slip and a stamped addressed envelope to be used by parents who did not wish to participate. Letters were translated into five languages to reflect the cultural demography of the areas and were sent in a language other than English on the advice of the families' social worker. In fact only five families of those approached refused to take part. A scrutiny of their background from files suggested that they were very similar to those who had opted into the study.

Thirdly, if parents did not opt out, the researcher visited the family at their own home. At the beginning of the initial interview parents' contributions were outlined and issues of confidentiality and anonymity discussed. The issues to be covered in interviews with children were carefully explained to parents and they were given a short outline of the areas to be covered with the children. They were also taken through the test materials. In addition, their informed consent to interviewing their child was established. Since children were to be interviewed on a second occasion, parents had time to consider this further. Parents' permission to talk to social workers and carers was also established, outlining the areas to be discussed.

Fourthly, protocol was developed with the four agencies to deal with any revelations of possible child abuse. However, the research team was relieved to find it was not necessary to apply this in any case.

Piloting the study

The earlier study had informed the research team about the issues surrounding short-term accommodation which parents and social workers thought important in relation to service delivery. This helped to formulate ideas and hypotheses which would be tested out in the study. These ideas informed the development of the research instruments which were then piloted in a number of ways:

1   Draft interview schedules were tried out with six parents from two of the study authorities who had recently experienced short-term accommodation.

2   The adapted assessment and action schedules (see later) were piloted with a group of parents attending a family centre in one of the study locations. This was desirable because the schedules had originally been designed for looked-after children. At the beginning of this study, the extensive testing of the assessment and action schedules on a wider population had not been completed (see Ward 1995).

3   Four social workers from agencies included in the earlier study but not in this one were consulted over both social work schedules and how best to access children.

4   Finally, materials for children were piloted in children's own family homes. The children's questionnaire was piloted with four children over the age of seven who had experienced overnight stays with child-minders in the belief that this respite experience was similar to the experiences of children accommodated short-term. Additionally, the games and toys used with very young children were piloted with three under-fives who had also been child-minded overnight.

The information gained from piloting the different research instruments helped shape the final version of interview schedules or tools used in the study.

Interviews

Interviews were conducted with parents, social workers, carers and children. When considering parents, the interview was carried out with the parent who considered him/herself more responsible for child care. Parents, social workers and children were interviewed at two points in time:

1   when the offer of short-term accommodation had been made and had been accepted by the family; and

2   at a re-testing after at least nine months had elapsed and the accommodation was ongoing, or sooner if the arrangements had ended earlier.

In the latter case this proved to be not less than seven months. It was felt that to leave some gap for reflection after the service had ended would be desirable in the shorter term cases plus the fact that seven months would allow for changes to have been consolidated. In the piloting it had been established with social workers that the majority of cases in study areas would have ended their episode of short-term accommodation within nine months. All ended within the time-scale of the Children Act Regulations. In 97% of cases, children were accommodated for two or three days over the weekend. Only two children had longer periods with the carers, and none for more than four days at a time. All interviews where arrangements had ended were conducted within three months of the ending. The span between first and second interview is shown in Table 2.2.

Table 2.2 *Intervals between initial interview and final interview (n=60)*

Interval	Number of arrangements	Percentage
7 months	8	13
8 months	11	19
9 months	35	58
Over 9 months	6	10

Carers were interviewed only once to coincide with the second interview with families and social workers. As with the parents an index carer was identified as the one who considered him/herself most responsible for child care.

Style and content of the interviews

The interviews were conducted informally following the guidance of Hammersley and Atkinson (1983). This style allows families to see the interview as an extension of normal conversation. The parents found this method facilitating and most were able to talk at length about their circumstances, their problems and the service.

In a proportion of cases early in the study, at least two members of the research team worked together interviewing the same family to develop a consistent pattern of interviewing and to prevent distortion (Glaser and Strauss 1967).

One prominent issue was recognising the importance of being sensitive to cultural and linguistic issues in families of Asian origin. Accordingly, in these cases there was always a female member of the research team taking the lead. Additionally, in four cases, the services of locally based interpreters were used in interviewing parents whose first language was not English. The research team spent time with the interpreter before the interview familiarising her with the research schedules. After the interview the interpreter and research team member spent time checking the accuracy and meaning of any qualitative comments.

After seeking permission, all interviews with parents, carers and children were tape-recorded. It was important to impress upon parents and children that they could have the tape recorder turned off at any time. After the interview was completed parents and children were given the opportunity to listen to as much of the tape as they wished. Many of the children were much amused by the sound of their voice: 'It was like being on the radio.'

The research interviews were not without incident, some amusing. There was one occasion where two members of the team were happily interviewing the parents when there was a knock at the door and in walked a woman police constable and a social worker from the child protection enquiry team. The research team offered to depart but were firmly invited by both parents to stay. Some heated exchanges took place in the kitchen between the mother and the visitors for about ten minutes, after which the child protection team departed. The family reassured the research team, which was somewhat bemused, that this was a fairly frequent occurrence, related to the finding of bruises at school on the eldest child. It was a nuisance but a fact of life that the visits occurred from time to time. Nothing resulted from them and more importantly, no help was given to the family who had much to say in the rest of the interview about the difference between the family support workers and the child protection workers!

A second incident caused the research team to reflect on the value of team members' past history as very experienced child care social workers, taught not to panic in strange circumstances. Arriving to interview a mother, the researcher was greeted by her at the door carrying a baby: 'Just look after the baby and the others will you while I go to get my giro.' Before the researcher could draw breath, the baby was deposited in her arms and Mum disappeared for twenty minutes only to reappear with a packet of tea bags and milk. 'Now I can give you a drink and we can talk'. The relieved researcher, whose child care and play skills had been well tested, was more than eager to comply with the parent's wishes.

Interviewing children: issues

As discussed earlier, parents gave their informed consent to participate in the study, having been given two opportunities to opt out. By contrast, the research team was aware that children agreed to be involved without really knowing what they were agreeing to. Young children would not be able to understand the implications of the research but did give agreement to take part in the study. In seeking children's assent the research team was aware that, while it is possible to match adults for social characteristics, the disparity of age when interviewing children cannot be overcome (see Mahon et al. 1996).

When seeking children's agreement, the research team emphasised the limits to confidentiality, discussed by Morrow and Richards (1996). Children were assured that information given to the research team would be kept confidential but at the same time it was made clear that they were free to share with their parents and others what had taken place. The research team was helped in interviews by the fact that it had acquired many skills in talking to children through many years of working professionally in social work with children.

There was awareness of the importance of talking to children in private. Children may conceal some of their feelings from parents because they do not wish to hurt them. Parents were aware that children might have a different perspective on the service and in all but one case parents were happy to arrange for the child to be seen in private.

The factors that influenced the interviews with children were similar to those with adults. It was important to establish a rapport, and in this the research was helped by the fact that most children were in the house while their parents were being interviewed. Thus they became familiar with the interviewer and also saw that the researcher was accepted by the parents. This had a normalising effect on the situation. Children were always seen on a second occasion and parents were urged to contact the research team if they or the children had any misgivings about the interview. In fact, there were no refusals.

Great effort was put into preparing for children's interviews using the skills of the research team to develop scene-setting explanations for children which took account of their cognitive development and linguistic ability.

Although an interview schedule could be used with older children, the research team developed a number of methods drawn from direct work with small children to gather information from young children. These included games, play materials and glove puppets. All of the children over five were interviewed, and three of the younger ones. The decision to interview children or to use play techniques was made in consultation with parents.

Throughout the interviews, researchers were very concerned not to lead children and to empower them not to feel inadequate if they could not answer a question. In addition, the team was highly sensitive to points when children were uneasy about answering a particular question and reassured them that it was perfectly acceptable to do so. The team also gave children opportunities to end the interview at any point, a facility taken up by five children. On these occasions researchers empowered children to curtail the interview and negotiate its continuation at a later time. The careful approach to children helped to ensure a 100% response rate.

Pen picture of the family

To add a further context to the interviews, the research team wrote up a short pen picture of the family and their home at the end of the interview. This helped the researchers to recall families at the analysis stage and was especially useful in developing profiles and typologies of families and their problems.

Tests

Two standardised tests were used, one with parents and one with children, to serve as outcome measures.

Psychometric data from parents: Levinson's tri-dimensional locus of control test Parents completed a psychometric test at both the interview stages, aimed at estimating where they perceived the predominant influences which shaped and controlled their lives to lie. The test used was an adapted form of Levinson's tri-dimensional locus of control.

The hypothesis underlying the Levinson's tri-dimensional locus of control test is that control in the lives of individuals is experienced predominantly in one of three ways:

- ♦   in the self as the main agent of control – described as *internal*;

- ♦   in other people, either as individuals or as organisations – described as *powerful others*; or

- ♦   it is assumed to be due to random, and largely uncontrollable factors – described as *chance*.

It is anticipated that the dominant way of perceiving where control lies in each individual's life will strongly influence that person's view of their life and the capacity to influence its course, and hence their characteristic behaviour in dealing with life.

The literature on stress and strategies of coping indicates that beliefs about locus of control can influence all aspects of a person's life (Beresford 1994), and that an internal locus of control is associated with greater resilience and adaptability in the face of stress. When the locus of control is felt to be outside the self, an individual feels less confidence in influencing living circumstances. In general, Beresford points out, related research finds a positive association between an internal locus of control and measures of parental adjustment or well-being. Beresford stresses that the relationship is a complex one, but observes that people with a sense of control in their lives are more likely to make use of resources available to them.

While it is the overall trends which are useful in describing the group, and the perception of each parent at a particular point in the intervention, the more detailed breakdown of the score is useful in looking at movement within the perception of individual parents over the intervention period.

The Kovacs children's depression inventory The psychological well-being of the children was measured at the beginning and end points of the study using the Kovacs children's depression inventory. The test is a well-validated and reliable instrument which has been developed and used extensively with normal child populations, children attending for treatment of mental health problems and in studies of child protection.

The test is a self-rating instrument which has proved a reliable measure of affective disorder in childhood and adolescence. The test is standardised for children aged 8–13 years and was therefore applicable only to this age group. Where there was uncertainty concerning the child's ability to read the test items, this was done by the researcher. Inclusion of the test was important to allow a comparison to be made with other children who had been referred for enquiries because of suspected child abuse (see Farmer and Owen 1995; Sharland et al. 1996).

It is important to stress that the test is an indication of depressive disorder, and not a precise diagnostic instrument. For example, a study which explored the relationship between childhood depression as measured by the Kovacs inventory and academic performance concluded that there was no direct association between the two, so that depressed children might be functioning adequately in other areas of their lives (Fundudis et al. 1979).

Information on the child schedules

Developmental data about the children gathered from their parents formed the study's 'Information on the Child' questionnaires. These were based on the Department of Health's Assessment and Action records for looked-after children. The aim of these was:

> to provide a method of assessment that covered all those milestones in growing up which are informally monitored and promoted by 'reasonable' parents. (Ward 1995)

The Assessment and Action Records were developed to help plan for the needs of children 'looked after' by the local authority (see Parker et al. 1991; Ward 1995). The version used in this study was the prototype designed by Parker and colleagues. This has been developed and tested widely by Ward (Ward 1995) and is now being used substantially by local authorities in the UK and by social work agencies in at least 13 other countries.

Seven developmental dimensions were identified in the prototype: health, education, identity, family and social relationships, social presentation, emotional and behavioural development and self-care skills. Key questions were selected from the Assessment and Action Records, after consultation and piloting with a group of families using a play group in the community and families using an 'open' family centre. As in the original format, age-related versions of the schedule were prepared.

The questionnaires in the short-term accommodation study were answered by the children's parents.

Payment of families

To emphasise the business nature of the research interviews and to make a tangible gesture of appreciation to parents and children, parents received a small payment at the end of the second interview. Children were given pencils on this occasion.

Feedback to families and agencies

The research team provided regular feedback to social workers on the progress and shared with them some of the preliminary findings. A newsletter was sent to families three months after the first round of interviews had taken place to report on progress and remind them that the research team would be contacting them again. Social workers also received copies of the newsletter.

Managing the data

It had been suggested by the Department of Health at the commissioning stage that the study should not see itself as evaluative but rather as exploratory since new legislation was under scrutiny. This enabled the research team to use a combination of quantitative and qualitative data.

The qualitative data were used in several ways:

1   It was used in conjunction with the quantitative data from the questionnaires and tests. In this respect the quantitative data created a basis on which to test the reliability of the qualitative comments (Bullock, Little and Millham 1993; Cleaver and Freeman 1995).

2   Comments from parents illuminating the findings of the standardised tests provided concrete examples from everyday life, for example, to give meaning to parents' degree of control over their lives in the Levinson test.

3   Using both quantitative and qualitative data provided a richer and more reliable basis from which to develop theories, concepts and typologies. The process of developing typologies was similar to that used by Cleaver and Freeman (1995), developed from Loftland (1971). It involved the following stages:

     ♦   considering how a problem is dealt with by the subject under study;

     ♦   constructing the typologies, allowing for modification as the study progressed from stage one to stage two;

     ♦   looking at whether the typologies would apply to different situations of both families and family support social work; and

     ♦   refining the concepts and typologies through consultation with research respondents and other researchers.

The coherence of the study, in that it was rooted in testing the application of legislation in practice, helped to anchor the findings conceptually. The research team was constantly aware of the fact that it was testing the hypothesis that, under the Children Act 1989, family support intervention could and should be used to help prevent family breakdown. Further, the concepts of parental responsibility, consultation and partnership informed the development of a typology of social work processes designed to achieve this aim.

The comparison of parents, child, carer and social worker on certain dimensions also helped in two ways:

1   by showing the degree of congruence between the professionals and the users of services on important theoretical dimensions; and

2   by testing the veracity of Children Act theory.

The validity of data is always a problem especially when attitudinal data are sought. The emphasis on a prospective approach helped to overcome problems of using retrospective data identified by Quinton and Rutter (1988).

Quantitative data were analysed using standard statistical packages. The service of an NHS statistician was enlisted in help with the quantitative analysis. She also validated the Levinson and Kovacs tests. Together with her help, the research team decided which dimensions leant themselves to quantitative analysis. One of the unexpected problems was the homogeneity of the sample of families. This had not been anticipated because four geographically diverse research sites were being used. Although this limited the complexity of statistical analysis, it did help to reinforce both the reliability and validity of the data across the areas.

Finally, the study makes no apology for a heavy emphasis on the perspectives of parents and children. As users of the service, they have much to contribute to the refining and development of services from their observations of the fit between agency activity and the meeting of their needs. Similarly, carers' views are also pertinent to service development. Indeed, recognition of the importance of users' views in research greatly influenced the evolution of the Children Act 1989 itself (see DHSS 1985b). To preserve the anonymity of families and children throughout this study the names have been changed.

Summary

This study aims to explore the use of short-term accommodation as a family support service to help prevent long-term family breakdown. It studies the service from the perspectives of all those involved in it – social workers, carers, parents and children – and explores the implementation of Children Act law and theory.

The study is intensive, tracing the progress of 60 children and their families who were recruited sequentially to the study in the four agencies. There was an excellent response rate. Data were gathered at two points: from children, parents and social workers just before the service commenced, and from children, parents, social workers and carers at a point either when the service had ended or no later than nine months from its start.

Families were representative of those using the service in the areas studied but, because of the limitations of agency records and the complexities surrounding the development of a new service, the study was not set in a wider extensive sample. Rather, it confined itself to an exploration of the meaning of short-term accommodation for the families using the services and the social workers and carers providing it.

Both quantitative and qualitative data were used to explore the process and outcome of the service for all concerned. Qualitative analysis was used to support quantitative findings using theory, concepts and typologies developed during the study.

3 *Family matters*

Introduction

Before exploring the impact of the short-term accommodation service on families, it is important to locate the families using the service in this study within a general context.

The Children Act emphasises two important factors in relation to family support:

- the 'new concept of parental responsibility'; and

- 'the local authorities' duty to give support for children and their families'. (DoH 1989, p. 1)

To these are added the principles of the normality of problems and the reasonableness of all families turning to the state for help at some time.

However, although it may be normal for all families to have problems some may be more susceptible to family breakdown. As Utting (1995) points out:

> Family life does not exist in a social vacuum. Nor can parenting be considered in isolation from the many social, economic and environmental influences to which families are exposed. (p. 32)

This is a factor to be accounted for seriously when local authorities attempt to identify children in need in their area. That need does not exist in a social vacuum either, but is related to the circumstances in which children grow up and the way in which their parents are able to exercise their responsibility to promote children's welfare. Utting further remarks that this is not the whole story:

> Interest in the direct responsibilities of individual parents for their children is a valid point of departure for debate. Its weakness is that it can too easily be slanted to avoid considering what responsibilities belong to government or to the wider community. A more balanced discussion needs to take account of the indirect and external influences on family functioning. These range from

questions of public health to wealth and without considering them no realistic understanding of ' family breakdown' or 'parental responsibility' is likely to be achieved.

Quoting Rutter, he goes on to say:

> Good parenting requires certain permitting circumstances. There must be necessary life opportunities and facilities. Where these are lacking even the best parents may find it difficult to exercise their skills. (Utting 1995, pp. 32–5)

Much research has catalogued the characteristics of families whose lack of 'permitting circumstances' has led to family breakdown. This is perhaps the best context for considering the characteristics of the study families whose children were classified by social workers as being in need of services to prevent family breakdown. From Gray and Parr's first study of characteristics of children in care in 1957, through to Packman's seminal study of the 1960s (Packman 1968) and Aldgate's Scottish study in the 1970s (Aldgate 1977), to Bebbington and Miles' study of 2,500 children in care in the 1980s, the picture of families living in a complex matrix of adverse circumstances remains relatively the same. Bebbington and Miles (1989) reported the characteristics of children in care in their sample:

> Only a quarter were living with both parents;
> Almost three-quarters of their families received income support;
> Only one in five lived in owner occupied housing;
> Over one half were living in 'poor' neighbourhoods. (Bebbington and Miles 1989, quoted in DoH 1991c, p. 6)

Bebbington and Miles (1989) discuss the links between family breakdown and certain adverse family circumstances. Their findings are echoed by those of Belsky and Vondra (1989) and Gibbons (1992) who emphasise the stresses and supports in the surrounding environment as important forces likely to influence parental functioning.

There has to date, however, been far less information from research on the characteristics of families who have sought family support help but remained intact. What there is suggests that they may have similar characteristics to the families described by Bebbington and Miles. Packman et al. (1986), for example, found little difference between the circumstances and characteristics of children in and out of care. Aldgate and Heath (1992) found that the families of children living in the community receiving help from social services were on low incomes, had few supports and were living in homes which compared unfavourably with a group of long term foster carers from the same area. Smith (1992) describes a sample of 125 households using family centres as largely unwaged, with 29% of children growing up in a lone family and with 46% of households containing an adult or child with a specified health problem (pp. 10–12). On the positive side, over 80% felt they did have adequate social supports from family or friends unlike the families in Gibbons' two-area study of prevention. Gibbons (1992) found families referred to social services were:

> more likely to be coping alone, to have financial and housing problems, to be lonely, anxious, and depressed and to be burdened by a range of non-financial family problems to do with relationships and health. (p. 27)

There follows a brief outline of the characteristics and social circumstances of families participating in the study. Where relevant, comparisons are made with the findings from other studies.

Households and characteristics

Type of household

The Children Act 1989 recognition of the diversity of family life (DoH 1990) is reflected in the different types of families in this study. Thirty-eight families (62%) were living in households headed by a single parent. Twelve of these were unmarried women and 26 were separated or divorced, of whom 23 were women. The proportion of one-parent families in this study is also considerably more than the national average of one in four but reflects the pattern reported in other studies of similar families seeking social work help (Aldgate and Heath 1992; Gibbons 1992; Smith 1992). It is rather higher than 46% of similar households reported by Packman and Hall (1995) in their study of full-time accommodation. The pattern suggests that, overall, the study families were living in well-established units. The remaining 22 were families who had two carers in the household. Of these 22, 19 were families where both carers were the biological parents of the index child. The remaining three were reconstituted families with one carer being the biological parent. Rather fewer children in this study were living either with both biological parents or in reconstituted families than those in Packman and Hall's study (1995).

The families showed a fairly high degree of stability with two-thirds (41) having been established in their present form for at least two years and 20 of these having been stable for at least five years. Only five families had established themselves in their present form within the last year.

There was some variation in family type within the areas covered by the study, with parents from Midcity living in co-habitation more frequently than in marriage but this seemed related to the fact that often they were younger parents with fewer children.

The stability of families was reflected in the age of the main caring parent. More than three-quarters of parents were in their mid-twenties or older (see also Chapter 6).

The ethnic origins of families

The ethnicity of families was explored with reference to whether households contained one or two parents. Of the 22 two-parent households, there were four with both parents of Asian origin, two where one parent was white and one black and the majority, 16, where both parents were white. Within the 38 lone-parent households, five were black and 33 were white.

This meant that of the 60 study index children, 49 were Caucasian, four were of African-Caribbean origin, four were of Asian origin and three were of dual heritage (African-Caribbean and Caucasian).

The social workers told the research team that the number of minority ethnic families did not reflect the population distribution in their areas, a factor identified in other studies of family support (see Gibbons et al. 1990).

The reasons for low take-up were not clear but social workers were aware of the lack of take-up in minority ethnic families and were consulting with community leaders and families in the area. One problem might have been lack of appropriate publicity. The importance of reaching minority ethnic families appropriately has been highlighted by Amin and Oppenheim (1992) whose research stresses their vulnerability. They suggest that families of Bangladeshi, Caribbean or Pakistani origin do 'face a much higher risk of a life marked by a low income, repeated unemployment, poor health and housing, working for low wages with few employment rights and being . . . [reliant] on social security benefits' and 'for an Afro-Caribbean or Asian woman, the chances of being poor are even greater'. (p. 34)

Household size

Eighty per cent of families had two children or more living in the household. There were eight larger households, of which seven had five children and one had six resident. The number of children in the household was a fair guide to family size. Only five families had children living elsewhere, three who were young adults living independently and two families where children lived permanently with other adults – one with a grandparent and one with foster carers on a care order.

Children in the families

Age and gender of the children

The age banding of the children was based on the criteria used by the Department of Health's Statistical Service (1995b). Figure 3.1 reveals that short-term accommodated children in this study show a rather different profile from children 'looked after' nationally. In terms of who gets services there are clear differences with regard to age. The government's latest national figures show children aged 10–15 account for the largest proportion (43%) of those 'looked after' (DoH 1995b). In contrast, of the study population of 60 children, those aged 5–9 made up over half (31) receiving short-term accommodation. The second largest group (22) were children under 5 years, while children aged 10–15 accounted for 12% of children receiving short-term accommodation. These figures also differ from those in Packman and Hall's (1995) study. They found a larger proportion of teenagers and a smaller proportion of children under five were accommodated full-time. The difference may well reflect agency policies with regard to full-time and short-term accommodation with

Figure 3.1 *Children receiving short-term accommodation by age and gender (n=60)*

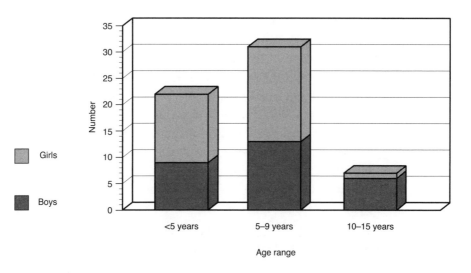

the latter being targeted at families with younger children. This would be consistent with the use of short-term accommodation as part of a strategy to prevent family breakdown.

There were also differences in terms of gender as Figure 3.1 reveals. Slightly more girls (54%) were accommodated short-term than boys, a picture opposite to that found for children 'looked after' where the proportion of boys (53%) was slightly higher (DoH 1995b), and also differing from Packman and Hall's (1995) sample of accommodated children where there was an equal distribution of boys and girls. The prevalence of girls in this study, however, does not apply to children over 10 years: six of the seven children aged 10–15 were boys.

Where the family contained more than one child (48), in only a quarter of cases were all the children offered short-term accommodation. Where only one child in the family was accommodated (36) the greatest influencing factor was the decision made by parent and social worker concerning which child would benefit from the service. For 58% (21) this was the oldest child, suggesting that ordinal position affected which child was accommodated. This was borne out by parents' comments which revealed that often the oldest child was thought to be the one who could cope most easily with being away from home. For the remaining single accommodation cases, 28% were made up of the youngest child and in 12% of cases a middle sibling received the service.

Social circumstances

Income

Families were asked about the level and the source of their income. Table 3.1 represents the amount of money families had available after housing costs had been met. Two-thirds of the families were living on a disposable income of £120 or less per week. Clearly, these figures on their own are meaningless without some context. The Rowntree Foundation's Family Budget Unit calculated that, in 1992, £105 a week was insufficient for a family with two children to live on modestly (Utting 1995). At least half the families in this study were living on the equivalent amount or less, calculated for four individuals in a family. These findings reflect those of Packman and Hall's study, where 'financial difficulties were judged to be a significant issue for more than half the families' (Packman and Hall 1995, p. 61).

Table 3.1 *Family income (n=60)*

Net weekly income	Number	Percentage
Less than £80	11	18
£81–£120	30	50
£121–£150	8	13
£151–£200	6	10
Over £200	5	9

To interpret the meaning of living on a low income, it is useful to refer to Amin and Oppenheim (1992), who describe material disadvantage as:

> a kind of partial citizenship, since the effects of material deprivation make it very difficult to participate in society as a full member . . . this exclusion may be experienced particularly strongly . . . the marginalisation of whole groups of people from mainstream society. (p. 36)

Table 3.2 *Family income according to family type*

Net weekly income	Parents with partners		Parents alone	
	Number	Percentage	Number	Percentage
Less than £80	2	9	9	24
£81–£120	7	32	23	61
£121–£150	4	18	4	10
£151–£200	4	18	2	5
Over £200	5	23	0	0
	(n=22)		*(n=38)*	

As Table 3.2 shows, lone-parent families were considerably worse off than two-parent families, with over 80% of lone parents living on £120 a week or less, mainly accounted for by the fact that only two lone parents were in full-time employment, compared with nine two-parent families. This reflects national trends of the employment patterns of lone parents and the concomitant financial disadvantage pointed out by Utting (1995).

Employment

Table 3.3 shows that over half the families (31) were totally dependent on income support, a finding echoing the 53% in Packman and Hall's (1995)

Table 3.3 *Employment (n=60)*

Employment in families	Number	Percentage
One adult – full-time	11	18
One adult – part-time	13	22
Two adults – full-time	0	0
Two adults – part-time	5	8
Household wholly on income support	31	52

study of full-time accommodation. In 11, just under one-fifth of the families, at least one adult was employed full-time. There were no full-time dual worker families in contrast to the national average of six out of ten (Utting 1995) but in five families both parents worked part-time. Part-time income to supplement income support was earned by 18 families, in five cases by both parents undertaking part-time work. In the remainder one parent had a part-time job. The comments of two parents, a student nurse and a 'lollipop lady', illustrate the importance of work to them despite the considerable difficulties they had in finding work compatible with their home responsibilities:

> My work is hard, but I love it. And I feel like a . . . well, a person! It's going to help us for the future, too. It is complicated, and she [social worker] has been a real help with child-minders and so on.

> I just love to get out of the house. There are times when I just need to see the back of everything – kids, cooking, all the little niggles and moans. Everyone knows me and I get to know all the mums and kids . . . a breath of sanity, really!

Housing

The majority of families, 51, (85%) lived in local authority housing, a higher figure than the 60% of families in Packman and Hall's (1995) study. Only a small number (five) were living in houses they owned, or in privately rented property (four). Scrutiny of the patterns of accommodation across the four study areas showed little difference and patterns of use were similar for each scheme.

Thirty-six families lived in houses, 20 lived in flats and the remaining four in shared accommodation. Compared with families in the study by Bebbington and Miles (1989), the accommodation in this study was good although the material standards of furnishing in two-thirds of the homes was judged by the research team to be rather impoverished.

Health and illness

The association between low income and ill health in both children and parents is well known (see, for example, Bradshaw 1990; Gibbons et al. 1990). Low family income and social class have been found to be factors which adversely affect the well-being of new-born infants, and their subsequent developmental problems (Woodroffe et al. 1993).

Poor physical living circumstances such as run-down, cold or damp housing are associated with the incidence or exacerbation of some chest complaints in both adults and children. Chronic or recurrent upper respiratory complaints are more frequent in children, and these may also affect hearing. Arthritic or rheumatoid conditions are likely to be more troublesome in both adults and children (Platt et al. 1989; Bradshaw 1990; Beresford 1994).

Gibbons (1992) adds a third dimension to this equation – social support. She asserts:

> Adequate social support may have a direct effect on individuals' mental or physical health, so that people lacking support are likely to develop illness. (p. 25).

Gibbons' view is reinforced by the literature on health and social inequalities which shows an interaction between physical and social components of ill health or sickness (see, for example, Kumar 1993).

To explore the prevalence of health problems in the study families, parents (main carers) were asked to self-report on significant health problems. While these perceptions were not verified by others, the perceptions themselves give a profile of how healthy families perceived themselves to be and are valid in their own right. When parents were asked about their health, 26 (44%) said that some form of chronic illness had been diagnosed in the last year. This definition covered chest, intestinal and skin problems as well as recurrent mental health problems. Twenty-two parents (37%) had been in hospital for treatment within the last five years (excluding childbirth). Some of these hospital stays were related to the fact that 17 parents (28%) had been diagnosed and treated within the last year for some acute illness, for example, kidney or heart problems. In addition to these diagnosed illnesses, 36 parents (60%) felt that stress had exacerbated their illness at some point.

Partners also suffered ill health with 13 of the 22 partners diagnosed with chronic illness, 11 having been in hospital and five having experienced acute illness. In 13 cases, partners' illness was thought to be exacerbated by stress.

There was, therefore, a high incidence of health problems in families, which reflects findings from other studies on the association between living circumstances, stress and health. The short-term accommodation families also resembled those of children accommodated full-term with respect to ill health where Packman and Hall (1995) reported:

> parental ill health and in particular mental ill health were a key problem in half of all cases and the vulnerability of mothers was of great significance. (p. 62)

Family support systems

There is a considerable body of literature and research on the definition and value of social support which it is beyond the scope of this study to enter into in detail (see for example, Wilcox and Vernberg 1985; Barrerra 1986; Argyle 1992). The research of Gibbons et al. (1990) and Gibbons (1992) on families receiving preventive social services help is especially relevant to the current study in drawing attention to the importance of family and community support systems as a buffer against adversity and both from within and without the family. Gibbons (1992), for example, believes:

> It is reasonable to suppose that families in need who are linked with sources of support in the community will be more able to overcome difficulties than families lacking support. (p. 25)

Gibbon's study looked at who families turned to for support, and drawing from Caplan (1974), used the definition of a 'supporter' as someone who may offer 'supplies of money, materials, tools, skills and cognitive guidance' which may help that person to deal or cope better with life and its difficulties' (Gibbons 1990 p. 112). This definition is developed further by Wilcox and Vernberg (1985) who talk of behaviour that 'helps the person cope with difficulties and develop new competencies' (p. 5). Clearly, the potential for the development of new competencies through social work intervention has relevance for this study.

There seems to be general agreement in the literature that social support may broadly be divided into practical and emotional support (see, for example, Wilcox and Vernberg 1985; Gibbons et al. 1990). In this study, *practical support* was described as ' advice or information and/or help with minding the children, shopping, housework, or providing transport'. *Emotional support* was described as 'having someone you feel accepts you and you can trust to talk to about your concerns and worries'.

Child care arrangements in families

In order to set the context for exploring social support with the study families, index parents and, where present in the household, their partners were asked which adults held responsibility for the day-to-day care of their children. In all families only biological parents were perceived as main carers; in 58 families this was the mother, and in two the father. No families divided care jointly between two adults. Families' views are represented by two lone parents and the mother in a two-parent family:

> I am the one who looks after them . . . all the usual things, clothes and food and school. Their dad helps . . . Yes. He comes most weekends to see them and they like that . . . playing, going out sometimes. And he helps with big things . . . coats and shoes sometimes.

> It's difficult for me on my own since the wife left. I had to learn a lot – how to use the washing machine for one thing.

> I'm the mum, so I take charge of all the everyday things. He is at work [part-time factory worker] and then he has other things to sort. I could do with a bit more help.

Fourteen of the 22 families (64%) where partners were in the household said their partners offered some aspects of material, practical and emotional support. In addition two mothers said their ex-spouses contributed practically to the care of the children.

In the remaining 38 families headed by lone parents, only 12 said they received material, practical or emotional support from their ex-partners.

Families tended to stereotype roles by gender. Women expected little support from partners in either a practical or an emotional way, whether they were the biological fathers of their children or not:

> Terry wouldn't help . . . he wouldn't know how to!

Extended family and community support systems

There is a wide definition of what constitutes the family in the Children Act, and includes extended family members as well as the immediate nuclear family (see DoH 1989). With this in mind, the study sought to explore the role of extended kin in supporting parents.

Proximity of family was an obvious starting point. Two-thirds of the families (67%) lived within five miles of their relatives. Eleven lived within ten miles and of the remaining seven who had relatives, only two lived further than might quite easily be reached for a day visit using public transport. Distance itself is, of course, not an accurate indicator of accessibility. Parents did indicate that most of their relatives within five miles could be reached either on foot or by public transport within half an hour.

Alongside relatives, Gibbons (1992) believes that the use of other supports in the community can do much to buffer families against adversity. Accordingly, parents were asked to indicate what sources of practical and emotional support were available to them regularly (defined as at least monthly).

Table 3.4 Sources of regular practical support (n=60*)

Source	Number	Percentage
Relatives	21	35
Friends	29	49
Neighbours	19	32
Family centre	11	19
Child-minder	8	14
Primary health care team	13	22

*Categories are not mutually exclusive

Table 3.4 shows that, despite the fact that relatives lived within fairly close proximity, only just over one-third of parents (21) used relatives for regular practical support. (It is difficult to make direct comparisons with families in Packman and Hall's (1995) study because of differences in measuring support but the findings do seem comparable.) A similar proportion of families in this study (32%) turned to neighbours for support. By contrast, friends were the most frequent source of practical support depended upon by nearly half the families (29).

There was some dependence upon practical support from commonly used professional sources, much of it universally available to all families in the community. Family centres and child-minders helped by giving some assistance with looking after the children. Finally, over one-fifth of families (13) relied on primary health care workers, principally health visitors. Parents defined the advisory and liaison role of the health visitor as a 'practical' help, rather than an 'emotional support' because their advice related directly to the care and management of children:

> If I am stuck with what to do about James being naughty or when he is ill,
> I always know Mrs Evans [health visitor] will have a sensible suggestion.

In many families practical support was obtained from more than one source. Although families felt fairly well supported in terms of sources they could turn to for some practical help, they made it clear that help from friends, neighbours and relatives was confined to short spells, hours at the most. The day care from child-minders or family centres was greatly appreciated by the minority who used them, but the attraction of the short-term accommodation arrangements was that it would give families a longer breathing space – not simply advice, or the odd hour of baby-sitting.

Emotional support in the community

Gibbons (1992) reflects the view of other researchers in the social support field by suggesting that:

> one of the most powerful kinds of social support in its effects has been shown to be the availability of a close, confiding relationship with another person. (p. 25)

In this study, it was, therefore, not surprising that the absence of emotional support was more keenly felt than a short supply of practical help, particularly among the lone parents:

> After a hard day, when you'd love someone to give you a cup of tea and tell you you're not so bad after all – someone to talk over all those little worries with – and a few big ones! That's when you feel it.

Table 3.5 shows the sources of regular emotional support.

Table 3.5 *Sources of regular emotional support (n=60*)*

Source	Number	Percentage
Relatives	22	37
Friends	33	55
Neighbours	23	39
Family centre	9	13
Child-minder	3	5
Primary health care team	17	29

* Categories are not mutually exclusive

As with practical support, only just over one-third of the parents (22) felt they had an emotionally supportive relationship with their relatives. Friends were turned to in over half the families (33) and, to a lesser extent, neighbours (23). Family centres and child-minders were primarily seen as offering practical support. But the primary health care team, both general practitioners and health visitors, provided emotional support to over a quarter (17) of parents.

The extent to which the primary health care team was turned to for practical help and emotional support may be partly due to the fact that this resource is universally available and one of the few community resources to which there is relatively easy, unrestricted access – particularly for families with children. The general practitioner may also be the first port of call for emotional distress for both the men and women. Studies of men under stress in divorce, for example Ambrose et al. (1983), have described the important de-stigmatising role of the general practitioner in providing someone to whom men may turn to discuss their feelings, while studies of women under stress report a similar role for the general practitioner. The universal role of the health visitor is clearly important here for families with young children.

Using social services

In theory, social services should be part of the 'enabling authority' (Hardiker et al. 1996), a personal social service to which families can turn in times of difficulties. However, it has been suggested that dependence on social services is an indicator of serious need (Dartington Social Research Unit 1996). Recent research on families involved in child protection enquiries reinforced this view. Cleaver and Freeman (1995), for example, found the majority of cases in their sample had been known to social services for over two years.

However, it is important to disaggregate the different types of interventions offered by social services. Dependence on support services may not necessarily be negative. The continuing use of family support services may prevent the need for more intrusive interventions at a later stage (see Hardiker et al. 1996). In this study, for example, while three-fifths of families had been known to social services for over two years, only a minority (six) had come under suspicion for abuse while a further four had children who had been taken into care or adopted. In contrast, just over one-quarter of the families (16) had first used social services within the last six months, ten of these being new service users.

What is significant is that the majority of the families in this study, irrespective of whether or not they had a history of contact with social services, were about to receive social work help which could be classed as 'family support' rather than 'child protection enquiries'.

Summary

Families in the study were representative of those in other studies of children looked after.

The families represented a diversity of arrangements but it was striking that over three-fifths of families were living in a household headed by a lone or single parent.

Family units had a high degree of stability, with two-thirds established in their current households for over two years.

Black families were under-represented even though three of the four study areas were in multi-racial locations.

Short-term accommodation presented children with a different profile from those accommodated full-time. The children in this study were younger, possibly reflecting agency policies to target young families. More girls than boys were accommodated short-term in contrast to full-time accommodation.

The families' social circumstances revealed them to being living mainly in local authority housing on very low incomes, with over half solely dependent on income support.

There was a high incidence of health problems among the families, ranging from chest and intestinal complaints to mental health problems. Over one-third of parents had been in hospital as an in-patient over the last five years (excluding pregnancies).

Of particular note was the social isolation of families and their lack of emotional and practical support networks. Friends and neighbours provided more support than kin.

Families used public services such as child-minding and family centres as sources of support. Community health practitioners were also an important source of help.

There was evidence of positive dependence on social services. Three-fifths of families had previous contact with social services but the majority of these had been in contact with social services for family support rather than child protection enquiries.

4 Expectations and outcomes

Introduction

In trying to make sense of any social work service, it is essential to consider the question of the aims and outcomes of that service. A clear sense of what the service aims to achieve helps planning and inspires confidence in users of the service. What 'problems' will be addressed? For whom? How far are aims shared between the givers and receivers of services? Thoburn et al., for example, have suggested that families are more likely to be responsive to intervention in child protection work when they have a shared agenda with social workers (Thoburn et al. 1995). Common expectations at the outset and a shared agenda for action are also components of the Children Act's philosophy of partnership. When children are to be accommodated, *Guidance and Regulations* specifies the translation of expectations are into a written child care plan, which makes it clear what the expectations are of the service on offer and the anticipated participation of individuals to effect a favourable outcome.

Much has been written about the nature of services, and how the agenda for social work action should be developed. Services which seem to be offered more for the benefit of the providers than the users have been heavily criticised (see DHSS 1985b). It has been argued that the development of services should be led by potential users of those services (Webb and Aldgate 1990). A synergy between user and social work aims, expectations and evaluation of outcomes is clearly to be the goal of a service which enhances parental responsibility.

Another important aspect of efficient service delivery from the social worker's point of view is the extent to which the likely outcome of the service can be predicted and evaluated. How will changes be evident? What will be the actual experience in people's lives that reflect these changes? How will service providers, managers and practitioners know what the links have been between 'input' and 'output'? Yet, as Parker et al. (1991) suggest, the increasingly pressing need for thoughtful and apposite assessment of outcome in social work is a fairly recent phenomenon.

When the child care services were first established, few doubts were expressed about the appropriateness of social work interventions and the question of outcomes did not arise. Recently, research into modern social conditions, the emergence of theories about prevention, the weakening of confidence in the public care of children following a number of well-documented tragedies, the attention given to consumer views and the emphasis on cost-effectiveness have all served to produce a climate in which the development of reliable means of assessing outcome is increasingly seen as a necessity.

Assessing outcomes is, however, a complex matter. As Parker et al. (1991) suggest there are at least five kinds of outcomes in child care that reflect different perspectives and interests. These are:

- public outcomes;
- service outcomes;
- professional outcomes;
- family outcomes; and
- child outcomes.

Parker et al. (1991) begin by describing how powerfully public expectations influence what will be offered to children and families in need. This is 'the broad political framework from which the evaluation of child care cannot be divorced'. They suggest that service outcomes – often presented in terms of numbers of referrals and rates of referral – though important, can be misleading if not clearly set in the context of salient demographic features relating to families, localities and service provision. They then talk of professional outcomes as a 'reflection of professional interventions' or the tool with which social workers evaluate the effect of the work done with and for their clients. They go on to discuss family outcomes and raise the question of difficulty in selecting appropriate measures of change for individual families, according to input and aims, and the varying influence of intervention on individual family members. They conclude with a consideration of outcomes for individual children, and stress the importance of working from the child's perspective on the changes, costs and benefits of an intervention.

Analysing the gains and losses from any intervention is fraught with problems. Human perceptions may not always reflect observed changes in problems or behaviours. Who is to say that an outcome is less valid when an individual feels better at the end of any intervention but there is no measurable change, compared with cases where measurable change occurs but the individual fails to feel the benefit?

Additionally, measuring outcomes in social work is a muddy business. It is impossible to know categorically whether a specific intervention has brought about change or whether an individual is feeling better because of, say, a positive life event. Administering social work is not the same as administering a pill, where the effects can be clearly tracked.

These complexities notwithstanding, this study is concerned with the last three definitions of outcome as defined by Parker et al.: outcome as experienced by the users of the service, both parents and children, and outcome as perceived by the 'direct' providers of those services, carers and social workers.

The protagonists

There were four main protagonists involved in the exploration of expectations and outcomes in short-term accommodation:

1   parents;

2   children;

3   social workers; and

4   carers.

This chapter explores the expectations and outcomes of short-term accommodation from the perspective of parents. Chapters 5 and 8 explore the contribution of social workers and carers to the service and their impact on both service outcomes and user outcomes. Chapter 9 deals with the expectations, processes and outcomes for the children.

To provide data for the task of investigating expectations and outcomes, parents, children, carers and social workers were interviewed as soon as possible after the joint work of planning and setting up the arrangements had begun. All participants were re-interviewed either when the arrangements finished or within nine months of the start of the arrangements (see Chapter 2).

Measuring parental expectations and outcomes

From the first phase of the study it was quite clear that parents saw the short-term accommodation service firmly embedded in family support services. Thus, one of the important aspects of exploring expectations and outcomes was to see what families thought the service might offer in order to prevent family breakdown. There are three dimensions to the exploration of expectations and outcomes for parents:

1   A baseline for looking at change was to gain from families a profile of the problems they thought might be addressed by social work intervention.

2   Clearly, families who approach social workers for help are under stress. The fact that they need to turn to the state for help instead of finding this within their own families and communities is in itself evidence of their difficulties. Crisis intervention theory, for example, suggests that when individuals are under stress they may not be functioning at their optimal level and may feel that, to a greater or lesser extent, their lives are out of control (see Compton and Galloway 1989).

    To provide a second baseline from which to examine outcomes for parents, it was decided to use a psychometric measure of parents' sense of locus of control which would be supplemented by details of life events prior to the intervention and during or after the arrangements that were felt to be significant by the parents. This test could be used alongside parents' perceptions of their problems.

3   A third dimension for measuring parental outcomes was to ask parents what they expected from the service, what changes might occur in their families and what reservations and fears they had about approaching social services. At the end of the arrangements parents were re-visited to explore perceived short-term and long-term gains and unfulfilled expectations.

Profile of family problems

A starting point for exploring the impact of short-term accommodation on families was to elicit from them details of their current problems.

As suggested in the last chapter, the study families were living in circumstances of considerable stress. It was therefore hardly surprising that the problems which had brought them to seek help from social services reflected those circumstances and the impact of those stresses on parents' personal relationships with children and partners, and extended kin. The original data were collected in the form of a five-point scale for each variable. Where problems were cited by parents, they were given the ranking of severe or very severe in over 80% of cases. As a result of this clustering of severity and the small size of the sample, we were advised to collapse the table to a simple

Figure 4.1 *Severe problems identified at first interview (n=60*)*

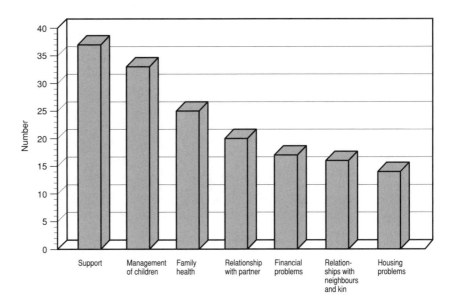

*Categories are not mutually exclusive

dichotomy between problems rated by parents as at a high level of severity or above, and the rest. Figure 4.1 outlines the problems rated as severe by parents at the beginning of the study.

The last chapter gave a profile of the two-thirds of study families having some difficulties related to social isolation. Not surprisingly, absence of support was therefore the most frequent problem which had brought families to social services, rated by over half the families as a severe problem. The essence of lack of support is summed up by one mother:

> I think my biggest worry is not having anyone I can rely on to help. The kids aren't any worse than any others – sometimes they're better! But we get worn down – worrying and fretting.

The second problem was management of children, identified as a serious problem by over half the parents. It must be stressed that the emphasis here was very much on management of children, which parents related to a lack of support rather than seeing the problem as child centred. The state of the family's health was a cause of serious concern for two-fifths of parents. Relationships with partners was on the agenda for just under one-third of families. Of the 23 families who were living in two-parent households, 18 of these had problems with their partners. Moreover, 12 families had difficulties with kin or neighbours with whom they had fallen out; thus, previous offers of support were now not available.

At this stage of the study few parents (27%) felt dissatisfied with their financial situation, this despite the fact that 95% were living on benefits. Many families at the beginning of the study seemed to accept their poverty as inevitable:

> It's a fact of life. I don't think there's much I can do about it . . . not at the moment. It's bad enough without worrying about what you can't do anything about.

Finally, housing was a problem for just under one-fifth of families. These cases were evenly distributed between the four local authority areas. In 11 of these 13 families, parents said that lack of space exacerbated problems of child management.

In control of their lives?

The Levinson test of locus of control explores perceptions of being in control. As outlined in Chapter 2, the hypothesis underlying the Levinson's tri-dimensional locus of control test is that control in the lives of individuals is experienced predominantly in one of three ways:

- ◆ in the self as the main agent of control – described as *internal;*

- ◆ in other people, either as individuals or as organisations – described as *powerful others;* or

- ◆ it is assumed to be due to random, and largely uncontrollable factors – described as *chance.*

It is anticipated that the dominant way of perceiving where control lies in each individual's life will strongly influence that person's view of their life and their capacity to influence its course, and hence their characteristic behaviour in dealing with life (see Table 4.1).

The findings from this test at the point of the first interview are noteworthy. Over half the parents felt in control of their actions at this point. A further 11 attributed the source of control to others. Only a quarter felt their lives were governed solely by chance events. The results suggest that at this point parents had considerable inner strengths and potential to change their approach to their problems. Whether they actually did so will now be discussed.

Table 4.1 *First locus of control score (n=60)*

Perceived control source	Number of cases	Percentage
Internal strong	27	44
Internal moderate	7	12
Internal basic	0	0
Powerful others strong	9	14
Powerful others moderate	2	4
Powerful others basic	0	0
Chance strong	12	20
Chance moderate	3	6
Chance basic	0	0

Expectations of short-term accommodation

Immediate benefits

In spite of the fact that well over half the parents felt that the control of their lives was mainly within their own hands and minds, the parents were experiencing major stresses from a range of sources. In these harassed circumstances, the anticipation of some temporary relief from looking after children was to parents almost the promise of paradise. Parents developed expectations about how they might use the service. These expectations were, however, not ambitious but very straightforward and simple. Parents anticipated that they would use the time in three ways – to rest, to reflect and to begin to address their problems.

Although at this early stage the service did seem to parents to be primarily to relieve their stress, their responsibility towards their children was generally impressive. Nearly all parents emphasised to the research team that if the time away from their children was going to be useful for them this had to be set in the context of knowing and being reassured that any benefits of the service to them would not be at the expense of their children. Figure 4.2 shows the distribution of parents' hopes and wishes in respect of how they might use the time away from their children, at the start of the arrangements.

Figure 4.2 ranks the expectations according to popularity and shows the range of hopes and expectations which parents had. Some parents had several expectations and most gave two.

Figure 4.2 *Expectations of short-term accommodation (n=60*)*

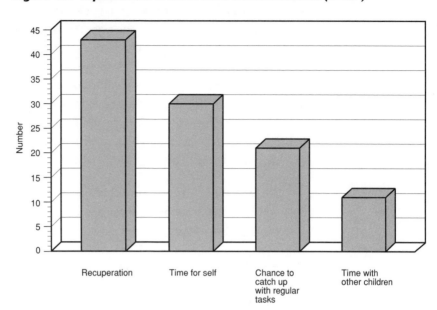

*Categories are not mutually exclusive

Recuperation Given the stresses many parents were under in the management of children, it was hardly surprising to find that almost three-quarters of parents hoped that the accommodation arrangements would give them respite from the full-time care of their children, a 'breathing space'; time to recuperate from the demands and responsibilities of child care:

> What you long for is the chance to put your feet up . . . go out for a drink, shop . . . or window shop! You want to flop . . . to feel like a human being, as much as a 'mum'. If that's possible, and they're having a nice time . . . it would make a lot of difference, I think.

Another parent, who had suffered from a long period of depression, valued the time to recuperate:

> What I think it would do is give me time to think. I know that sounds funny – especially since I have kept it together . . . but I could now use some time to think about things . . . for me and for the kids. Feeling a bit better . . . I think, well I've got a chance . . . you've got to think.

Time for self Half the parents hoped for time for themselves which they would use constructively to address longer-term personal needs:

> What do I hope for by having respite for the kids? What don't I hope for! Meet people . . . maybe Mr Right, but especially friends. Seriously, though . . . a bath, do my hair, watch a late night film without nodding off after ten minutes . . . you could say I hope for a bit of life.

Some parents hoped the breaks would allow them an opportunity to go away. Parents were not thinking of weekends in hotels – but more that they could take the opportunity to visit friends and family, and stay longer than usually possible when they had their children with them or had to return to take care of children at home. This reflected parents' feelings of isolation:

> I'd like to be able to visit Sue [friend] and really relax – even stay over. Maybe you shouldn't, but sometimes you just long to think entirely of yourself . . . what you want, what you need . . . no rushing here and rushing there.

Two parents had other hopes – one mother was a student nurse and hoped to have time to catch up with her studies. The other was the father of three children and he hoped:

> To have time off from being both mum and dad.

The kinds of things that parents hoped to do while their children were staying with carers are on the whole, the sort of self-caring and self-maintaining things that all parents need in order to keep going. What had happened to the study parents was that the balance that most parents strike between their own needs and those of their children had been lost. In many ways the need for respite was similar to that found in studies of families with disabled children (see, for example, Stalker 1989) but the factors that triggered short-term accommodation were more diverse.

Chance to catch up with regular tasks Over one-third of parents hoped the breaks would offer them the chance to catch up with everyday tasks:

> I'm really hoping for the chance to catch up with myself . . . there's always a million things that need doing . . . that pile of ironing, for example . . . never gets any smaller! But really it is the time to think straight that'll be good.

Time with other children Finally, twelve parents hoped the service would give them time to spend with their other children:

> With the younger ones going to Mrs Smith, it'll give me some time to spend with Sam . . . she's a good kid, a real help . . . but they still need their mum, don't they? Then we get a take-away . . . no cooking . . . and we settle in.

Figure 4.3 *Hoped-for long-term benefits of service at first interview (n=60*)*

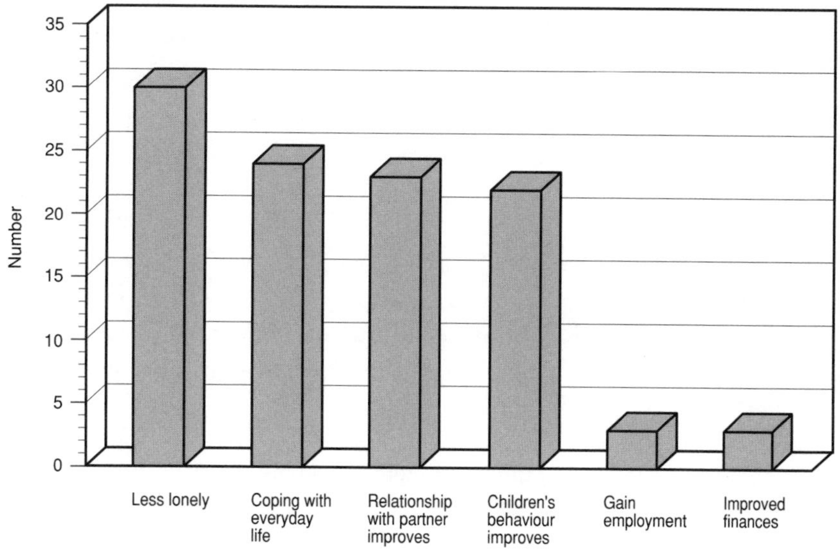

*Categories are not mutually exclusive

Longer-term benefits

Turning to the potential of longer term benefits, Figure 4.3 shows parents' wishes were closely related to the current stresses.

Less lonely Once again, social isolation was highest on the list. Several parents spoke of their hope that the time spent away from their children would lead to new friendships. Five or six also hoped that grandparents and other relatives could be persuaded to visit more often:

> I sometimes feel I'm that woman in the film who talks to the wall [*Shirley Valentine*]. I never see anyone for days. I shouldn't think I'd have the chance of a romantic holiday but I hope that the break will let me get out of the house and meet new people.

> I never see my mum. I fell out with her over him [partner]. It's silly really, my sister is just up the road but I never see her. One thing I'm going to do is go to see them.

Coping with everyday life Many parents felt overwhelmed by the stresses and demands of everyday life. However, many felt that the period of recuperation would allow them to gather strength and cope better. By contrast with those who felt isolated, there were some single mothers who felt put upon by a constant stream of demanding friends:

> I'm sure the break will make me feel better. If I'm less tired things won't get on top of me so easily. I think we'll all get on better.

> 'There always seems to be an extra body sleeping on the sofa. If only I felt stronger. I'd be able to say no – get out, but I haven't strength to argue, so I give in. Things just get worse. It's not that I don't like them but I just can't cope.

Relationship with partner improves If they were feeling better about life, parents thought that there would be a positive 'knock-on' effect on their relationship with partners:

> If he gets more of my time, we won't argue so much and it will be easier all round.

Children's behaviour improves Over one-third of parents anticipated better behaviour from their children. This would occur for several reasons: parents would feel more in control, carers might have 'sorted them out' and children might appreciate parents more after a spell away from home:

> It will do them good to go away and see they can't get their own way all the time. Then they will appreciate us more.

> What Jason needs is a dad. He needs a man to tell him off. He just runs rings round me. I can't get him to do anything for me. Paul [carer] is strict. He'll sort him out.

Gain employment There were two parents who wanted to have time to look for a job and one who wanted to finish her training. All three hoped that at the end of the breaks they would have realised their ambitions:

> If I can get the time to look for a job, I think I can get a part-time one to fit in with school. It was great when I was in the factory. Pity they closed. Life was more fun when you had a laugh with the girls.

> I know I can get a job if I can get my qualification. Everyone needs nurses. I feel I have a lot to offer.

Improved finances Apart from raising self-esteem through being employed, one realistic outcome of being in the labour market for two parents was to improve their income. What was surprising was that in spite of the fact that the majority of parents in the study were living in financial hardship, only two parents looked for an improvement in their finances as a result of having time way from their children:

> I must get more money. The kids deserve better. It breaks my heart when the kids want something and I can't give it to them.

As the quotes show, parents' aspirations were very normal. They looked for a level of family support which many would expect in order to achieve the balance between adult needs and being a parent. What was unusual was that these parents needed to turn to the state for help. Not surprisingly, in the light of recent research findings about the concentration of activity on child abuse enquiries (DoH 1995a) and the media representation of social workers as child rescuers, the approach was made with some trepidation.

Reservations and fears about using short-term accommodation

In spite of the fact that parents anticipated positive gains from short-term accommodation, two-thirds of parents had worries about using the service. These were evenly divided between those who had previously used social services and those who were new clients.

Parents' fears fell into three main categories:

1   fear of losing their children;

2   fear that they would be categorised as failed parents; and

3   fear that the intervention would turn their children against them.

Fear of losing their children

Parents were often anxious about 'becoming involved' with social services for fear of losing their children. Many parents felt that the decision to seek help was finally prompted by desperation, even when the need for support had been urgently felt for some time. Two things fuelled parents' anxiety – one was a belief that services for families were in short supply, and that 'you had to be desperate before you qualified for help'; the other was fear that the agency would remove children from home if parents were found to be struggling:

I felt as if they wouldn't even hear me unless I said I'd thumped him . . . and God knows, you feel like it often enough. Not knowing if I should show the best or the worst of it . . . and not knowing what they were thinking.

You wondered if you were actually mad to go there . . . sort of, into the lions' den! I think we both 'pussyfooted' round each other for a while . . . 'what's she really thinking?' in both our minds.

Fear of being categorised as failed parents

Over and above the considerable ambivalence with which parents first viewed the agency, there were frequently great worries about being seen as failed parents. Parents worried that they would be seen as incompetent, uncaring or even bad parents:

I dreaded to think what they thought about me. Couldn't manage . . . selfish . . . shouldn't have them if she can't cope . . . who does she think she is?

Such concerns extended well beyond what the social workers might think. Parents were extremely sensitive to what they thought carers might think of them. In this respect, the parents in this study were not dissimilar from those in earlier studies of full-time accommodation. Aldgate, for example, found that parents of children in care were very anxious about judgemental attitudes from residential and foster carers and that it was a factor influencing both contact and restoration (Aldgate 1980). A similar finding in relation to the loss of contact was found by the Dartington Social Research Unit several years later (Millham et al. 1986). In the current study, the sensitivity is well illustrated by one mother:

I think if she'd given a hint of 'looking down on me', I'd have gone straight home. There she is . . . looking after mine as well as hers . . . getting it right. But she never did, and when I got to know her better . . . she gave me a lot of confidence. And common sense.

Fear that the intervention would turn their children against them

Finally, there was concern for the children. Would they settle, would they behave themselves? Above all, would they turn against their parents for sending them away:

I do worry about Mrs Wright. Her house is so nice, fresh, you know. Tracy is old enough to see the difference. I worry it might turn her against me, make her realise what we don't have.

Influence of previous social work encounters on parents' fears

Another issue influencing parents' perceptions was previous contact with social services. Over two-thirds of families had previous contact with social services as suggested in Chapter 3. The length of time parents had been known to agencies was not found to influence their perceptions. Rather it was the nature of their previous contact which had an impact on their current attitudes. Positive experiences left parents with positive expectations:

> I knew the social would help. See, they sorted me before when he left.
> They were good to me, got me a place in the [family] centre.

Conversely, parents with previous negative experiences had considerable anxieties about returning to social services. For example, the compulsory admission of children to care had been a real possibility for four families and for a further three, child protection enquiries had been instigated in the past. These parents originally thought the accommodation service had a hidden agenda of child rescue. However, with clear and sensitive social work approaches, such families became receptive to family support even if previous experiences had been negative. This reflects the findings of Cleaver and Freeman (1995) which show that, even in cases of suspected child abuse, sensitive intervention and much-needed services could change the perceptions of parents. Further, parents were able to distinguish between different services offered by social services, a feature illustrated by the following case:

● ●

Mr and Mrs Williams had three children. The eldest, aged 9, was accommodated in short-term foster care, while her younger brother and sister stayed at home. The two younger children aged 6 and 7, were 'a real handful' while the oldest was described as 'withdrawn and isolated'. Heavy-handedness by the parents in an attempt to control the children's behaviour had resulted in child protection inquiries but no further action had been taken. Parents were now receiving family support, including short term accommodation for the oldest to help improve their parenting skills:

> They seemed to think we needed help. I wondered if it was . . . well, to keep tabs on us. We were a bit surprised . . . that they didn't offer the arrangement for the two young ones. They are a real problem – headstrong, little devils sometimes. But Susie's always been such a good girl. She [social worker] said

it would be a good idea, and it has been. She loves it. We miss her, but we've had time to sort out the young ones. It did make us realise that they aren't always out to get you.

● ●

Factors ameliorating parents' fears

Although two-thirds of parents were initially anxious about approaching social services, this still left one-third of parents who said they had few anxieties about the arrangements. This finding is in contrast to much previous child care research on full-time accommodation (see DHSS 1985b). This may owe much to the fact that the majority of parents with few anxieties (18 of 20) were involved in a scheme which had grown out of extended child-minding. There are three aspects related to this mode of provision which affected parents' perceptions:

- ◆   some parents already knew carers in their role as child-minders;

- ◆   the majority of carers lived in the same or similar communities (see also Chapter 8); and

- ◆   because the carers were seen as child-minders the service was seen as an extension to child-minding rather than as an aspect of the local authority care system.

The difference between these arrangements and those organised as part of family placement work was quite marked in this respect. Parents felt less under scrutiny, more in control of arrangements and clearly perceived services to be family support.

Outcomes

Outcomes are based on the experiences of only 59 of the original 60 families receiving short-term accommodation because one family moved to Scotland during the study period.

Amelioration of family problems

The first outcome explored was whether parents believed that the short-term accommodation had alleviated the problems they had identified at the beginning of the intervention.

Figure 4.4 *Comparison of severe family problems (n=59*)*

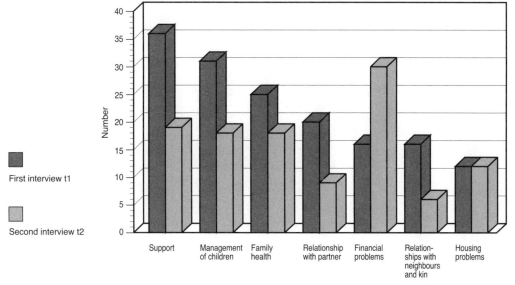

First interview t1

Second interview t2

*Categories are not mutually exclusive

Figure 4.4 shows that there had been shifts on several dimensions. Some were statistically significant, on Wilcoxon two-tailed T tests. For example, shifts in perceptions of support were significant at the 0.001 level, changes in relationships with neighbours and kin, management of children and perceptions of financial needs were all significant at the 0.01 level. Relationships with partners also changed although the shift was not significant (p=<0.07). There was little change in parents' perceptions of family health or housing problems.

Figure 4.4 shows the degree and direction of change in parents' perception of their problems. However, it is also important to understand the context of the results. To what degree was the shift brought about because parents felt problems had diminished, had got worse or remained the same?

Support

At the beginning of the study, 36 parents identified the need for support as a severe problem. By the end, only 19 parents identified support as a major problem. These were made up of 16 of the original 36 plus an additional three for whom support had become a problem by the end of the study.

In Chapter 3, parents' support systems were broken down into two dimensions: practical and emotional support. These two categories were revisited at

Figure 4.5 *Sources of regular practical support (n=59*)*

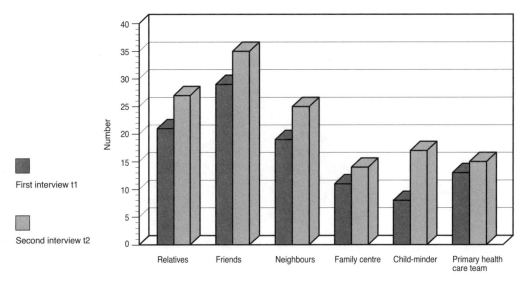

*Categories are not mutually exclusive

the second interview. The findings (which show an increase in both practical and emotional support from a variety of sources) complement parents' perceptions of the improvement in their support systems.

Figure 4.5 shows that, although practical support from relatives, friends and neighbours had increased, the greatest change was in the use of child-minders.

As Figure 4.6 shows, changes in parents' emotional supports showed a similar pattern to that found for practical supports. Parents were more inclined to seek emotional support from all sources, but the greatest increase was in the use of child-minders (by 22%).

The experience of short-term accommodation gave parents the confidence to ask for help from relatives and friends. By and large, parents received a positive response to their requests. This positive response built upon a similarly positive attitude they had experienced from social workers and carers and did much to reinforce their self-esteem. By the end of the intervention parents had learned from their experiences with professionals that they had a right to ask for reasonable amounts of help. Further, the experience of short-term accommodation helped to empower them to use their own informal support networks more appropriately.

Figure 4.6 *Sources of regular emotional support (n=59*)*

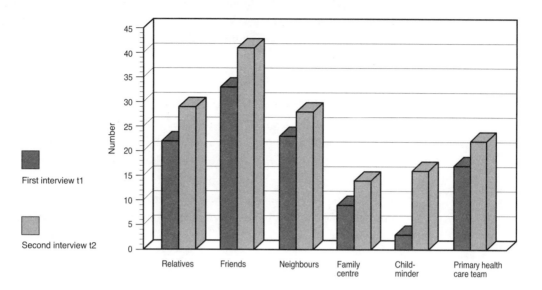

First interview t1

Second interview t2

*Categories are not mutually exclusive

Management of children

Parents found by the end of the study that the management of children was less of a problem overall – 18 of the original 31 felt things had improved. In comparison, five families who had not perceived child management to be a severe problem at the outset now saw it as one. Two of these children were accommodated full-time during the study because their behaviour was out of the control of their parents. But as shown in the following quotes, it was not the children's behaviour itself that had changed but parents' perception of their ability to cope with their children, helped in large part by advice from carers:

> She used to get on my nerves, always asking questions and wanting attention. But when Janice [carer] said 'Isn't Amy a bright spark?' it made me think. Now, I feel better, I can see she [Amy] just wants to know things.

> I was surprised how naughty Joan's [carer] kids were sometimes, but she doesn't give way like I do and it seems to work. She taught me to stick to my guns and take a deep breath when they try and wind me up.

Family health

Twenty-five parents thought health was a real problem for the family at the beginning of the study. Only 18 parents held this view at the end. There was no particular trend in either direction. Four parents felt the families' health had improved, three thought family health problems were now severe and the majority saw no real change. What had changed, as shown below, was parents' motivation to address family health needs.

Relationship with partner

It will be recalled that only 23 of the 60 families were living in two-parent households. At the beginning of the study, 19 of these had identified their relationship with their partner as a severe problem. At the second interview, only nine of the 23 parents thought their relationship with their partner was still a severe problem. As might be expected changes had taken place both ways but the strength of the direction was towards reducing problems with nine believing their problems had reduced compared with three who thought they had risen.

Financial problems

There was a contrary trend in relation to financial problems. Practically twice as many parents saw their financial problems as severe at the point of the second interview (31) compared with perceptions at the outset (16). Eight of the parents who said finances were a problem at the outset did not rate them so at the end compared with 23 who did not rate finances as a problem at the beginning but did so at the end. This was an important finding, in the light of the fact that, as reported in Chapter 3, over half the families were living on benefits and most were on low incomes. It suggests that parents now had a more realistic view of their financial situation. A major factor influencing this change was that parents identified themselves with the carers on many counts and aspired to their higher standard of living (see also Chapter 8).

> She's just like me but she's got it together. Made me think I need to sort myself out and get a job. Maybe I could do the breaks for other parents.

Relationships with neighbours and kin

Relationships with neighbours and kin had improved significantly. Twelve of the 16 who had reported this as a problem at the outset were not doing so by the end. This compared with an additional two cases which had become a severe problem by the end.

> The break let me see my mum without the children. It's funny, we got on so much better. We sorted things out and I feel I can ask her to take the kids for the odd day. She was pleased I was more relaxed. Told me I should put my feet up more.

Housing problems

There were 13 families who had identified housing as a problem at the outset. There was no change in the overall number of families who identified this as a severe problem at the second interview. None the less, there were changes within the group. Three families who originally saw housing as a problem were moved to better accommodation during the time of the study and one moved to live in a spacious house with a new partner. By contrast, one lone parent acquired a partner with three children with the result that her previously adequate accommodation had become overcrowded. More interestingly, as with their finances, three parents re-evaluated their housing situation in the light of visiting the homes of carers.

Feeling more in control

By and large, parents felt there had been positive shifts in their problems or they felt more capable of dealing with them. An examination of results of the locus of control tests at the first and second interviews shows if parents' feelings about their ability to handle their problems were reflected in the scores. While it must be remembered that over half the parents had attributed the locus of control within themselves at the beginning, there were 16 parents who located control outside themselves.

At the beginning of the study 34 parents believed they were in control of their lives (internal locus of control dimension). Twenty-seven of these rated themselves to be strongly in control, and the rest moderately so. Eleven parents felt that much of what happened in their lives was decided by others and 15 believed things happened by chance. All parents scored moderately or strongly on all the dimensions – no parents scored on the basic level. At the end of the study, as Table 4.2 shows, there had been some changes.

Overall, at the second interviews, as Figure 4.7 shows, the number of parents who felt in control of their lives had increased. The increase appears to be at the basic level of internal control. There is a drop in the number of parents who felt that control lies with powerful others. There is also a reduction in the number of parents who felt their lives were ruled by chance. One parent moved out of the area and was not re-tested.

Comparing the 59 families at the beginning and the end of the intervention showed that 27 of the 34 remained within internal control. Five changed to chance and one felt the control now lay with others. The internal control

Table 4.2 *Second locus of control score (n=59)*

Perceived control source	Number of cases	Percentage
Internal strong	26	44
Internal moderate	10	17
Internal basic	4	7
Powerful others strong	5	8
Powerful others moderate	3	5
Powerful others basic	0	0
Chance strong	10	17
Chance moderate	1	2
Chance basic	0	0

Figure 4.7 *Comparison of parents' first and second locus of control scores (n=59)*

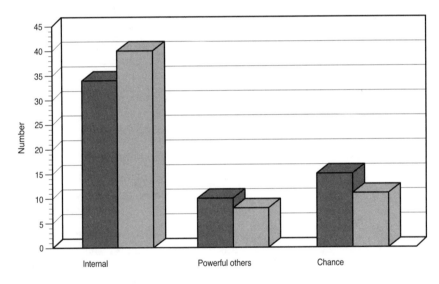

category gained seven from an original locus of powerful others and six from the chance category, making an overall increase of 34 to 40.

In the powerful others category, the pattern of changes led to a decrease from 11 to eight. Similarly, in the chance category, although there were some gains, overall, there was a decrease from 15 to 11.

The shift in locus of control should be set in the context of the fact that over half the parents scored highly on this test in the first place. What the test perhaps showed was that where the potential for change exists, then strategic input of services may help empower parents. As will be shown in subsequent chapters, social workers had some misgivings about targeting families for the services who were, in their judgement, unlikely to be able to manage partnership arrangements or for whom short-term accommodation alone would not be enough. The success of the service for parents must be seen in this context.

Of course, there is no way of knowing from the re-testing of parents of any causal relationship between intervention and changes in how parents scored on the locus of control test. Other events could have had just as much of an impact on parents' perceptions of their ability to control their lives as did any social work intervention. Any conclusions drawn from changes can at best be speculative, but they are grounded in parents' own accounts of the influences on their lives during the period between our two interviews. Parents were asked at the second interview to recall any major events which had had either a positive or negative impact on their lives during the research period. Any reported impact of the experience of short-term accommodation should therefore be seen in this context of personal life experiences.

It emerged that, during the period under review, the majority of parents' lives had been remarkably stable with few changes in partnerships, few traumatic events and few changes in their health status or income. There were two cases where negative changes had taken place. These were the cases where children had come into full-time accommodation. Additionally, in two families, there had been separations from partners. On the positive side, one mother had qualified as a nurse, two had obtained part-time employment and one parent had married. In one family, there was a new baby.

Realising expectations of short-term accommodation

In general, family problems were alleviated or were seen more realistically. Clearly, parents' perspectives of problems had shifted and some parents felt more in control of their lives. But had their expectations of the service been met? We revisited at the second interview the three dimensions of expectation explored at the beginning of the study.

Immediate benefits

In the earlier sections of this chapter, the study explored parents' expectations about how they would use the time away from their children. This section examines how far those expectations were met. Table 4.3 shows the proportion of expectations of immediate benefits arising from the short-term accommodation service which had been met.

Table 4.3 *Proportion of immediate benefits met (n=59*)*

Immediate benefit	Number of expectations	Percentage met
Recuperation	42	86
Time for self	30	93
Chance to catch up with regular tasks	21	66
Time with other children	12	58

*Categories are not mutually exclusive

What was extremely heartening was the fact that the service had fulfilled parents' expectations to a large degree. The following illustrations show the immediate impact of the service on parents:

Recuperation Parents clearly valued the break away from the children. During the first break, many parents were so tired that they could do little other than sleep and rest:

> I can't tell you how lovely it was to stay in bed on Saturday morning without feeling guilty. The first two weekends I did nothing. Then I thought, this is silly. I should do something with the time.

> It was great to have a bath without the children hammering on the door or fighting.

As parents felt stronger they were more able to think about addressing their problems:

> I went to stay with my mum. Once the kids were gone I just collapsed, I felt so tired. I hadn't realised how tired I was. My mum looked after me for that first weekend – that made me feel much better.

Time for self After the initial recuperation parents began to use the time away from their children constructively to address their problems. Parents used the time in a variety of ways, for example, some took stock of their lives, other renewed links with family and friends, a few sought to improve relationships with partners, other to improve their financial circumstances. Finally some parents used the time to sort out their health problems:

> I wrote to Sue [old friend] and asked if I could visit her. We had such a good time. She made me remember what it used to be like – fun and laughs. The breaks helped me laugh again.

I took a good look at my life and decided I had to sort something out.

I went to the doctor about my backache, she listened to me and sent me to the physio. I always knew it could be sorted but I never seemed to find the time to go.

Chance to catch up with regular tasks Many parents felt that their child care duties had so overwhelmed them that little attention had been given to the upkeep and general care of their homes:

We had a great weekend, clearing out all the rubbish.

For the first time I managed to iron his shirts and her dresses, it made me feel really good.

I'd been ashamed of our front garden, ours is a dump compared to all the others. At least it's tidy now.

Time with other children Several parents felt that it was difficult to give enough attention to all their children. Weekend breaks allowed some parents to devote more time to younger children:

I never seem to have enough time to cuddle her, we had a great time just the two of us. She been a lot less demanding since.

Longer-term benefits

Many of the changes parents had hoped for were accomplished but not in all areas (Table 4.4).

Table 4.4 *Proportion of longer-term benefits met (n=59*)*

Longer-term benefit	Number of expectations	Percentage met
Less lonely	40	96
Coping with everyday life	52	76
Relationship with partner improves	10	60
Children's behaviour improves	30	25
Parent can go to work	3	100
Family finances are improved	2	50

*Categories are not mutually exclusive

Less lonely Undoubtedly the most significant shift was that parents felt less lonely. The pattern of social isolation which had been so marked at the beginning of the study had begun to change. Half the parents had originally hoped that a consequence of having their children in short-term accommodation would be that they would feel less lonely. The follow-up shows that 96% thought this aim had been achieved. As will be shown later in the chapter, parents' account of this change was supported by an increase in social networks:

> Having been to see my sister we've started to see each other regularly, she's got lots of friends and now they're mine too.

> I still go round to see Tom and Mary [carers]. Mary's my friend now, I know I could turn to her if I needed some help.

Coping with everyday life Coping better with everyday life had been identified as a hoped for benefit for 40 parents. Although three-quarters of those who hoped they would be coping better did so, it is of concern that a quarter of those who wished for an improvement were still under considerable stress. Some parents however, did feel that they were now more able to balance competing demands within the family. Of equal if not more importance was the success of those who had used the time for themselves to develop strategies to allow them to continue to find space to address their own needs. The strategies involved renewing links with friends and family and learning from carers the importance of developing a wider, supportive social circle:

> Nothing much has changed, I still haven't got a housing transfer, but I feel more on top of everything.

> It hasn't really made any difference, a few weekend breaks was not enough. It was great while it lasted but now I feel just as tired as before.

Relationship with partner improves Ten parents wanted to use the breaks to improve relationships with their partners. Of these, six believed the short-term breaks had enabled them to build bridges with their partners and were determined to sustain the improvement in their relationships. None the less, this left four parents dissatisfied:

> I hoped the social worker would sort him out, I need him to help me with the kids more, but it's made no difference.

Children's behaviour improves About half the parents had hoped the breaks would 'improve' children's behaviour. In fact, at the end of the study, only 25% of these saw any improvement in their children's behaviour.

None the less, many of these parents felt better able to manage their children. A significant factor in this reappraisal had been the part played by carers, who had helped them recognise behaviour which required professional intervention:

> I'd always blamed myself, especially when he started stealing. Joyce [carer] said they couldn't manage him either, that made me feel better that it wasn't just me.

Gaining employment Three parents who wanted to use the arrangements to find work did in fact do so and were all very pleased with their progress. The student nurse had completed her course and was working nights with the help of the carer who volunteered to take the children three times a week. One mother found a part-time job in a shop manageable with extra support from her mother who agreed to collect her child from school and another was working at a day centre as a cook.

Improved finances Only two families were hoping to use the breaks from their children to improve their finances. One father had hoped that the breaks would allow him to increase his part-time job in a car factory. In fact this did not happen because there was no work. As shown earlier in this chapter, one unexpected outcome in relation to perceptions of finance was that by the end of the study many parents who had not originally seen finance as a problem started to compare themselves with carers' families, and were resolved to improve their circumstances.

Conclusions

Looking at the changes that had taken place in the context of the data presented, there are four important trends:

1   Overall, the position of strength from which families started had been maintained and strengthened as evidenced from the Levinson test and from parents' accounts of how they saw the management of their lives. Parents were feeling better.

2   There had been considerable shifts in parents' support systems and in the nature of their personal relationships. To a large extent the two are intertwined.

3   With extra support parents were able to attend to other matters in a more assertive way, such as health and child care problems.

4   A minority of parents had shifted their perceptions about the structural problems in their lives: finance and accommodation.

Parents feeling better

What stands out from each area of exploration, whether it was a shift in parents' perceptions of their problems, fulfilling expectations of using time away from children or changes in parents' locus of control, is that over three quarters of parents were feeling better at the point of the second interview. So, although statistically the sample is small and purposive, the results of the psychometric tests are consistent with parents' own *perceptions* of changes.

Several parents talked of a rise in energy, more enthusiasm to tackle problems and a reframing of their attitudes, especially towards their health and finances.

Increases in informal support systems and changes in relationships

One major outcome for the study parents was the changes which had taken place in their support systems with a clear move towards using more informal support networks. This change was borne out by parents' views on the changes that had taken place in the regular sources of practical and emotional support during the time of the study.

The development of networks for support also achieved the desired goal of reducing loneliness. In one or two cases, friendships at a distance had been rekindled by parents having time to travel to see friends and some reconciliations had been made with relatives. Loneliness had also been reduced by keeping in touch with carers.

Not surprisingly, with some resolution of the support problems, parents then felt better able to manage their children's behaviour. As suggested earlier in this chapter, it was not that behaviour had changed but that parents had shifted their perceptions. They could now see the difference between 'normal' naughty behaviour that could be changed by a modification of their own responses and, in a minority of cases, behaviour which was seriously awry and needed professional help. Often, the parents' shift in attitude towards normal behaviour problems in their children was influenced by talking to carers, who had their own 'little horrors' and who helped parents recognise that parenting was a difficult task in the best of circumstances. Carers helped parents to remember that the combination of attention and clear boundaries could give children the confidence and security they needed. Carers also gave parents practical tips on how to manage children's behaviour.

Managing relationships with partners is another 'normal' problem. The give and take of close adult relationships requires much diplomacy and energy. Improvements in relationships were attributed mainly to two factors. First, parents had felt able to give more time to partners during the time the children were away. This space had in itself been therapeutic to partnerships. But over and above this, parents were determined to preserve this adult time as an outcome of their experiences. They recognised how much the balance between their needs and their children's had become skewed. Social support from relatives, friends and child-minders was all important to this end.

Addressing health and child care matters

With increased social supports, parents began to think about how to tackle more entrenched problems. Ironically, because parents were feeling more on top of life they were better able to address chronic physical health problems, such as gynaecological problems, backaches, intestinal problems and headaches.

Hence health visitors and GPs were turned to more often for a solution to both adult and child problems. With more energy, parents seemed to have more interest in their children's health, asking health visitors for guidance on specific issues. This assertiveness seemed to be related to a transfer of learning. Having been empowered to use social services, as will be shown in the next chapter, parents were more ready to make their needs felt to other professionals.

Additionally, from what parents said at the end of the study, it might well have been that the wheel had come full circle and that health visitors, having referred families elsewhere were once again carrying the primary support which had been carried by carers during the accommodation arrangements. This finding supports the view that services for children should be organised in a multidisciplinary way by design and not by default.

The use of short-term accommodation had also helped parents to gain access to other services, particularly family centres and child-minding. In around ten cases, family centre support had been built into the short-term accommodation package. The positive experience of using carers led families to recognise that child-minding could continue to give them the space which had been created by short-term accommodation. In around ten of the cases where child-minders were used, these were carers who had continued to help parents under another role.

Addressing financial and housing problems

More parents now rated their financial difficulties as serious. This change did not result from a sudden surge of 'retail therapy' on the part of parents during the time their children were accommodated, but rather was as a result of a change in perceptions, a move from resignation to recognition of reality. Contact with carers undoubtedly influenced this change. Not that carers were considerably more affluent, but rather that carers presented a picture of similar living styles to parents without the problems parents seemed to have. This contact raised the aspirations of some parents, who compared themselves unfavourably to carers in terms of income and standards of accommodation. Further, there may have been some influence from social workers here. As Chapter 6 will show, social workers rated parents' financial problems far more highly than did parents at the beginning of the study.

In short, the short-term accommodation service was a resounding success for the parents in this study. Whether their children held the same view is explored in Chapter 9 but, before hearing the children's story, the next two chapters look at the input of social workers and carers.

Summary

Parents liked the services they were offered and used them well.

By the end of the study more parents felt that the locus of control in their lives lay within themselves rather than with others but well over half the parents entered the study with considerable potential to ameliorate their problems.

The service met parents' expectations to a large degree and gave them enough help to begin to tackle their major problems.

By the end of the study parents had improved their social support systems, and were managing the relationship with children and partners in a more constructive way. They were more aware of their health problems and actively began to seek help to improve these. They also began to recognise that they were in reality living in poverty. A minority of parents became more aware of their accommodation problems.

Social work and short-term accommodation: a trilogy of activity

5 *Access and accessibility*

The positive outcomes of the short-term accommodation service for the majority of parents in the study could not have been achieved without the activities of social workers and carers. This chapter examines the contribution of social workers to those outcomes. It discusses the social work role in the short-term accommodation service, the social work processes by which that role was translated into practice and parents' perceptions of key aspects of the social work service in which they were involved. Children's perceptions of the service are dealt with in Chapter 9.

The social work role in short-term accommodation is led by *Guidance and Regulations* and by the underlying philosophy of the Act, namely, of enhancing parental responsibility by working in partnership with parents:

> One of the key principles of the Children Act is that responsible authorities should work in partnership with the parents of the child who is being looked after and also with the child himself, where he is of sufficient understanding, provided that this approach will not jeopardise his welfare. A second, closely related principle, is that parents and children should actively participate in decision-making process. (DoH 1991a, p. 4)

Much has now been written about the nature of partnership. Marsh (1993) has no doubt that:

> a partnership-based service is in part a practical response to the real circumstances of the job. It is about recognising barriers to communication, different levels of power, and the need to develop a working relationship within constraints that both parties may be unable to alter. Partnership forms the basis of realistic negotiations between user and worker. (p. 42)

Ryan (1991) believes that any inequality in levels of power between workers and families can be addressed without undermining the fundamental principle of partnership, that is, working together towards a mutually agreed goal:

> Partners may have different amounts of power, but partnership will involve a genuine commitment to open negotiation with clients about how best to

promote and safeguard the welfare of children. Clients need to be empowered to engage in this negotiation by having easy access to clear information about services and about ways in which services can be delivered. (p. 5)

Further, Tunnard (1991) spells out the mechanics of partnership in practice:

The essence of partnership is sharing. It is marked by respect for one another, role divisions, rights to information, accountability, competence, and value accorded to individual input. In short, each partner is seen as having something to contribute, power is shared, decisions are made jointly, and roles are not only respected but are also backed by legal and moral rights. (p. 77)

As the Social Services Inspectorate points out in relation to child protection, 'partnership should not be an end in itself' (Social Services Inspectorate 1995, p. 11), a view applicable to the provision of services for any child 'in need'. Rather, it is a means to achieving the general goal of promoting the welfare of children. In relation to short-term accommodation, offering the service in partnership is one means by which the aim of strengthening parental responsibility can be achieved.

The Social Services Inspectorate (1995) groups the reasons for working in partnership in child protection under four headings:

- ◆ effectiveness;

- ◆ families as the source of information;

- ◆ citizens' rights; and

- ◆ empowering parents.

These headings are equally applicable to all children in need, including those accommodated.

Effectiveness

For children who are accommodated, the endorsement of 'a co-operative working relationship between the helping services and families' (Social Services Inspectorate 1995, p. 9) is no less essential than in child protection enquiries. As shown in Chapter 4, some parents in this study initially harboured fears that short-term accommodation was really a child rescue service masquerading as a benign family support service. Only by establishing a shared agenda and trust will an effective service be established. If trust is established, parents can overcome their fears, free themselves from feelings of guilt or failure, use time away from their children to strengthen their sense of self-worth and consider realistically how they might tackle some of their problems.

Families as the source of information

Studies that pre-dated the Children Act drew attention to the enhancement of self-esteem that could result from recognition of parents as experts about their children (Aldgate 1976; DHSS 1985b). So with short-term accommodation, the central tenet of the Children Act about preserving continuity for children accommodated (see DoH 1990) cannot be fulfilled without parents making their knowledge about the family and their community available to family placement workers.

Citizens' rights

The legacy of research showing the negligent lack of attention to the needs of parents of children in the care system led to the insistence in the Children Act that arrangements for accommodating children are made in voluntary partnership. As those holding parental responsibility for their children, parents have a right to ensure that they are given every opportunity of maintaining that right while their children are looked after by others, however briefly. Children accommodated also have the right to expect that the state ensures the promotion of their welfare while they are looked after.

Empowering parents

As the characteristics of families in this study demonstrate (see Chapter 3), lack of control over their lives is as much a feature for some families whose children are accommodated short-term as it is in child protection enquiries. This is an important common thread between services supporting and protecting children:

> The fact that they can take part in decision-making helps build up their self-esteem and encourages adults and children to feel more in control of their lives. Professional practice which reduces a family's sense of powerlessness, and helps them feel and function more competently, is likely to improve the well-being of both parents and children. (Social Services Inspectorate 1995, p. 10)

A theoretical framework: the ecological model

To ensure that the Children Act is firmly translated into practice, its philosophy of working in partnership with parents needs to be grounded in a theoretical framework which encapsulates the important concept of parental responsibility. One model that sits easily with the Children Act philosophy is the ecological model, first developed by Bronfenbrenner and adapted to child care practice by Maluccio and colleagues in the USA. Maluccio (1981) puts forward the idea of families as *expert information givers*, while his work with Fein and Olmstead on permanency planning (Maluccio et al. 1986), a title tainted in the UK context by an equation between permanence and adoption, offers the theoretical underpinning for a family support service.

The essence of the ecological model is a belief in working to families' strengths, using community resources to supplement and complement family care and ensuring there is harmony between a family and their surroundings. In many ways the model has much in common with a systems approach, but the difference is that it purports to build on existing strengths of individuals and their emotional and physical environments. The model adapts well to the provision of short-term accommodation.

The family is the unit of intervention. The family identifies problems to be solved. Account is taken of parent and child strengths, for example, attachments, coping skills, sense of control over the immediate environment (that is, neighbourhood and social networks). The environment is assessed for nurturing qualities. Lack of emotional support from relatives may be identified as a problem for the family, for example. Can this be temporarily replaced by carers? The management of children is another source of stress. The accommodation services provide children with a positive alternative source of attention, and allow parents rest and space to realign their strategies in relation to child management. The role of the worker is that of facilitator and enabler. Participation of parents and children in decision-making, and the offer of realistic choices over which users have control, increases their sense of self-esteem. The model offers services in the partnership mode.

This model has much in common with Children Act philosophy. One of the aims of practice under the Children Act has been 'to establish an environment in which partnership with families can thrive, and in which adults and children are enabled to contribute ideas about the development of services appropriate to their needs' (Social Services Inspectorate 1995, p. 7).

The rhetoric of the ecological model is appealing but, as Marsh (1993) points out, translating 'partnership theory' into 'partnership in routine services' is not straightforward (p. 39). Barriers may come from entrenched attitudes on the part of workers, such as applying a model of assessment to families which emphasises dysfunction rather than achievement, not recognising the normality of families' experiencing problems from time to time, not being willing to communicate to clients the difficulties of trying to operate a system of choice in the context of hardly enough resources and, above all, denying the power imbalance between workers and families and the impact this will have on attitudes towards social services.

The tone for a service offered in partnership can be set at the first point of contact with social services. Therefore this chapter begins the exploration of the social work contribution to short-term accommodation by looking at the accessibility of social services, the nature of the referral process, and parents' response to these.

An accessible service?

Under Schedule 2 of the Children Act, local authorities have a duty to publicise services available to families with children in need. Further, *Guidance and Regulations* states, 'as far as possible, the relevant publicity should encourage parents to seek help if it is needed' (DoH 1991c, p. 13). Ryan (1991) has commented on the value of easily accessible services which help empower parents to make an informed choice about what is best for them. This in itself can set the tone of a partnership model of practice.

Gaining access to the short-term accommodation service in this study was not entirely straightforward. Accessibility was far from the model envisaged by Ryan. Indeed, all families had to overcome three main hurdles.

Hurdle number 1: the search for social services

The first hurdle to be overcome was finding out about services on offer and accessing them. Two-thirds (39) of parents told the research team that they knew before they approached social services that some family support might be available. This knowledge was based on previous contact which had resulted in family support, such as day care or child-minding or casework in relation to family problems. Twelve of these 39 families were currently using a family centre and had been informed about other family support services there.

By contrast, the remaining one-third (21) were unsure about where to turn for help or what social services might offer them. Half of these had prior contact with social workers but mostly with regard to suspected child abuse and had been surprised that social services might offer supportive services. The rest had no previous contact with social services.

It appears that without previous knowledge of how the system worked, a third of parents experienced a variety of barriers in reaching social services.

First, 17 parents reported difficulties getting information about family support services which was easily available to the family:

> It was a real struggle at that point – I didn't know what to do. I thought I knew what I needed, someone to help me get started with thinking . . . but how do you know where to go for that?

> When you don't have any idea what there is, and you know you haven't any money . . . it doesn't spring to mind that you could ask a social worker . . . I'd have said before, that it was asking for trouble to let a social worker in.

A second issue for those who did not know their way around the system was an initial, off-putting response to their first contact with the agency, only to be mediated later by the intervention of a health visitor:

> Someone said 'the social' could help, and I rang the main office. I said we needed some help . . . but when I couldn't say what exactly, he put me off . . . said he didn't think we needed their help . . . What about Midcity Aunts [baby-sitting service]. Couldn't our family help? Well, then I thought if I said we don't have any relatives nearby, they'd think we couldn't manage at all. I didn't want any trouble. My health visitor was wonderful. She got me a place in the breaks scheme.

The initial perception of social services by one third of families was of an inaccessible agency but this left two-thirds who spoke positively about access:

> I've had help from them for a long time. They have always been there when I really needed them. They have bailed me out with money and emergency child-minding in the past. I always know I can phone up Martha and she'll listen.

It is reassuring that so many parents found social services so approachable. Moreover, there was no statistically significant association between parents' rating of their satisfaction with the quality of the service and their perceived level of difficulty in accessing social services. Nor was there any statistical association between accessibility and parents' later participation in the planning and decision-making phase of short-term accommodation. Any initial barriers did not subsequently influence the process or outcome of the service offered.

Given the overall positive view of social services, there were two factors that increased accessibility. The first was previous positive contact with social services, which has already been discussed. The second was the role of health visitors in referring families to social services.

Health visitors: a positive force

The role of health visitors in helping families gain initial access to social services merits special attention. Health visitors had suggested to families that social services might help in 44 cases and, in 15 of these cases, had referred families to social services directly themselves. It is worthy of note that the 15 cases were all in one authority where health visitors had direct referral lines to the short-term accommodation team and were able to bypass access teams. This simplified the system for families as the following case study shows.

● ●

Mrs Blake, a single parent, and her three young children had little contact with their extended family who lived over 50 miles away. She found child care took up all her time and deprived her of any social contact with other adults. She became lonely and depressed. Her GP suggested she should discuss what help might be available with her health visitor. The health visitor referred her to the short-term accommodation scheme in Midcity. The scheme social worker explained:

Mrs Blake turns to her health visitor quite a lot . . . advice about the children . . . and someone to reassure her from time to time. She [health visitor] suggested the breaks – which Mrs B didn't know about, and said would she mention it to us at our monthly meeting? Mrs Blake was only too pleased . . . she trusts the health visitor . . . thinks she's sensible.

● ●

Although it was outside the scope of the study to look at interagency collaboration at a strategic level, this close liaison at the grassroots was heartening and reflects the Children Act philosophy of promoting working arrangements between agencies in relation to children in need. Community-based health services, such as GPs and health visitors are universally available and are likely to be regularly used by families with children. When professionals are aware of the circumstances of their clients and similarly knowledgeable about the services that are available direct links can be arranged. In all the study authorities, local liaison meetings were held regularly between social workers and health centres, and individual contact between health visitors and social workers was frequent. This interagency working was an essential part of helping families access the short-term accommodation service, as one social worker explained:

> People have got to know about it before it'll be much use. You have to be careful because it's not something everyone can have . . . it can't be. But what is important is to get the information to the people that families will see regularly and who understand what they need . . . and what we can and cannot do . . . it's vital. (River Town scheme leader)

A resource-led service

Knowledge about short-term accommodation schemes was clearly in the hands of health visitors and other professionals and the widespread availability of information on family support services, in the public domain, as suggested by Ryan (1991), was noticeable by its absence. Even where access to services was via a drop-in family resource centre, there was little publicity about other services on offer.

There was an unspoken policy in all the agencies not to advertise services, borne out of fear that giving wide publicity to services would result in an overwhelming deluge of applications for help. Each service had a finite budget. Social workers told the research team that they faced a real dilemma. Should they maintain a service which, in their view, was barely enough to have an impact upon families or offer a watered-down service to more families which might achieve little success for the majority? The outcomes described in this study showed that the present system of targeting quality services rather than watering them down was working. Only a controlled experiment could test further assumptions about the need to control quality by controlling intake.

Hurdle number 2: the gatekeepers

It was clear that once the majority of parents managed to open the door of social services and were assessed for support, there was no guarantee that this resulted in automatic access to short-term accommodation. Those who had direct access to schemes via health visitors were more likely have to have their requests accepted because health visitors were familiar which eligibility criteria. In other cases, access workers, acting as gatekeepers, were firmly in control of the limited resources on offer. This may be representative of the way general respite care has been offered in the past (see Aldgate et al. 1989). Discussion with social workers in this study reinforced this view. Indeed, the power over access social workers as gatekeepers had was formidable. The notion of an agency offering clients a choice between different types of family support service was still hypothetical.

Broadly, the referral processes of the four agencies could be represented by three models.

Traditional access to services

The first model placed considerable power in the hands of access team workers, backed up by a children and families operations team member. There was a linear gatekeeping system:

- ♦ **Stage 1** access worker assesses for eligibility;

- ♦ **Stage 2** locality social worker, for children and families, makes general assessment that child is in need and refers to family placement team for short-term accommodation; and

- ♦ **Stage 3** short-term accommodation scheme leader (located in family placement team) consults child and parents and arranges placement.

Access from attending family centre in a children's resource centre

Figure 5.1 shows the system of referral via the family resource centre (FRC) in Ferryport.

The referral point was generally the family centre housed in the same building but other professionals or social workers from another area could access the family resource centre. Families would then be referred on for assessment by the provider of the service, the family placement team. The scheme was characterised by the easy access to the service through the family centre. It was also helped by the good communication because all the relevant workers were in the same building. Another excellent feature was the monitoring and evaluation of the service which was built in alongside staff development.

Referral from local area team or health visitor

Figure 5.2 shows the third model of referral. This had a more simplified system of access than the others with well-established and broad criteria for admission to the short-term accommodation scheme. There were two facilitating features worthy of note: health visitors had direct access to the project

Figure 5.1 *The family resource centre model of referral*

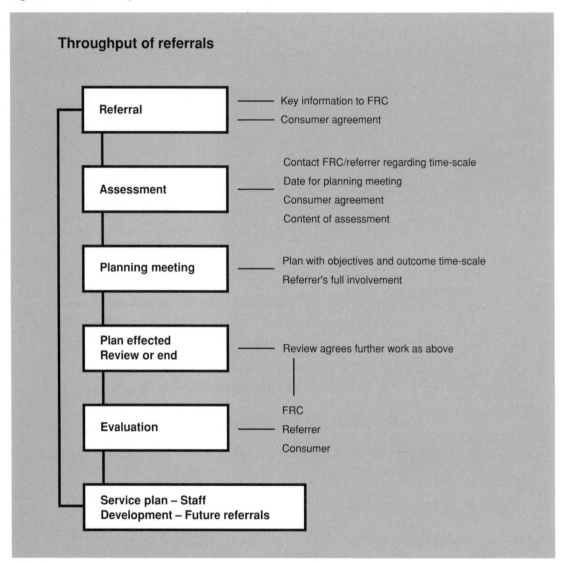

co-ordinator, who was in charge of the whole process, both supporting families and carers. The project co-ordinator shared an office with the local area team which also facilitated communication.

All three referral models worked well because of the clear systems and the dedication of the staff involved. All the agencies had strong gatekeeping either at access or by those running the schemes. All the schemes were very much resource-led. Workers controlled who received the service. Once they had been accepted for access as potential clients, the final hurdle for families was to establish their eligibility for short-term accommodation.

Figure 5.2 *Referral accessed through local area or health visitor*

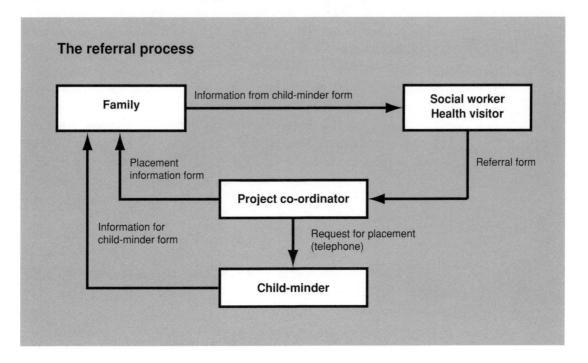

Hurdle number 3: eligibility

The concept of eligibility does not sit easily with the Children Act philosophy of parental responsibility and consumer choice. It is, however, a concept which has been a part of welfare services for several centuries. Although notions of 'deserving' and 'undeserving' are clearly out of line with equal opportunities thinking, eligibility for family support services is accepted in the philosophy of Section 17. Local authorities do not have a duty to meet all need but can set priorities for groups of children to gain priority access to services. Everitt and Hardiker have suggested that confining family support services to a restricted group of children defined as 'in need' is 'clearly a mechanism for residualising services' (Everitt and Hardiker 1996). Much hangs on how authorities define children in need, as Aldgate and Tunstill (1995) found in their study of the first 18 months' implementation of family support services.

The social services departments in this study may not be representative of the national scene at the time (see Aldgate and Tunstill 1995). All four social services deliberately set their criteria for eligibility for Section 17 services within a broad-based definition. This encompassed a range of family problems including parental illness, financial stress, marital problems and children's behaviour.

Chapter 3 showed the characteristics of families who were accepted for services. Further, Chapter 4 showed that over half the parents felt in control of their lives but had problems serious enough to define them as being in acute or chronic distress (Cleaver and Freeman 1995).

On pressing social workers responsible for short-term accommodation, it emerged that criteria for eligibility for the service are not easily defined. Social workers were concerned to include a broad range of families who came with an equally broad range of problems. Those who were scheme leaders were particularly concerned not to impose simplistic categories for inclusion but rather lay down guidance for access social workers and themselves about which families might be excluded. This resulted in decision-making being led by professional judgement.

The main criteria for the service were that children were within the agency definition of 'in need' and that the provision of services at this point would prevent 'more intrusive interventions' at a later stage (Hardiker et al. 1996). There was another important criterion related to professional assessment. Workers were looking for families who could respond to the service offered. Did they have the potential to use the time away from children profitably? Would children and parents manage the coming and goings of respite arrangements?

It was significant that criteria were held in the minds of social workers and were not accessible to families. Parents and children had no overt part in defining their eligibility at this point. Social workers felt that, had access to criteria about eligibility been open to families, it would have been more difficult to take risks about who was included. As it was, there were certain families whose potential they considered to be limited but who just might make use of the service. The pros and contras of this approach can be debated at length. In the context of the service offered, the resources available and the outcomes achieved, it was the view of the research team that social workers were acting as fairly as possible to target those most likely to use the service responsively.

Each of the schemes saw itself as part of a range of social services' resources for family support. Although a great deal of individual judgement, borne of experience, was evident in deciding who *gained access* to the short-term accommodation services, the study found considerable agreement across the four authorities on criteria used for exclusion. There were a number of circumstances which, in the opinion of social workers, rendered families ineligible. Most schemes, for example, specified the age groups of children they could take. Additionally, there were several factors which were regarded as possible contra-indications for short-term accommodation.

No emergency arrangements

Social workers were firm that short-term accommodation should not be offered as a crisis resource. However, short-term accommodation might be triggered by an emergency placement, although the service itself would not be offered until a formal assessment had taken place.

Families subject to Section 47 enquiries re. alleged physical or sexual abuse or where there continued to be suspicion of significant harm

It was felt that short-term accommodation would be unsuitable for children and parents during any period of formal enquiry. More specifically, the arrangements might prove insufficient to keep children safe if they were used as an alternative to full-time accommodation. This view was shared by the four study authorities. However, this may have been a characteristic of the particular schemes in this study. Thoburn has recently suggested from her ongoing study for the Department of Health that there can be successful use of short-term accommodation for children who are at risk of significant harm.

Short-term accommodation as a therapeutic treatment for children with severe behavioural difficulties

All short-term accommodation social workers expressed considerable reservations about including these children because, in their view, carers had not been trained to meet such needs. In fact, there were a handful of children in the study who came into this category. It is noteworthy that two of these children were transferred to full-time accommodation during the course of the study.

Families with a history of disorganisation and difficulties

A third group excluded were those whose lives were described by workers as 'chaotic'. The Spire City family placement social worker commented:

> People don't suggest it to parents who are chaotic and having endless difficulties coping . . . I imagine they don't want to raise their hopes and disappoint them. But it's more complicated, even. Such families make you worried . . . and you wonder if it could possibly be enough. When we [social workers] feel confident that it can support families in greater difficulties, I think we'll get this across to other professionals and to parents. I think more will ask then, and . . . we'll see, I hope.

She elaborated to say that social workers' anxiety about extending the range of families offered short-term accommodation was compounded by worries about funding restrictions, and the capacity to build and sustain the professional networks needed successfully to support families in greater distress. In a different financial climate, where funding would allow for more intensive support alongside short-term accommodation, routine expansion to these families was thought possible.

Families unable to sustain themselves without substantial organising help

The strongest contra-indication put forward by social workers was the lack of potential for parents exercising responsibility and establishing a working partnership between parent and agency. Parents chosen to participate had to take an assertive part in maintaining the arrangements. Parents who would be too dependent on carers or those who would find it difficult to stick to arrangements without fairly minimal help were likely to be excluded. This was because, as will be shown in Chapter 7, social workers often withdrew substantial support once the placement had started, although they did retain a monitoring function. Thus, parents needed to be more responsible than was usual in cases of full-time accommodation for the 'upkeep' of the partnership through their contact with the carer. This in turn demanded from parents the potential to cope with the management of arrangements. Indeed, as the results of the Levinson test showed (see Chapter 4) this policy was being implemented with over half the families scoring that they felt in control of their lives.

The exceptions that proved the rules

In spite of these guidelines, it was clear that considerable individual judgement was exercised by scheme leaders about admitting families to the service so that even some families who in theory might not be eligible, because of serious concern about children's welfare, were offered the service. Some of these families might well be described as 'families low on warmth, high on criticism' (DoH 1995b, p. 19). Two case studies follow.

● ●

In one family, the oldest child had been removed because of emotional abuse. The parents were struggling to meet the emotional needs of their two remaining young children. The primary aim of the short-term accommodation was to give the parents time for their marital relationship, and to reconsider their parenting strategies. They were also receiving some intensive casework help on parenting alongside the accommodation for their children.

Another family with three children, between 9 and 14, had had two other children removed some years ago on the grounds of neglect. Although fears of emotional and physical neglect tended to resurface from time to time, a great deal of intervention had been undertaken to strengthen their parenting abilities, and the short-term breaks were arranged as part of an ongoing and, to date, successful strategy of support for both children and parents.

Parents' strategies for getting through the gate

Families were aware that a gatekeeping process was in place. Several adopted strategies to ensure they were chosen for priority services. The trick, they thought, was to strike a balance between showing that they were caring parents of children in need, under enough stress to warrant the short-term accommodation service, but not in any way putting their children at risk of significant harm. Though none of the families had, to the research team's knowledge, read the Children Act, they had an uncanny sense of the difference between Section 17 and Section 47:

> See, I'm on my own since the wife left. I need help but I don't want to lose the kids. They get a bit out of hand. With not being well, I can't cope. You have to make sure you pitch it right to get help. It's the kids who need the break.

> My kids really get me down but I love them. How do you tell the social workers you are a good mother? I was really scared going there. My doctor said I needed help. I told them I thought the kids would like a break but I didn't say I smacked them when I was tired. Well, they can take them away, can't they?

Parents' reactions to the access hurdles

Parents' comments about the access process reveal a good deal of scepticism about the motives of social services. There was a distinct feeling of suspicion initially which was only overcome by the assertive, reassuring attitude of individual social workers, and, of course, by the trust some parents placed in health visitors. The research team was left with the view that social services had a long way to go at the access stage to advertise that they were offering support not child rescue. It was perhaps significant that the least sceptical parents were those who had experienced a positive response in the past. Newcomers and those subject in the past to child protection enquiries were most dubious about what might be offered to help them:

> I expected they would give me a grilling to make sure I wasn't harming him. I didn't believe all the dross – wanting to hear my side . . . no one ever wanted to before! Get on with it, I thought . . . but actually what she said we were doing was thinking together. Come off it, love – that was my reaction. Afterwards, when we had met Susan [carer] I felt it might be alright.

> The woman I saw at first was a bit offhand. If I hadn't been so desperate I wouldn't have gone back. But the other [family placement worker] she was lovely.

> You are always worried that 'the social' will take the kids away. That happened to my friend. But Mrs Park [health visitor] persuaded me. I wasn't sure. But she kept telling me they were there to help me keep the kids.

> I didn't know what to expect . . . I thought, it's not like going to the doctor . . . you tell them the problem and you get a prescription. The social worker said she couldn't have managed like I had.

> To be honest, I thought they would put up barriers. You can't have this, you haven't enough points – like the housing. It took me a while to realise this was just what he didn't want. I have dealt with them before . . . but more about matter-of-fact things . . . practical things, the money not arriving. The way he talked, I thought, yes, he does want to help.

> She listened to my problems. I thought she'd think I was hopeless but she didn't. She said she had helped lots of parents like me.

Summary

Accessibility to social services was variable. Parents new to social services found it hard to get information about family support services. There was little publicity available.

Although some parents found the initial contact with social services off-putting, two-thirds had little difficulty finding social services.

Two factors influenced accessibility positively: previous family support contact with social services and the role of health visitors as referral agents.

There was a strong resource-led system of gatekeeping at the point of access.

There were three modes of referral; all three had in common the fact that one of the alternative routes to services was through generic children and families' access teams.

Two scheme-based services also had direct access: one through a family centre in the same building, the other directly from the community through health visitors. This access seemed to facilitate the process.

In spite of the gatekeeping, there was a broad spectrum of eligibility criteria for short-term accommodation, provided children were within the agency's definition of children in need. This enabled families with a range of problems, from early to severe stresses, to use the service. In contrast to Thoburn's ongoing research, all agencies believed the service was not suitable for children who were at risk of significant harm.

Where resources were scarce and social workers had to justify the offer of short-term accommodation, parents and social workers adopted explicit strategies to overcome gatekeeping by pitching the request for service at a level that was serious enough to gain priority access but avoided any question of significant harm.

6 *Processes and participation*

Once families were accepted for short-term accommodation, the aim of the service could be defined and the essential social work processes to achieve a successful outcome could begin.

This study did not set out explicitly to investigate social work methods and processes, but it did set out to see how the implementation of the Children Act 1989 might have affected child care practice. Short-term accommodation is a service designed to promote the welfare of children primarily by facilitating family preservation. It aims to achieve this by offering parents space to examine and address some of their own problems, while children's needs are met and, ideally, enhanced by their stay in another family. In short, it is not seen just as relief from stress for harassed parents but as a social work service which offers an opportunity to strengthen families. The Children Act places an emphasis on working in partnership with parents and children, helping them to define their needs and to take an active part in designing services to meet those needs. Such an aim is not unrealistic, provided that everyone is clear about the expectations and limitations of the service offered.

To be most effective, social work services should be offered through a series of social work processes that include making plans, taking action and effecting endings. Child care social work places considerable emphasis on the first of these activities but the other two are no less important in promoting children's welfare. It is, for example, held to be potentially harmful to children to subject them to sudden separation from significant adults to whom they are attached without providing some ameliorating support (see, for example, Jewett 1984; Aldgate 1992).

There are four dimensions which, in principle, should underpin social work practice in relation to the provision of accommodation:

1   the legal framework, especially the relevant *Guidance and Regulations*;

2   theoretical models of social work processes;

3   the organisational framework in which social work is practised; and

4   partnership theory.

The successful provision of the short-term accommodation service demands an integration of these four elements.

The legal framework

The *Guidance and Regulations on Family Placements* is comprehensive in its instructions about planning for accommodation (DoH 1991a, pp. 11–12). There is then a further series of activities which include preparation of child and parents for the placement, work to be undertaken with child and parents during the placement, including reviews, and termination of the placement. *Guidance and Regulations* do not give details of the social work methods by which the processes will be carried out, but rather outline the different stages which must be gone through to promote children's welfare. To translate the guidance into action, social workers need to draw on social work methods. They need to know about direct work with children, and about social casework and other therapeutic intervention processes that may strengthen parental responsibility.

Theoretical models of social work processes

There are many models of social work intervention which could be adapted to this service, but the social work processes involved in the short-term accommodation service seem to fit most happily within the framework of a general problem-solving approach. It is important to find a model which allows the social work processes to be meshed with the legal requirements and recommendations for good practice included in *Guidance and Regulations*. It also requires a model which emphasises the promotion of parental responsibility as defined in the Act. Perry (1995) describes Compton and Galloway's model of problem-solving:

> The model makes the assumption that each human being wants to be active in their own life and that social work involves a partnership arrangement with clients to engage in problem-solving. The worker starts with the client's purposes. Practitioner and client may work on a variety of problems at the same time. The model is based on a systems perspective whereby social work interventions are aimed at the interface between the client and the environment. Intervention may not just be with the client system but also with resource and support systems in the client's environment. (p. 11)

Compton and Galloway (1989) identify three phases in the problem-solving process:

- ♦ **Contact** involves engagement and definition of the processes to be worked on;

- ♦ **Contracting** includes assessment and goal-setting; and

- ♦ **An action phase** involves carrying out the action plan and termination.

The first two parts of this method of intervention can be intertwined with the necessary actions described in *Guidance and Regulations* in relation to planning and setting up a child care placement. Grounding the legal requirements, which incorporate many principles of good practice, in well-tried social work methods and superimposing upon them theories of child development provides a framework for exploring the social work practice in this study.

The organisational framework

There is another dimension to be included: the organisational procedures and processes which demarcate the boundaries of individual social work posts and drive accountability in agencies. Some social services departments deliver their services by dividing roles between purchasing and providing services in line with the philosophy of the Community Care Act 1990. Such a model which splits the delivery of purchasing and provision does not sit easily with child care practice. This is because the service has always required a multi-faceted social work approach with a continuity of adult input to monitor and safeguard children's welfare. Some community care writers have argued that a similar organisational model is also advantageous for adult services. Challis (1986), for example, describes the *complete care management role* in which, alongside service arrangements and co-ordination, counselling and advice are part of the main tasks. The complete care manager role allows for the support of those providing the care in the community as well as for a mediation role between the interests of different parties.

This integrated role is especially relevant to the parents/child/carer constellation in accommodation arrangements. The superimposition of a comprehensive role in short-term accommodation allows for clear complementary juxtaposition of different professional tasks, where the social worker initially is assessor, facilitator/broker and social caseworker. It does not preclude a substantial supportive input by carers or the bringing in of more specialist help for parents or children during the course of the arrangements. What is important is that *one* worker is responsible for the setting up and carrying through of the whole process.

The role described by Challis is, in fact, little different from the classic role of child care social worker, which has obtained for three decades. The text-books which predominated when the idea of 'preventive social work' was introduced with the 1963 Children and Young Persons' Act are relevant today. The legal context is different but the practice, grounded in child development theory described by Timms (1962) or Pugh (1968), is reassuringly similar to the 'complete care manager' concept. The Children Act has added a more sophisticated dimension in the concept of parental responsibility, the explicit expectation for services to be offered in partnership with parents and children and the formal requirement to consult both. In making these additions, the Children Act 1989 both builds on and extends the mandate for good practice. In short, there always has been, and still remains, a place for the complex and comprehensive role of the social worker, perhaps better renamed the *family support social worker*.

The family support social worker works in partnership with parents, has been trained to undertake direct work with children and casework with parents, can organise and support the placement and work collaboratively with other professionals on behalf of the family. The role is underpinned by a philosophy that reconciles the promotion of children's welfare with the support of parents and other significant adults.

Partnership theory

Finally, the accommodation service must be offered in an ethos of partnership. *Guidance and Regulations* states:

> One of the key principles of the Children Act is that responsible authorities should work in partnership with the parents of a child who is being looked after and also with the child himself, where he is of sufficient understanding, provided that this approach will not jeopardise his welfare. A second, closely related principle, is that parents and children should actively participate in the decision-making process. (DoH 1991a, p. 4)

Translating theoretical processes and roles into practice

Translating these theoretical processes and roles into practice is no easy matter. The real world of social work is considerably more complicated than that espoused in the textbook. Nevertheless, throughout the course of the study, it emerged that there was a pattern of organisation and processes which enabled the service to be offered efficiently. Consequently, it was possible to explore the content of social work practice within the framework of legal requirements, roles and processes already described.

The chapter now explores how the theory was translated into practice. The scene is set by the organisational context. This is followed by discussions of the planning process, beginning with exploration of the assessment process and its use as a vehicle for partnership between parents and social workers. There follows consideration of the nature of consultation with parents and others specified in *Guidance and Regulations* and some exploration of parents' participation in planning and decision-making. The chapter ends with parents' views on the social work input at this stage.

Organisational background: the family support social worker

As shown in Chapter 2, there were two patterns of organisation offering short-term accommodation, one organised as a discrete scheme and the other organised as part of family placements. Both had in common a social worker who co-ordinated and delivered an individual service for families and supported carers. All the workers saw their role as that of family support social worker, undertaking the social work processes of contact, contracting and action. They informed parents and children about the service, helped them to think through what they wanted and reach a decision about the best arrangements for children and parents. They also linked families with carers and prepared parents and children for the placement.

In the 'action' phase of intervention, there were three variations to the family support social worker. The first was targeted at families where there were 'early stresses' identified (see Hardiker et al. 1996 and Chapter 8) and where social work aims were addressed towards acute need (see Chapter 7). Variations two and three were concerned with children or parents where 'serious stresses' had been identified and social work aims were targeted at chronic family need, and more serious problems to do with children's development or behaviour (see also Chapter 7). All three variations were within the Children Act definition of Section 17(10). What distinguished them was the degree of severity to which children's health and development was, or might be, at risk without the provision of services.

In the first variation, the aim of the placement was to address problems which represented a temporary set-back in families who usually coped well with their lives, although the loss of coping skills was sufficiently serious to deem children to be 'in need'. Once the placement had begun, social workers continued to keep an eye on the course of the arrangements through letters and phone calls to families but delegated to carers the responsibility for any counselling of children and parents and for ending the placement. Social workers provided some support for carers to enable them to carry out their tasks.

In the second variation, a one- or two-worker approach was adopted to address parents' chronic personal needs and their severe problems with parenting. Here, intervention centred on building parents' self-esteem, mediating in spouse or partner relationships or in attempting to modify parents' attitudes and behaviour towards their children, in other words, enhancing parenting skills. This intensive casework with parents during the placement was separated from the task of facilitating and maintaining the placement. In some cases, the whole process was undertaken by the family support social worker. In others, the more intensive work on parenting or relationships was separated from the family support social work role. The decision depended more on the skill and experience of individual family support workers than on agency policy.

In the third variation, which represented a minority, the focus of the placement was strongly targeted towards meeting the developmental and behavioural needs of children. The main focus of the service was to provide children with a weekend environment to supplement parental care. The family support social worker continued to provide casework for parents and support for carers but, while the child was in placement, additional direct work with the child was undertaken by a second social worker, a specialist in working with children. Specialist social workers and carers worked closely in these cases to develop a programme of intervention to improve children's behaviour. The family support social worker continued to monitor and end the placement.

Further discussion of the different variations of intervention and their relationship to social work aims takes place in Chapter 7. Here, the general framework for intervention and the influences upon it have been outlined. It cannot be stressed enough how much parents and carers valued the role of the family support social worker during all phases of the arrangements. This role contributed substantially to the building up of trust in all the participants in the service and their positive evaluation of the social work input.

The planning processes to set up short-term accommodation

There are four discrete tasks to be undertaken in the planning process for accommodating children: 'inquiry, consultation, assessment and decision-making' (DoH 1991a, pp. 11-12).

To a large extent, the initial process of enquiry corresponds to Compton and Galloway's (1989) first social work process of 'contact', whereas consultation, assessment and decision-making are all part of the process of 'contracting'.

As always, the real world of practice does not necessarily follow the textbook. Because the eligibility of children and parents for short-term accommodation had been established early on and, because parents were eager to receive the service, the processes of enquiry and consultation were usually conflated within the same interview between parents and the family support social worker.

Similarly, consultation, assessment and decision-making within this phase were often confined within a single planning meeting. Workers felt that the nature of the service did not call for a more elaborate process. So long as workers both at access and within the complete care manager role were assured parents could make good use of the service and suitable carers were available, arrangements could proceed fairly quickly. It was difficult in practice to disaggregate each element; they were often discussed together. However, it was possible to look at how much the planning stage served as a vehicle for implementing partnership theory.

By the time parents met the family support social workers, they were already beginning to shape their ideas of what the service might give them. Every family had at least one initial interview with a family support social worker. The interview generally had a threefold purpose:

- ◆ to assess children's needs and families' problems;

- ◆ to consult parents about their wishes in relation to service delivery; and

- ◆ to engage families in decision-making.

Assessment of family problems: a shared agenda for planning

In order to tailor any social work service to help families best, the problems families are facing need to be identified and needs assessed. The manner in which that assessment takes place in any case is likely to influence the course of intervention at a later stage. So in short-term accommodation, joint assessments of problems to be addressed by parents and professionals are one way whereby partnership theory can be translated into reality. As studies on child protection have suggested (Thoburn et al. 1995 ; Cleaver and Freeman 1995; Sharland et al. 1996) a shared agenda for action is more likely to lead to plans and actions executed in partnership.

Because of the truncated nature of the planning process in short-term accommodation arrangements, and the fact that some preliminary assessment of eligibility for the accommodation service had taken place at the access stage, it was difficult to identify the steps or components included in assessment of children's need for short-term accommodation although, as shown in the next chapter, the outcome of that process was evidenced in clear social work aims for intervention once the arrangements had been set up.

However, one way forward was to look at the degree to which social workers and parents shared a common view of problems to be solved. In other words, how far was assessment needs-led in the eyes of both parents and social workers? The following series of Venn diagrams illustrates both the congruence and dissonance of social workers' and parents' perceptions with regard to severe family problems at the start of the intervention. The diagrams are quantitative in that the regions, with the exception of the white outer area which represents the number of cases where 'Neither parent nor social worker' thought there was a problem, have areas proportional to the number of cases. Thus the larger the circle, the greater the number of parents or social workers identifying the issue as a problem. In the diagrams, the area within the rectangle represents the entire sample of 60 cases. The two overlapping circles represent the number of parents or social workers who see a particular issue as problematic.

In Figure 6.1, for example, parents and social workers agreed that lack of support was a severe problem for parents in 29 out of 37 cases. In the other eight cases, although parents thought it was, social workers did not. Additionally, workers attributed support as a problem in 20 other cases where it had not been so defined by parents.

Figure 6.1 *Venn diagram of support (n=60)*

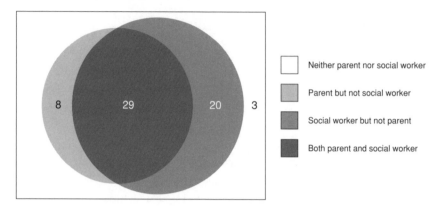

Workers also ascribed problems of child management to 17 additional families but failed to agree with parents in seven cases that child management was a severe problem (Figure 6.2).

Figure 6.2 *Venn diagram of management of children (n=60)*

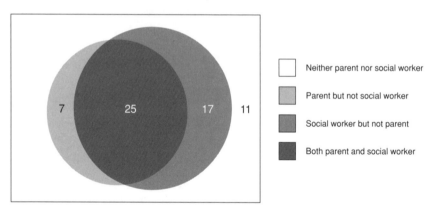

In both these instances, it was clear from talking to workers that they were assessing families against a wider context, informed by theory on family functioning and child development. Social workers were assessing children's behaviour and management against a general assessment standard, usually the so-called 'Orange Book', (DoH 1988), and their practice wisdom borne out of considerable experience of working with families. By contrast, at the beginning of the study, parents were judging their problems far more by their own experience.

The same pattern was repeated in relation to family health. Parents identified health as a problem in 25 cases but in five cases social workers did not agree with parents. Conversely, social workers identified health as a problem in 21 cases where it had not been identified by parents. This difference is attributable to the differing priorities given to problems. At the beginning of the study, many parents accepted ill health as a fact of life, and were far more concerned about their children and their loneliness. Social workers were placing parents within the wider context of their knowledge of a range of families. Conversely, in the five cases not acknowledged by workers, parents were thinking about stress-related minor illnesses not revealed to workers (Figure 6.3).

Figure 6.3 *Venn diagram of family health (n=60)*

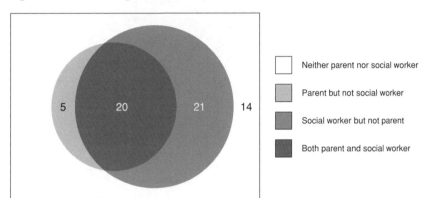

Problems with partners loomed larger in the minds of parents than they did for social workers. Partnership problems were identified by parents in 29 cases but social workers only identified problems in nine of those cases. An additional 17 cases were thought to be problematic by social workers where parents saw their behaviour as normal. It may well have been that in these cases, social workers were applying a different meaning to partners' interaction with each other. These couples tended to shout a lot to each other, a form of communication generally employed by them on many occasions, including responding to the research interview (Figure 6.4).

Figure 6.4 *Venn diagram of relationships with partners (n=60)*

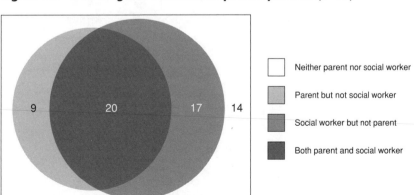

Conversely, social workers rated difficulties with 'others' – mainly neighbours, friends and extended family – as greater than did parents. Thirty-eight families were assessed by social workers to have problems but only 12 parents agreed with this assessment. Conversely, a further four parents perceived problems not rated by social workers (Figure 6.5).

Figure 6.5 Venn diagram of relationships with neighbours and kin (n=60)

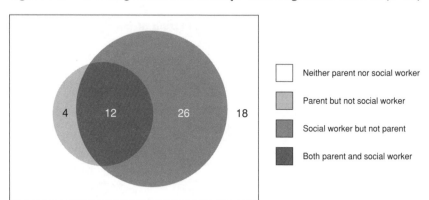

	Neither parent nor social worker
	Parent but not social worker
	Social worker but not parent
	Both parent and social worker

Differences may reflect social workers' conflation of partners with 'significant others'. The *Guidance and Regulations* does not specifically designate for attention partners who do not hold parental responsibility. Rather they are included under 'others who play a significant part in the child's life' unlike other extended family members who are designated as significant in their own right (DoH 1991a, p. 13). Many partners do not have parental responsibility and yet their influence in the household can be critical to the family's well being as recent child protection studies have shown (see Cleaver and Freeman 1995; Farmer and Owen 1995). Certainly in this study, positive relationships with partners were important to both men and women.

There were also discrepancies in perceptions of financial problems at the beginning of the study with social workers attributing problems to parents in 41 cases but, of these 41, only 13 parents felt there was a problem. Once again the difference can be accounted for by social workers judging problems within a wider perspective of relative poverty. By contrast, at the beginning of the study, as suggested in Chapter 4, many parents were resigned to their poverty (Figure 6.6).

As one parent put it:

> Money worries? Well, yes of course. But not that kind of worry . . . I mean . . . I can't do anything about that . . . not now. It's more a fact of life.

Figure 6.6 Venn diagram of financial problems (n=60)

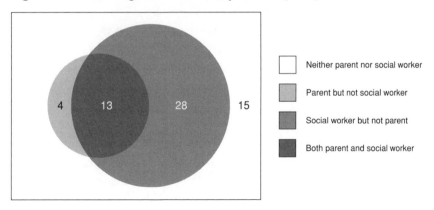

Neither parent nor social worker

Parent but not social worker

Social worker but not parent

Both parent and social worker

Fourteen social workers thought housing was a severe problem. Only four parents agreed (Figure 6.7). Where disagreement did exist it was again in the direction of workers seeing parents' living conditions as worse than they were perceived by parents. This was accounted for by the fact that for parents there were more pressing matters on the agenda. This is succinctly caught by one parent:

> The flat? Not a problem. Could do with a bit more space . . . who couldn't, but it's fine. I don't worry about that. It's the kids and him who get on my nerves.

Figure 6.7 Venn diagram of housing problems (n=60)

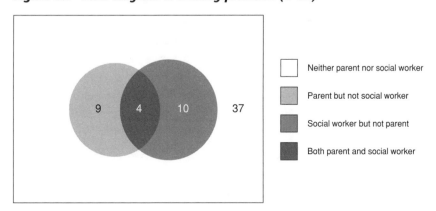

Neither parent nor social worker

Parent but not social worker

Social worker but not parent

Both parent and social worker

Consultation

The second aspect of the planning process considered was consultation about the service. *Guidance and Regulations* state that:

> The responsible authority should obtain and take account of the wishes and feelings of

(a)　the child;

(b)　his parents;

(c)　any person who is not a parent but who has parental responsibility for him; and

(d)　any other person whose wishes and feelings the authority consider to be relevant. (DoH 1991a, pp. 12–14)

Consultation prior to accommodation is a significant concept in the vocabulary of the Children Act. Consequently, in this study, consultation with both parents and children is considered but, because of the importance of considering children's views in their own right, consultation with children is given its own place within the discussion of children's experience in Chapter 9. Here, there is consideration of the meaning of consultation with parents and others in preparation for receiving the short-term accommodation service.

With parents

Consultation was explored in the study by asking parents whether they had been given the opportunity to air their views and explore matters which were important to them during the planning process, after the decision for accommodation had been made.

Forty-nine parents felt that they had been given a full opportunity to discuss their problems and the options the accommodation services could offer them. Because they knew that they had been accepted for access to the short-term accommodation service, and were generally pleased at the prospect of what the service might offer them, they saw consultation as an opportunity to concentrate on a more focused agenda.

Aspects of consultation that were valued included:

♦　time to think;

♦　time for questions; and

♦　reassurance about anxieties.

Examples were:

> I wasn't rushed. I kept asking the same questions until I was clear about how long the respite would be. Sarah never made me feel stupid . . . just kept giving me facts.

I was worried that the kids would never forgive me for sending them to someone else. She kept telling me about other families and how it had worked for them. She said it would be alright when I met Gwen and Chris [carers] and it was.

Parents felt consultation had been most satisfactory when they had a shared agenda with workers about the problems to be addressed. Those who appeared most satisfied had in their minds a clear idea of how the jigsaw of service delivery would fit together and they felt very much that they had a measure of control in putting the pieces together.

Conversely, consultation was deemed unsatisfactory when parents did not feel they had been given the opportunity to talk in full about the problems that were important to them. There were 11 families in this group who gave a range of reasons for their discontent. Most had previous dealings with social workers and expected the worst. For five families, the image of social workers had been tainted by child protection inquiries, by having children removed into care and by what had been perceived as unhelpful responses to previous requests for help. Two young single parents had been consulted in the presence of their own rather domineering mothers. Both expressed considerable resentment and felt consultation had been swept away by their mothers' desires to control the course of actions. Four parents, all mothers, considered that their relationships with their partners contributed significantly to their stress and felt strongly that more time should have been given to discussion of this problem. They were looking to social workers to 'sort things out' for them but social workers were equally clear that they did not wish to be placed in a coercive role in relation to any adult members of the household.

There was no significant statistical association between the satisfaction with the consultation and parents' overall assessment of the quality of the service because of the high level of satisfaction with consultation irrespective of perceived outcome. Eighty-one per cent of 'satisfied' parents felt they had been fully consulted, with an even higher proportion, 88%, less than satisfied with the outcome of the service. Thus it may be concluded, in this service – short-term accommodation – the very success of working in partnership with parents precludes us from exploring the effect of partnership on outcome.

It was clear from parents that the consultation process, in the form of the planning interview with family support social workers, had established three important ground rules of working in partnership:

1   social services could offer a service which was supportive not punitive;

2   parents would retain total responsibility for their children; and

3   parents and children were party to any decisions about arrangements.

With extended family

Finally, under the umbrella of consultation with family, there are discussions with the extended family. *Guidance and Regulations* states:

> The child's family, including parents, grandparents, and other relatives involved with the child should be invited to participate actively in planning and to make their views known . . . In drawing up a plan, therefore, responsible authorities should ensure that the parents of the child, the child himself and other significant persons are given the opportunity and appropriately helped to express their views on the objectives of the plan and on how the responsible authority proposes the objectives should be achieved. DoH (1991a, p. 13)

There were consultations with extended family in around a quarter of cases (14). These were often about practical arrangements in relation to taking children to and from carers. As shown in Chapter 3, it was of note that many parents felt unsupported both emotionally and practically by their kin. Whether an opportunity was missed at this stage in the consultation process for social workers to act in a mediation role is difficult to assess and beyond the scope of the data. What is clear is that extended family was not seen as a natural source of communication at this point.

With professionals

Guidance and Regulations states that:

> To meet the requirements of the Act [Section 22(4)(d)], responsible authorities will need to use their discretion to consult all the relevant statutory agencies which are and have been previously involved with the child and his family and other relevant agencies before a child is looked after. (DoH 1991a, p. 13)

Consultation with these bodies took three forms:

1   gathering information to aid in decision-making;

2   clarifying the detail of arrangements, often with a view to offering other services simultaneously with the short-term accommodation; and

3   information-giving by social workers to others about specific arrangements that would involve relevant agencies.

In ten cases, for example, general practitioners were asked to comment on the length of accommodation needed for parents with health problems such as heart conditions, complicated kidney treatment, or their views were elicited on whether mental health services should be part of a package of services. In just over one-third of cases (21) health visitors were similarly consulted about children's needs. Though direct referrals did not come from family centres or day care facilities for the under-fives, just over a quarter of social workers (18) consulted centres or nurseries which were either already being used by families, or which might be able to offer services in conjunction with short-term accommodation. In one-fifth of cases (20), teachers were approached because carers would either be collecting children from school on a Friday or returning them to school on Monday mornings.

Decision-making

Having set the scene for arranging the service, the next activity for parents and social workers was to construct a plan for the placement. This in itself continued the process of assessment of need. It involved decisions about the length of placement, the specific arrangements for each stay with carers and any decisions about additional services to be provided alongside the accommodation. The part played by parents in this process was important as tangible evidence of working in partnership but, as the Social Services Inspectorate has pointed out, it may be helpful to distinguish between involvement and participation:

> Although involvement and participation in decision-making are closely related activities, a distinction is made between the two. Involvement may be predominantly passive and amount to little more than receiving information, having a non-contributory presence at meetings, endorsing other people's decisions. However, when involvement becomes more active and when family members are asked to contribute to discussions and decision-making on key issues, they can be said to be active participants. (Social Services Inspectorate 1995, p. 11)

Even if parents do actively participate, it is possible to undermine them without positive support from workers, as Marsh (1993) points out:

> Participation, as an element of partnership, must be based on respect for the user-partner's view and respect must be appropriately conveyed. (p. 48)

There were three aspects to participation in decision-making that were explored:

1   attendance by parents and children at planning meetings;

2   parents' and social workers' perceptions of parents' participation in planning meetings; and

3   parents' and social workers' overall rating of their respective impacts on the decision-making process.

It emerged that all parents had attended formal planning meetings with social workers. Carers had been present in 70% of cases and older children in 13 out of 41 cases. The absence of children is entirely consistent with *Guidance and Regulations*. The significance of older children's participation will be discussed in Chapter 9.

Many parents were rather matter of fact about planning meetings. Some could compare them favourably with child protection case conferences; others, for whom this was a first experience of participating in a social work meeting, were pleasantly surprised. A minority (8) said they had been extremely anxious about the meetings. Success depended heavily on the skill of the family support social worker to prepare parents for the meeting and to hold meetings in an informal manner generally within agencies, but occasionally at the parents' home (four cases) or at the carers' home (three cases).

Three out of the four parents where meetings had been held in their homes found the experience comfortable and empowering. Parents felt social workers saw the true extent of their problems:

> I was glad they could see what it was really like for me and how I couldn't control the kids. I had to laugh. Jenny [social worker] went away looking as frazzled as I usually feel.

They also felt it was a great relief not to have to arrange child care or negotiate public transport.

The parent who did not appreciate the holding of a planning meeting in her living room felt it had been an intrusion of her privacy and was worried that there was a hidden agenda. This inhibited her participation in the planning process:

> You never really know if it's up front or they are really using the meeting to pick out your weak spots. Is your home clean enough? Do you have enough food? You know what I mean.

Parents' perceptions of planning meetings

It was quite astounding that 56 out of the 60 parents felt that they had fully participated in the planning meeting. The research team was concerned to test the reliability of this view, recognising that, with the exception of a few individuals who had experience of child protection conferences, parents had no baseline against which to set their judgements. However, when parents' views were compared with social workers' assessments of parental participation there was a very high level of agreement between them.

It was, however, noteworthy that in 13 cases social workers underestimated parents' perception of their participation. This may be because social workers reflect the Social Services Inspectorate view that the verbal articulation of issues is a sign of active participation whereas simply being present is no more than involvement. It was clear that parents did not entirely share this view. Some parents were content to be involved without having to have a strong spoken input into proceedings. Simply being at a planning meeting was enough to show they were partners. The fact that many parents had never had this participatory experience in previous dealings with social workers speaks for itself. The opening of the door to participation, however inadequate it might have been in social workers' eyes, was an act of empowerment that many parents valued highly. In this instance, social workers were underestimating the impact of consultation during the meeting on less articulate parents:

> *Social worker:* She didn't say much at the meeting. It was difficult to tell if she was happy about things.

> *Parent:* I didn't say much because it was difficult in front of everyone. But they kept asking me if I agreed and I said I did. It was OK. I was asked and I agreed. It was difficult to say more. I left it to them to arrange everything.

Although some were content with involvement, others remarked how difficult it was to be 'put on the spot' when they were not used to taking control of decision-making. These parents felt their contribution to be less than full while social workers thought it was significant. Invariably, differences were accounted for by parents feeling they had problems, such as their relationship with partners, which they would have liked to have been aired. There was no opportunity to integrate these issues into the agenda for the meeting:

> I wanted to tell them that one of my big problems was the way he upset us all when he came for his contact sessions, but somehow there was no space to say this. It was all about my health.

The vast majority of parents had felt able to put forward any points that were important and said that they had actively helped to shape the plan. It was clear from both workers and parents that any participation was set within fairly constrained boundaries. There was, for example, little choice between different carers and, in three of the four agencies, the maximum length of any placement was pre-determined by resources rather than need. However, these constraints apart, parents were able to influence how often and when children would be accommodated. The expert information they held about children's needs and habits was often brought out in meetings. This helped to enhance parents' sense of being in control. They also were used as 'experts' on their children's needs in many cases and contributed substantially to practical details. The following comments illustrate parents' experience of meetings:

> I was scared of going there but we'd talked to Sarah before and she said she'd be there. It was easy, it was all worked out.

> I was so pleased to have the kids away for the weekend I'd have done anything. They kept asking me if it was alright. I was that pleased to know I would have some time with Jason [partner], I was happy for them to arrange things. It was nice to be asked but not necessary.

> Last time there was a meeting was when they thought he'd done things to the children. That was horrible but this time it was friendly. They asked me when Jo should go [to the carers] I told them it was best from Friday to Sunday. They said 'Alright then'.

The relationship between consultation and participation

The experience of parents in this study suggests that there may be a place for both active participation and more passive involvement in enacting partnership theory. The essential feature is to be sensitive to parents' capabilities and prior experience of formal meetings. Some may need considerable help before they move from being involved to actively participating.

The individuality of circumstances is reflected in the fact that there was not always an association between consultation and participation in meetings. Three parents who felt they had only partially participated in planning meetings thought there had been satisfactory consultation. Conversely, 11 out of the 57 who had fully participated did not feel they had been fully consulted, mainly because of neglect of their agendas as described earlier. As Thoburn et al. (1995) have suggested, the issue of partnership is more complex in practice than in theory and cannot be imposed upon social work processes.

The social work task, as always, is not to mould individuals into an ideology-led framework, but rather to respond to their needs and wishes in a way that makes them feel valued and comfortable. This calls for sensitive assessment of parental strengths and styles. Social workers are coming to planning meetings with different knowledge and expectations from parents. These will influence professional perspectives of participation and how both parties see their role in decision-making. This is explicitly exemplified in the current study by the discrepancy between social workers' and parents' view of the power of social workers at the planning meeting.

To explore this issue parents and social workers were asked to comment on the impact of social workers on decision making in the planning meeting. Social workers saw their impact on decision making as less powerful than parents estimated it to be. All parents saw social workers as powerful contributors to the decision making. By contrast, eight social workers felt their power was limited.

Explanations lie in the fact that workers often felt powerless because the service was constrained either by its length, or because no choice of placement was offered to parents. In addition, social workers did not recognise the power that comes from holding knowledge and information not known by others. In short, they knew the system – when to speak, whom to contact if additional services were required and held in their hands the power to determine which carers would be selected for individual families.

The impact of social workers at this stage

The process of inquiry, consultation, assessment and decision-making requires considerable social work skills and the use of a casework relationship, such as that described by Perlman (1963) which is offered as a means of empowerment. It is difficult to identify the range of styles and actions which convey to parents the essence of a good social worker. Material from other studies about qualities in social workers which clients have found to be helpful, provided the research team with some clues. In *Social Work Decisions in Child Care*, for example, it was reported that:

> What was appreciated most was honesty, naturalness and reliability along with an ability to listen. Clients appreciated being kept informed, having their feelings understood, having the stress of parenthood accepted and getting practical help as well as moral support. (DHSS 1985b, p. 20)

Figure 6.8 *Parents' experience of social workers at start of intervention (n=60*)*

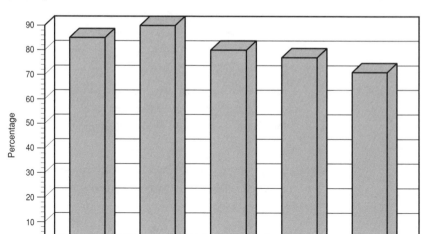

*Categories are not mutually exclusive

These qualities were discussed with parents in a family centre and, with their help, a typology of five major characteristics valued in social workers was developed. Parents were asked to rate their answers on a five-point scale. Figure 6.8 shows a collapsed rating of excellent or good.

It can be seen that, at the beginning of the study, parents rated family support social workers very highly on all dimensions. In fact they were positively glowing in their views. Well over four-fifths of the parents found the social workers highly credible on all of the measures, and very few (only one or two parents) found the social worker significantly lacking in these qualities. Parents' descriptions of the five qualities illustrate the findings.

Approachability

Approachability was described as being able to confide in workers about problems without this being interpreted as abdication of parental responsibility. Parents felt workers were trustworthy and would take what they said at face value:

> I don't like talking to strangers, but I could talk to her . . . she made me feel it was OK.

I felt that I could trust her . . . to know that when I said I needed a break that was what I meant and not that I was about to go nuts. I suppose I'd say I trusted her, you know, after I knew her a bit. Straight, you might say, that's what made it possible to approach her, as you put it.

I was ever so nervous, but she gave me a cup of tea and didn't rush me.

She said she didn't know how I managed . . . to make it so homely, and after that I thought – I could talk to you.

Honesty

Honesty in workers was perceived by the fact that the accommodation service was not going to be used as a way of observing their parenting capacity. The offer was 'up front'. Workers were being honest about resources and limitations:

You know where you are with him.

She set it out straight . . . we're here to help, not to take your kids into care.

They said we can't give you everything you want; we haven't got enough carers but we can offer help for three months. At least I knew where I stood.

Understanding

Understanding implies that social workers could empathise with parents' problems and make a realistic appraisal of what could be changed. Lack of a patronising attitude on the part of workers was essential to parents' perception of genuine understanding:

He made me feel he could see why I was so stressed with Jason getting into trouble in school and he offered the breaks to give me a break.

She helped me to see why things happened without blaming me.

I really felt overwhelmed . . . she said she wasn't surprised and she'd feel the same if she was me.

He thought I was really good coping on my own with no help from him [partner – a long-distance lorry driver].

Helpfulness

Helpfulness was strongly linked with the availability of workers. There was a sense in which parents felt able to hand over to workers some of their burdens and workers would come back with answers. This clearly raised the delicate balance that needs to be struck between parental participation and the relief that comes from a helping hand at times of stress. There was a sense of feeling in safe hands, where workers would hold together the arrangements. Although some parents were able to make links with carers themselves, the idea of a worker in the background as a safety net was most important and reinforces the necessity for a complete care manager role for workers:

> I was worried about Donna getting to school on the Monday and then Pauline [social worker] said she'd sort it with Sue [carer] and the school. I thought it would be difficult, but she organised it.

> I knew I could phone if it wasn't going well and Sharon was unhappy.

> I felt a wave of relief when she suggested the breaks. At last, some help. She just went away sorted it out and came to tell me about the carers, John and Susanna. Then we had the meeting. It wasn't really necessary but they made me feel I was the one who had decided. That was good.

> I never thought I'd get help but suddenly there she was telling me about the breaks and offering it to me. I couldn't believe my luck.

Reliability

Reliability was just that – being reliable. It was extremely important to parents that the rules did not change. What had been agreed would be delivered. Parents preferred to know about restrictions in service than to hope in vain for more than was possible:

> She came when she said.

> She said she'd find out about a house transfer for me and she did.

> I wasn't sure, I thought it might not turn out as she said, but she kept her word.

> It was good, I thought, I got what I expected.

> I was worried about what they would be like [carers]. She told me they were fine and she was right. They were really nice and wanted to help.

These findings are hardly surprising. To have overcome the obstacle course of lack of information and the stringent gatekeeping of access workers, and actually to have been offered a family support service without any visible signs of child rescue lurking in the background was indeed remarkable, in the current ethos of a service heavily prioritised towards children at risk of significant harm (Aldgate and Tunstill 1995). Undoubtedly, parents' perceptions of social workers at the start of the arrangements were influenced not only by their experiences in the processes of consultation and decision-making, but by what might be described as the exhilaration they experienced at being offered *any* family support service, and their anticipation of the relief the service would bring to the family. Not surprisingly, therefore, there was a significant statistical association between a composite rating by parents of the qualities of social workers at the beginning of the service and their anticipation that the service would meet their needs (p= <0.001, df=1, Chi square). The direction of that association was difficult to identify. What was important was that parents liked and trusted their family support social workers and were positively anticipating the short-term accommodation service.

Summary

The role of family support social worker was central to the successful delivery of the short-term accommodation service. The family support social worker worked in partnership with parents, undertook direct work with children and casework with parents, organised and supported the placement and worked collaboratively with other professionals on behalf of the family. The role was underpinned by a philosophy that reconciled the promotion of children's welfare with the support of families.

Social work was undertaken by one or two or more workers according to the severity of problems to be addressed.

Although broadly speaking, there was a shared agenda for intervention, parents' weighting of individual problems at the beginning of the study tended to differ from that of social workers. Both parents and workers agreed that social isolation was a major problem. Parents placed more emphasis on relationships with partners and the management of children. They were less concerned about their health, neighbours, housing and financial problems.

There was evidence that the consultation process with parents and others specified in *Guidance and Regulations* was being implemented well.

Parents felt they had been consulted properly. The majority felt there had been a full opportunity to discuss their problems and what the accommodation service might offer them. During the consultation process, parents valued time to think, an opportunity to ask questions and reassurance about their anxieties in relation to children being accommodated.

Parents felt consultation to be most satisfactory when they shared with social workers a common agenda for problem-solving.

The majority of parents felt fully involved in the decision-making process.

All parents had attended planning meetings. The success of the meeting depended on social workers' ability to create an informal atmosphere. In the minority of cases where meetings were held in the parental home, this provided a comfortable, unthreatening location.

Parents valued their attendance at meetings highly and generally found this to be an empowering experience.

Some parents who had never experienced the forum of a planning meeting felt inhibited and found it difficult to participate actively. Nevertheless, they perceived their presence at the meeting as a sign of their importance to the proceedings.

More thought needs to be given to the relationship between active participation and involvement. Some parents may be content to be quietly participating. Others may need to rehearse their views prior to the meeting so they feel confident to express themselves in public.

Difficulties within planning meetings related to the absence of a shared agenda where parents wished to address matters that had not been seen as relevant by social workers. There needs to be sensitivity to parents' agendas, especially their perceptions of problems.

Social workers were rated highly by parents at the beginning of the study on approachability, honesty, understanding, helpfulness and reliability. Their input in setting up the service in partnership was highly valued by parents.

7 Action and endings

The *Guidance and Regulations on Family Placements* suggest that the consultation and decision-making processes described in Chapter 6 should culminate in the writing of the child care plan. This is the specific blueprint for the next phase of delivering the short-term accommodation service. Additionally, *Guidance and Regulations* Volume 3 (DoH 1991a) is comprehensive in its instructions to social workers on implementing the plan through setting up, supervising and ending the placement. Although the Regulations apply to all family placements, there are certain aspects, such as contact between parents and children looked after, which seem particularly aimed at full-time placements. Accordingly, in this study, we decided to select areas of activity underpinned by the legislation which reflected the special characteristics of short-term accommodation.

This approach also allowed for inclusion of details of two other aspects of practice: the social work processes involved in this stage, which correspond to Compton and Galloway's (1989) 'action phase' of problem-solving casework (see Chapter 6), and the complex role of the family support social worker, on the one hand facilitating and on the other, undertaking direct work with parents and children.

The issues considered in this phase are:

- child care plans and written agreements;
- preparing for the placement;
- managing the placement;
- social worker evaluation of the short-term accommodation service; and
- parents' evaluation of social workers and their influence on the course and outcome of the service.

Child care plans and written agreements

Guidance and Regulations, Volume 3 state that 'there is no prescribed format for the child care plan' but it should be recorded and contain key elements concerned with the child's needs and the placement arrangements (DoH 1991a, pp. 15–16).

In 100% of cases, there was some form of written plan available. Plans did indeed vary in their length and presentation. Some were no more than one page of A4. Others were two or three pages of considerable detail.

The Children Act Regulations require that the child care plan should be translated into writing and be incorporated into a written agreement:

> Where a child is provided with voluntary accommodation the plan should form the basis of a written agreement between the responsible authority and the parents . . . Regulation 5(3) requires the responsible authority to produce a written copy of the agreement which incorporates the plan for the child and the agreement made. (DoH 1991a, p. 16)

There is some ambiguity in the *Guidance and Regulations* about the relationship between the plan and the agreement, which leaves latitude for interpretation. It is not specified whether the same document could be used to represent plans and agreement or whether they should be separate. In this study, both interpretations obtained, although it was only in a minority of the 60 placements, eight in all, that written agreements were drawn up separately from the child care plan. However, in all of the remaining cases, a child care plan was constructed jointly between workers and parents. In 51 cases (85%) parents had some details in writing but there were nine cases from two authorities where parents were not given copies of any plan in writing.

Reasons for the differing uses of plans and agreements seemed to relate to agency custom rather than to legal requirements. In one study authority, written agreements had formed part of any family placement arrangements well before the Act. Therefore this authority, which organised short-term accommodation within a general provision of family placements, had supplemented written agreements for parents with the detailed child care plans required by the Children Act to be held on file. The system was explained on the grounds that the plan required complex information which was not easily digested by parents. Having a separate agreement written in simple language highlighted for parents and children the information they needed but did not burden them with undue detail.

A second authority also organised its short-term accommodation through the family placements team. By contrast, its policy was to adopt agreements only in cases where problems of termination of the placement were anticipated. In one case, for example, workers worried about parents wishing to use short-term arrangements as a stepping stone to full-time accommodation. It must be stressed that using short-term accommodation as a back door to full-time accommodation was extremely rare, confined to this one case only. In two others, an agreement was necessary to allow for the review of open-ended placements.

In the third authority, social workers told the research team they thought agreements were a good idea but had not yet adopted them for every case because of resource constraints. In the meantime they were using the child care plan as the agreement but hoped to change the system within the next year. This authority did not always give parents details in writing.

By contrast, the fourth authority (described in Figure 5.2) had set up the short-term accommodation as a separate enterprise outside the usual full-time placements. Its planning processes were more streamlined and the agency workers considered it a waste of social work and parental time to provide a separate document. Plans were written in straightforward language and parents were always given a copy. Since all parents were included in constructing the plan, it was argued that the composition of a second document seemed superfluous. Both workers and parents were happy with this arrangement. It did not seem to inhibit the process of partnership but rather enhanced it. What made the partnership work was the fact that the purpose and details of the intervention were very clear and this was reflected in the content of any written document.

Because of the very short-term nature of some of the arrangements, the conflation of the two documents seemed appropriate and conserving of scarce social work resources. Conversely, where arrangements were complex, written agreements served to emphasise to parents significant points in the child care plan. They were particularly helpful in clarifying the basis on which any extensions of service might be given in open-ended arrangements.

Family support and child care plans

In all cases, there was an implicit assumption that the aim of short-term accommodation was to prevent family breakdown. The promotion of children's welfare was therefore inseparable from a broader concept of family support. Thus, although a child was defined as in need under Section 17 to justify the allocation of resources to the service provided, in order to meet that need, in all cases the family rather than the individual was seen as the unit of support. A systems approach (see, for example, Maluccio et al. 1986) was adopted by all four agencies whereby different members of the family could be targeted for social work action in order to achieve the overall aim of promoting the welfare of children 'in need'. So, in some cases, relieving parental stress would be enough to promote children's welfare. In other cases, where children's emotional health was of concern, any casework activity was focused on children during the accommodation arrangements. In others, parent–child interaction was seen as the cause of stress. This demanded intervention with both parents and children simultaneously. Finally, some families exhibited a multiplicity of problems which required an equally complex response from a variety of agencies.

Packages of intervention

In identifying the services accompanying short-term accommodation, two aspects of the provision were explored:

1   intervention or services offered or co-ordinated by social services; and

2   intervention or services offered by other agencies.

Intervention or services offered or co-ordinated by social services

The role of the family support social worker was to decide and arrange who should offer any package of services and if necessary liaise with other agencies offering relevant services. In fact, in 41 of the 60 cases, the managing social workers carried out all the social work activities themselves, but in the remaining 19 families, specialist casework services were used concurrently with accommodation, with the provision of these delegated to others within social services or other agencies. Most of these additional social work services centred on improving parenting skills, counselling parents on relationships with partners, or on direct work with children. Fourteen of these 19 families were also attending social-services-run family centres at the start of the study and 15 were using child-minding.

Intervention or services offered by other agencies

Additional to services offered by social services, the majority of parents (52) had been receiving some active help from other agencies at the time of referral for short-term accommodation. These included community health, mental health care for parents, use of playgroups or day care, housing, probation, services from education psychologists and social workers and a range of voluntary sector provision, such as Homestart. In only seven cases were the links with other agencies set up by social workers as part of the short-term accommodation package, two where children were referred to child guidance, one where there was liaison with education, and the remaining four where social workers were in touch with health visitors. In the rest contacts had predated the accommodation arrangements.

Table 7.1 shows the distribution of other services provided by social services and others.

Table 7.1 *Distribution of services provided*

Service	Provider	Number
Day care for under-fives	Social services	16
Child-minder	Social services	15
Family centre	Social services	14
Casework	Social services	10
Community health services	Other agency	42
Education	Other agency	30
Mental health services	Other agency	17
Housing	Other agency	11
Casework or counselling	Other agency	9
Probation	Other agency	5
Befriending services	Other agency	2

Main aim of social work intervention

Having explored the services which were included alongside accommodation, social workers were asked to identify the main aim of any package of intervention. From social work replies, it was possible to construct a typology of family problems addressed by the child care plan, in other words, a typology of the main aim of social work intervention. This typology has features in common with the typologies of social work support developed by Gibbons (1992) in her study of family support and by Cleaver and Freeman (1995) in relation to child protection enquiries. It has been adapted from previous studies to take account of service delivery under scrutiny in this study. The typology also reflected the management, provider and facilitator roles of social workers organising short-term accommodation. Broadly, the primary aim of social work intervention identified by family support social workers fell into five main categories:

- ♦ to respond to acute parental need;
- ♦ to meet families' chronic need;
- ♦ to ameliorate parent–child problems;
- ♦ to meet children's specific needs; and
- ♦ to address parents' health needs.

The distribution of these categories is shown in Table 7.2.

Table 7.2 *Distribution of aims between the different categories (n=60)*

Main aim of social work intervention	Number	Percentage
To respond to acute parental need	19	32
To meet families' chronic need	17	28
To ameliorate parent–child problems	15	25
To meet children's specific needs	6	10
To address parents' health needs	3	5

To respond to acute parental need

The primary aim of almost one-third of social workers when offering short-term accommodation was in response to acute parental need. For this group, the social worker felt that the family would be supported by strengthening the parent's abilities. In these families, social workers were responding to the acute needs of parents, recognising that these needs were impacting upon children's well-being.

In accordance with the principles underpinning Children Act practice, it was very much a case of recognising that parents have needs in their own right (see DoH 1991b). It was also recognised that attending to parents' needs would indirectly meet those of their children. Acute parental need also implied that parents' strengths were in existence but had been temporarily immobilised. With space for parents to attend to themselves, the family's well-being would be restored.

Examples of families' need for support were a student nurse given time to finish her studies following the breakdown of child care arrangements within the extended family; time for a parent to build a relationship with a new partner whose presence in the household was significant to the well-being of the children; and, in a family where the father was a long-distance lorry driver, a placement to provide relief from stress for the mother and attend to a 7-year-old's behaviour problems. In most cases, the family support social workers both arranged and delivered any direct services themselves.

To meet families' chronic need

The second largest category of social work activity is that of response to chronic family need, relating to just over a quarter of families (17). Workers described these families having multi-faceted needs, where there was a strong possibility of family breakdown. Short-term accommodation was rarely considered to be enough on its own. Consequently, complementary services were in evidence in this group. There were sometimes hints of children being at risk of abuse and more often neglect, but never enough to place the child within the Section 47 definition of being at risk of significant harm. Workers stressed the long-term vulnerability of families and believed that focused family support at this point in time was the best hope of preventing 'more intrusive intervention' at a later stage (Hardiker et al. 1996). By and large, these were families whose social problems were complex and more long-standing than the acute parental need category. They included parents with similar levels of stress but also with a long history of psycho-social adversity. Around two-thirds were headed by lone parents.

Although social workers had not singled out parental health as the main target of intervention, many of the 'chronic need' families were characterised by poor mental health. There was evidence of recurring bouts of mental illness, such as long-standing clinically diagnosed depression or anxiety. Because of the serious nature of the problems in six cases, short-term accommodation was offered alongside other services, including mental health primary care, casework for parents and direct work with children. Here, the family support social worker combined the roles of direct service and facilitation.

A good example was a mother living with three children on income support. Over the last five years she had experienced two periods in hospital for depression. She had recently been deserted by her partner. One child had been suspended from school and with his brother had been statemented under the Education Act 1991. During her last hospital stay, all the children had a brief period in full-time accommodation. The short-term accommodation was offered as a last attempt to keep the family together. The two older children were offered placements while the baby was left with his mother. Very experienced carers were chosen who could offer support to both mother and children.

To ameliorate parent–child problems

A quarter of plans (15) aimed to address the relationship between parent and child. There were cases where children's behaviour was troubling the family, for example, there was an eating disorder or children displayed 'tantrums' which parents could not control. In one case, workers felt the child needed the experience of spending time with a 'father figure.' Carers were selected who could simultaneously work with children and parents on the management of the parent–child relationship. This interaction was the main focus of the placement, held together by the family support social worker.

In one family, the separation of parents and the ensuing problems over contact had led to a rift in the relationship between mother and daughter with aggressive outbursts directed from the daughter to her mother. Both mother and child were being seen by child and family guidance. Short-term accommodation carers were found who could help the child come to terms with the loss of her father while the mother readjusted to her changed circumstances. At the same time, carers played a significant role in modelling appropriate parenting, helping the mother focus on her daughter's needs, and building up her own self-confidence.

To meet children's specific needs

Only six plans were couched in terms of primarily meeting the children's needs through short-term accommodation. All these children were living in families where there was also chronic family need but workers felt that the children's circumstances placed them specially at risk. These children were on the borderline of being at risk of significant harm.

They were a particularly vulnerable group. A scrutiny of individual cases shows two instances of potential neglect, three of potential emotional abuse and one where a 9-year-old was inappropriately acting as the main carer of her younger siblings. Four children in this group were receiving specialist direct work during the placement alongside the general support from the family support social worker. By the end of the study two children had come into full-time accommodation.

To address parents' health needs

In only three instances was parental health the main reason for the intervention. They were a single father with a heart condition, a mother with a kidney problem who needed hospital care from time to time, and a pregnant mother. Here the care for the parent was handed over to the health services while the family support social worker oversaw the placement arrangements for the children.

All three cases featured physical ill health, although as discussed earlier in the section on chronic family need, underlying mental health problems were an important factor for several families, but seen as secondary to other problems. This reflects the findings from several studies, which show that social workers experience difficulties in assessing risk in cases of parental mental illness (Cleaver et al. 1996).

Preparing for the placement

Preparing children and families for a placement has been an integral part of good child care practice for several decades. In the 1950s Charnley (1955) claimed: 'Children are least harmed when they are least surprised.' In the 1970s research suggested that the impact of placements was no less significant for parents than for children and that preparation could do much to allay fears and myths about carers as well as reassure children that their parents knew where they were (see Jenkins and Norman 1972; Aldgate 1977). Additionally, studies of children in hospital suggested that preparation was a factor influencing children's cognitive appraisal of treatment (Stacey et al. 1970). Attachment theory has changed its cultural context since the writings of Bowlby in the 1950s but, in the 1980s and 1990s, the principle of recognising the impact on children of separation from significant adults and siblings is no less important today than it was four decades ago (see Fahlberg 1981b; Jewett 1984; Aldgate 1992; Howe 1995).

Every parent had the opportunity to visit the carers' home before the placement. Fifty-one (85%) took advantage of this offer. Additionally, every child had met the carer before the first period of accommodation.

Parents suggested that visits to carers' homes did much to allay fears discussed in detail in Chapter 4 and reassure them that carers were not rivals for their children's affections. There were three main factors that reassured parents and helped them feel in control of the arrangements:

- ♦ proximity of the placement;
- ♦ carers seen as service providers for parents; and
- ♦ carers perceived by parents to be from a similar background to themselves.

Managing the placement

Social work input was an important part of the short-term accommodation service, with the role of the family support social worker central to sucess. It was most important to families that there was an identifiable worker who held the arrangements together throughout the placement. Although there was some additional specialist input in just under one-third of the cases, the family support workers were both facilitators and providers in relation to the placement. They steered the child care plan, prepared parents and children, linked families to carers, and undertook four main activities during the time the accommodation arrangements were in place. These were:

♦ formal contact – reviews and supervisory visits;

♦ informal contact with parents and children, mainly by letter and telephone;

♦ support and contact for carers (see Chapter 8); and

♦ ending the placement and the intervention.

The holding together of these activities between the triad of parent, child and carer is classic child care social work which has been described in the literature for many years and which has not been changed by the Children Act (see, for example, Pugh 1968; Thoburn 1988). In this area, the Act is building upon a well-developed knowledge base of child care practice.

Formal contact: reviews and supervisory visits

The welfare of all children looked after by the local authority must be monitored and reviewed at regular intervals. The Children Act tightened up the requirements in respect of the supervision and review of placements, putting all children looked after under the same regulations. Children Act Regulations specify clearly the requirements for supervising and reviewing all placements, including short-term accommodation. In relation to supervision, special arrangements have been made for short-term accommodation in the relevant statutory instruments but the Act requires they are regulated. In the case of short-term placements, the first visit must take place:

(a) during the first in the series of placements, and

(b) again, if more than six months pass from the beginning of that first placement when the child is in fact placed. (DoH 1991a, p. 155)

In addition to these supervisory visits, the Children and Young Persons' – Review of Children's Cases Regulation 1991 demands that:

3(1) Each case is first to be reviewed within four weeks of the date upon which the child begins to be looked after or provided with accommodation by a responsible authority.

(2) The second review shall be carried out not more than three months after the first and thereafter subsequent reviews shall be carried out not more than six months after the date of the previous review.

It is generally expected that, before conducting the review, the responsible authority will take into account the views of:

(a) the child;

(b) his parents;

(c) any person who is not a parent of his but who has parental responsibility for him; and

(d) any other person whose views the authority consider to be relevant. (DoH 1991a, p. 156)

In the study, each arrangement was reviewed shortly after the first break, as required by the Review of Children's Cases Regulations. A 'review' did not necessarily entail a specifically convened meeting and often referred to instances when carers, parents and some children were asked whether the arrangement had been satisfactory. In spite of the informality, parents and carers were clear that they had met to review the placement. Thereafter, many of the arrangements were reviewed 'as required', which generally meant at points where a change was requested or indicated. This happened in about one-quarter of the cases.

Given that 26 of the 59 arrangements followed up were of short duration (three months or less), this seemed to work quite satisfactorily. Three-quarters of those which lasted over three months were subject to a second review.

The implementation of the requirements was therefore encouraging. But there were some problems reported in relation to the timing of reviews. Workers said it was difficult to fulfil the law because how long placements would last was often uncertain. There was also some confusion about the interpretation of the law. Did three months mean three months of the calendar or did Regulation 9 allow for three months of placement days? A majority thought that it was the calendar months that counted but were clearly uncertain. The rest calculated placement time by the number of days in placement but this was not an easy task. (In only a handful cases were carers asked to inform workers formally of the days in placement, although this information was clearly made available to the finance department.) Additionally, apart from confusion about the legal requirements, if a placement was going well and was to end within six to eight weeks, even if it was over the limit for the second review, the urgency of reviewing arrangements was not so strong. Conversely, if arrangements had been in existence for well over six calendar months, this clearly signalled to workers that a review was due. The research team was left feeling that the organisation of reviews for short-term placements needed some clarification within all four agencies and that some modification to national guidance might be appropriate.

Supervisory visits were conflated with review meetings. It was clear that not all placements were actually visited, probably because placements occurred mainly at weekends. Consulting child, parent and carer sometimes by separate meetings or through review meetings was the norm. Again there was some confusion here about what was required but social workers did ensure that a 'review', formal or otherwise, was always conducted after the first weekend away, although they had not strictly adhered to the legal requirements by seeing the child within the placement, which was a worrying omission.

Parents and social workers always met together for the 'review'. Thirty of the 41 older children were present and most of the remaining children had been consulted in advance. Only ten carers, mainly from one authority, did not attend any review and a further five attended some but not all. This meant practically three-quarters of carers (44) attended every review.

Informal contact with parents and children

Informal meetings to monitor the placement were rare in all four authorities and occurred between parents and workers in only four cases. Because many families did not have a telephone, much informal contact was done by letter. Although the communication focused on the practical arrangements for the beginnings and endings of a particular break, as Aldgate et al. (1989) have pointed out, the contact by workers between placements in short-term arrangements can take on greater significance for parents in confirming the regularity of the placements. It also has a symbolic function. It seals the agreement made and can be instrumental in helping families 'hang on' until the next break occurs. This feature was clearly evident in this study.

It was of interest that while at least 30 children were over the age of literacy, letters were not a means of communication used by social workers. To test the impact of this on children was beyond the scope of the study and any conclusion of the omission of letters to children can only be speculation. To some of the older children, a letter might have done much to reinforce children's self-esteem by confirming that the placements were for them as much as for their parents. Only two children spoke to workers on the telephone.

Contact between carers and social workers was regular, although often face-to-face contact was confined to formal supervisory or review meetings.

Telephone contact was a frequently used means of communication which was appreciated by carers and occurred in all but one case. Much of the contact during the placement was to confirm practical arrangements but in about a third of the cases, it was clear from carers that discussion entailed support for carer families (see Chapter 8).

Clearly, what tended to happen in many cases was that carers took over a care manager role alongside any direct work with parents and children. For some carers this was acceptable; for others, as will be shown in the next chapter, it was a burden they had not been anticipating.

Summary of the family support social worker role

Managing the placement was important for parents, children and carers. The contact maintained by social workers made all parties feel that there was a safety net if things went wrong. For example, parents gained much encouragement from the formal meetings held to review placements and letters sealed agreed arrangements and boosted families' morale until the next break. Contact with carers was also an important part of the placement support system and will be discussed in the next chapter.

The management role was important to the success of the placement and to the impact of the service on parents and children. Above anything else it was the activity which made links between the social work processes involved in intervention, the legal requirements of regulation and guidance and the agency role ascribed to workers.

Once again, it was the continued presence of the family support social worker throughout these different stages that gave families confidence in the service and reassured most carers that support was available if it was needed. The same results would not have been achieved in a purchaser–provider culture or one which did not recognise the value of casework to allow parents time to reflect and re-adjust their lifestyle.

Endings

The family support social worker was less effective in ensuring a sound transition to end the intervention. Parents, children and carers alike commented on the fact that it was left to them both to effect an ending and say good-byes and to come to terms with the transition. Parents felt this was unsatisfactory, leaving them no time to reflect on the improvement sustained throughout the period of the arrangements.

Children comment about their feelings on leaving carers in Chapter 9. As will be shown in the next chapter, carers felt an unfair burden was placed on them to end the placement.

Comments from parents summarise the problem:

> It was awful saying good-bye to Alice and John. I felt they were friends. It spoilt what had been good that we couldn't keep up contact.

> She cried when she left. She kept saying why can't I see them. Marian [child of carer] is my friend. It's not fair.

Others kept in touch informally which helped ease the end of the placement:

> I still phone them and I've been round for tea a few times.

> Tessa sees Tony at school so we keep in touch. I do miss them.

Given the centrality of attachment theory in child care social work, it seems surprising that little was done to effect a formal transition (see for example, Aldgate and Simmonds 1992), although the lack of attention given to the ending of foster care placements has been reported elsewhere in research (see Aldgate and Hawley 1986). Perhaps workers underestimated the strength of the impact of the short-term accommodation service on parents and children. It may well have been assumed that, because children kept their home base throughout the service, the impact of living with others was not so great. This attitude has been found in research on respite placements for children with disabilities (Stalker 1989). Such assumptions fly in the face of theory and would not be endorsed by child care textbooks. Jewett (1984), for example, exhorts workers to recognise the impact of placement end on all concerned. Certainly the findings from this study would urge that more attention be given to this important aspect of child care practice. Also missing was any evaluation of the impact of the intervention on families in terms of feedback. This seemed strange given the considerable effort that had been put into the building of partnerships early in the planning stage and the emphasis on holding together arrangements throughout the duration of the placement.

Social workers' evaluation of the short-term accommodation service

As shown in Chapter 4, the study explored outcomes in terms of parents' satisfaction with the service. None the less it is important to explore two other measures of outcome:

1   whether the services ended as planned; and

2   whether social workers thought their aims had been met in full.

Did the service end as planned?

Most (81%) of the placements in all four agencies ended as planned or were continuing satisfactorily by the end of the study. It is important to note that of the 11 which ended prematurely, only two were categorised as failures by social workers in that they did not prevent family breakdown and children needed to be accommodated full-time. These are described fully in Chapter 4.

In the remaining nine cases parents and workers agreed that the placement should end early. In all cases, the experience had been beneficial for parents and children. For example, in five families, the accommodation had enabled parents rapidly to resolve their problems:

> Once we were on our feet, in charge of life again, you might say, I felt
> it was time to end, and so did Katy and Dean.

Two teenage boys requested an end to short-term accommodation because they were homesick and a return home was organised as soon as it was practically possible:

> Yes, it was good and I did enjoy it . . . but now that Mum is OK I want
> to be with her. I couldn't see my mates or go to the match.

Finally, there were two cases where unexpected problems in the carer family brought the placement to an early end. Rather than transfer the children to another carer, there was a unanimous decision, led by parents, to end the placement prematurely.

At the end of the study period nine cases were continuing satisfactorily. All of these were in Ferryport and reflected the policy of that particular scheme to offer a more open-ended service. In looking in detail at the nine cases, it emerged that five were cases of chronic stress, where families had multiple, long-standing problems. In two cases there had been issues of emotional neglect and social workers remained concerned about children's needs. In another two, social workers were concerned about the families' general management of children's behaviour. Eight out of the nine families were receiving at least three other services alongside the short-term accommodation, including mental health care for parents, casework and psychological services for children as well as a range of day care.

Did social workers think their aims had been fully met?

As suggested at the beginning of the chapter, exploring the role of the social workers concentrated on social work processes and their contribution to the impact of the service upon families. One major limitation of the study was the restrictions placed by agencies on the research team in relation to time spent directly with social workers. Accordingly, any study of outcome from the social work point of view was confined to two broad-based questions:

1   What were the main hurdles of delivering the service?

2   Were social workers' aims for individual families met?

What were the main hurdles of delivering the service?

One-third of placements (20) had caused social workers few difficulties in making suitable arrangements for children. Difficulties arose in cases where more specialist placements were needed. Workers were frustrated by not having enough time to recruit a range of carers to meet the diversity of children's individual needs. They found that much of their time was spent setting up individual arrangements or supporting existing carers to the detriment of recruiting new families and developing a wide range of resources. Equally frustrating was the scarcity of existing carers who were sufficiently skilled to work intensively with parents especially on improving their parenting skills.

A second difficulty, discussed from the parents' perspective in Chapter 5, was the image of social services as a child rescue agency. Social workers had to spend a unexpected amount of time reassuring some parents that the short-term accommodation service was not a back door to full-time accommodation or care. Though this was accepted as a necessary foundation for working in partnership with parents and children, it demanded more time and effort than they had anticipated.

Thirdly, there was a minority of cases which exemplified the tensions of taking into account the wishes of children as required by the Children Act, and meeting the needs of parents. Social workers thought that the only responsible action to prevent family breakdown with its concomitant adverse affects on children's welfare was to override the wishes of the children and arrange short-term accommodation.

Were social workers' aims for individual families met?

At the second interview, social workers were reminded of their stated aims of intervention at the start of the study and asked to say to what extent they believed their aims had been met. Overall, in practically two-thirds of cases social workers felt their aims had been fully met but, as Table 7.3 shows, there was some variation in successful completion according to the type of problem they had aimed to address.

Table 7.3 *Proportion of social work aims met*

Social work aims	Number of aims	Percentage met
To respond to acute parental need	18	72
To meet family's chronic need	17	65
To ameliorate parent–child problems	15	47
To meet children's specific needs	6	71
To address parents' health needs	3	100

To respond to acute parental need In families where social workers saw their task in terms of meeting acute parental need, their aims were broadly met in almost three-quarters of cases. A clear agenda and a short intensive period of weekend accommodation had helped parents regain their equilibrium enough to carry on supporting their families. There were a minority of cases where social workers felt their aims had not been met. This was unrelated to the needs of the family. The failure reflected social workers' guilt about the fact that money had run out before the agreed amount of short-term accommodation had been completed, resulting therefore in the premature ending of placements. None the less, even in these cases, parents felt the service had been beneficial.

To meet families' chronic need Where the aim was to address chronic family need, social workers' assessment of success related to the evidence of some change in behaviour or attitude on the part of parents or child. Even though these families still retained a high level of stress, social workers felt confident enough to terminate short-term accommodation although for some families, other family support, such as attendance at family centres, child guidance and family counselling continued. Workers in two authorities were in no doubt that problems might resurface for some families. As one worker said: 'We've only reached the tip of the iceberg but it's enough to keep them going for a bit longer.' There was a sense of crisis management in approximately half of the cases.

To ameliorate parent–child problems When social work aims focused on improving parent-child relationships, the key factor to success was brokering a better balance between adult and child need. Workers were especially pleased when parents had improved management of their children. Conversely, social workers felt their aims had not been met in cases where concern about potential neglect or emotional abuse remained. The findings here reflect those in other studies. In their study of teenagers, for example, Triseliotis et al. (1995a), found that the parent–child relationship was particularly resilient to social work interventions.

To meet children's specific needs Where children's specific needs were the target of social work aims, success occurred when parents responded by modifying their behaviour or children's behaviour appeared to benefit from the opportunity of living even for a short while in a different family. Where children exhibited behaviour problems, defined as severe by parents, social worker and carers, the placement did not seem structured or long enough to respond to their needs. As shown in Chapter 4, the two children who were accommodated full-time during the study period came into this group.

To address parents' health needs Where the service had given sick parents some respite so they might regain the full-time care of their children, workers felt a good service had been given.

Outcomes for parents and social work

Having examined social workers' evaluation of the completion of their aims, it is important to relate these to parents' view of the service.

Two measures of outcome were used to do this. First, a rating of the quality of the service: This was elicited through asking parents to rate the service on a five-point scale, ranging from excellent to very poor. Second, there was a rating of quantity of the service: was it enough to meet their needs? This was also elicited on a five-point scale. Subsequently, each scale was conflated to represent a rating of good or excellent against the rest.

Using this revised scale in relation to parental perception of service quality, Table 7.4 shows a high level of congruence between social workers believing their aim had been fully met and parents believing the service was of a high quality. Least satisfactory for both parents and social workers was where the aim of intervention had been to address difficulties in parent–child relationships. This is not surprising. The service was not specifically aimed to address these problems and, where there are entrenched difficulties, effecting change is notoriously difficult as suggested earlier.

Table 7.4 *Parental perceptions of service quality (n=59)*

Social work aim	Number of aims	Percentage of aims fully met	Percentage of parents rating service as good/excellent
To respond to acute parental need	18	72	90
To meet family's chronic need	17	65	71
To ameliorate parent–child problems	15	47	47
To meet children's specific needs	6	71	83
To address parents' health needs	3	100	100

The second aspect explored was the relationship between fully completed social work aims and parents' perceptions of whether the service was enough to meet their needs – the quantity of the service (Table 7.5).

Table 7.5 *Parental perceptions of service quantity (n=59)*

Social work aim	Number of aims	Percentage of aims fully met	Percentage of parents rating service as sufficient
To respond to acute parental need	18	72	66
To meet family's chronic need	17	65	57
To ameliorate parent–child problems	15	47	47
To meet children's specific needs	6	71	40
To address parents' health needs	3	100	100

In contrast to the congruence found between the meeting of social work aims and parents' perception of the *quality* of the service, Table 7.5 suggests that parents were less satisfied with the *amount* of service they received – they wanted more. Although parents could appreciate that social services were operating within finite limits, sometimes they felt thwarted by the amount of accommodation offered:

> The children really responded so well to being able to . . . just relax. Mrs R. sorted things out at home . . . she fairly blossomed. I just wish they could have had longer . . . but there isn't the money. Mrs. Clark [carer] said she will keep in touch, and they can pop in. I know she means it but I couldn't impose on her.

> Why did it have to end? It's not fair on parents like me who are looking after the kids on their own. I was just beginning to feel better. I hoped I'd look for a job but here I am again, looking after the kids and no money.

However, the wish for more accommodation was not related specifically to the actual amount offered in each case. There was no statistical association between the length of the service and parents' level of satisfaction with the amount offered. A similar proportion of parents who had less than three months accommodation were as satisfied with the service as those whose accommodation lasted more than three months. There are several factors that contributed to this finding. In part, it may relate to the different organisation of services. Parents who received short bursts of accommodation tended to be located in one of the authorities which organised its service within a ring-fenced scheme where plans were clear and the amount of service on offer was specified in the child care plan. As one parent said:

> I knew exactly what I was getting – six weekends. It wasn't very much but gave me the space to sort myself out.

By contrast, the other three authorities organised the service through their family placements service and placement lengths were more idiosyncratic. Sometimes it was hard to give up a good thing. At least one parent had resorted to subterfuge to ensure the service continued:

> The trouble is it's so nice having the breaks. They said they'd see how it went. I didn't tell them quite how much better I felt in case it ended. But the more you get the more you want.

The importance of the service to parents was further exemplified by the fact that, in 15 cases, where social workers aims had not been fully met, parents nevertheless rated the service as good or excellent. The reverse was less common when social workers felt the aims had been met. There were only six instances where parents were dissatisfied with the service.

Impact of social work on families' patterns of using social work and other services

A further way of exploring the impact of the accommodation service on families was to examine whether the service had altered the pattern of families' dependence on other services. In Chapter 4 it was shown that parents believed the service had helped to ameliorate some of their problems. There were, for example, reductions in parents' social isolation, resolution of health problems and management of their children. Would this be borne out by a shift in the use of other services? If parents were feeling better and had resolved some of their problems, might this be reflected in a different pattern of dependence on services?

Figure 7.1 and Figure 7.2 together show the changes in the distribution of services. Figure 7.1 shows other services provided by social services at the beginning and at the end of the study, while Figure 7.2 shows the concomitant use of community-based voluntary services.

Figure 7.1 *Family's use of social service provision at start and end of intervention (n=59)*

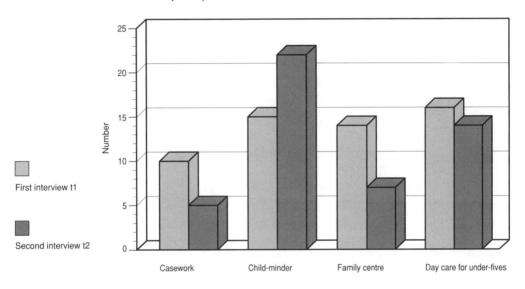

Figure 7.2 *Family's use of community-based services at start and end of intervention (n=59)*

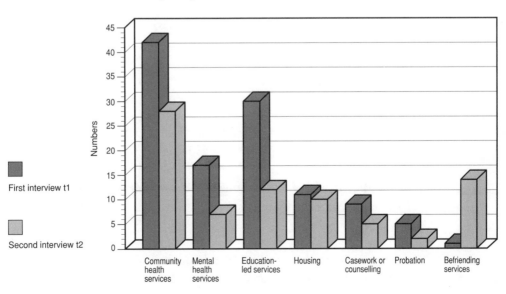

In relation to services under the umbrella of social services, there was a notable increase in the use of child-minders. This is consistent with the finding that parents valued having time for themselves. It also reflects the contacts made with carers, a proportion of whom continued to offer some day care after the short-term accommodation had ended. Conversely, casework services and use of family centres declined as parents began to feel better and turned to friends, families and voluntary arrangements for support.

In relation to community-based services, the most significant changes were the increased use of befriending services. These included a number of women's groups which focused on depression and loneliness, and groups such as Homestart which focus on the improvement of parenting skills.

The use of other community-based services had declined. For example the use of health services for physical ailments fell from 71% to 42%. The doctor's surgery is often used as a universal non-stigmatised point of access to services which may reflect psycho-social as well as defined medical needs. The decline in visits to GP surgeries complements the finding on the perceived reduction by some parents of health problems and the more appropriate refocusing by others on specific health issues (see also Chapter 4). The use of mental health services also fell, possibly because parents' depression or anxiety reduced as they felt more in control of their lives. Nevertheless, one-fifth of parents continued to have mental health problems requiring continued treatment. This finding is worthy of note and reflects that from recent child protection studies (see DoH 1995b).

There was also a halving of the use of education-related services. In a large part, improvement could be attributed to parents' perceptions of the management of their children. Where services continued, this reflected more serious psychological problems in children. Additionally, the use of counselling services to address partnership relationship problems had shown a similar reduction, being retained where problems were still intense. Three probation orders had ended within the period of the study.

Housing problems were static due to the structural problem of reduced housing stock in three of the four authorities. Waiting lists were very long and only parents with critical problems could contemplate a move within months rather than years. Two families, rehoused within the time of the study, were moved on health grounds.

Clearly, it is not possible to attribute the changes causally to the short-term accommodation service alone. Statistically, there are no significant associations between individual changes in service usage and parents' perception of outcome or decline in related problems. Nevertheless, the relative increase or decline in use of each service is consistent with the trend in parents' perceptions of changes in their problems.

Parents' experience of social workers at the start and end of the intervention

At the beginning of the study parents had been asked to rate their social workers along five dimensions. When parents were asked to re-assess their experience of social workers, as Figure 7.3 shows, there was still a positive attitude to social workers overall but the euphoria of the opening encounter had become calmed into a more realistic picture.

Figure 7.3 *Parents' experience of social workers at start and end of intervention (n=59)*

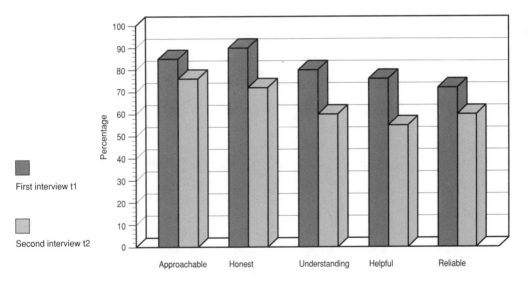

There are two reasons for this change. First, the initial ratings of social workers were given at a time of crisis, when there was a tendency to overstate their role. One is reminded of undertakers, nurses and doctors and occasionally the police, who enjoy a similar adulation borne out of relief and gratitude for responding positively and producing tangible evidence of help at a point of stress. At the second interview, the honeymoon period had ended. Nevertheless, the overall impression of social workers remained positive.

Secondly, the initial impact of social workers had waned because they had dropped away from the scene. As shown earlier, in the action phases of the arrangements, apart from supervisory meetings or reviews, the intensive activity of setting up the placement had been converted into an occasional meeting, letters and telephone calls. Important though these were, nearly one-fifth of the families had no ongoing social work contact at the second interview. Contact for the rest, except for the third who were receiving intensive casework, was confined to letters or, less frequently, phone calls. The initial impact of social workers as parents' champions had waned simply because social workers had faded into the background, although ther symbolic role as the manager of the arrangements had not diminished with lack of contact. However, the euphoria about social workers' direct contact with parents had died down somewhat, mainly because, as will be shown in the next chapter, new heroes and heroines had taken their place.

How parents evaluated their social workers was significantly associated with their overall rating of the short-term accommodation service. There was a statistically significant association between these two variables ($p=<0.04$, $df=1$, Chi square). Eighty-one per cent of parents who were fully satisfied with the service also rated their social workers as excellent. This shows that the service was highly rated by parents and that social workers were seen as significant catalysts in effecting change. The important part played by social workers in this study deserves serious consideration.

Summary

There was some form of child care plan in 100% of cases but considerable variation between the format, length and content. *Guidance and Regulations* were being implemented appropriately and creatively in this respect.

Written agreements were conspicuous by their absence and were often conflated with child care plans. Where arrangements for short-term accommodation are straightforward this may be a cost-effective and efficient way of fulfilling the legislation, provided documents are written in easily accessible language.

The aim of social work intervention was appropriately needs-led and in practically two-thirds of cases social workers felt their aims had been met.

There was a high level of congruence between social workers having attained their aims and parents' satisfaction of the *quality* of the service. The cases where short-term accommodation was judged to have been most successful spanned cases of acute need and chronic need. Cases least successful related to serious behaviour problems in children or serious parent–child relationship problems.

There was less congruence between social workers' views of aims completed and the *quantity* of accommodation. This judgement was based on parents' views of the extent to which problems had been solved rather than to the length of time involved.

From the point of view of social workers, difficulties in arranging placements related to a dearth of specialist carers and the disproportionate amount of time spent at the consultation stage on reassuring parents there was no hidden agenda of child rescue.

Families' use of other services had shifted by the end of the arrangement with a movement towards using more child-minding and befriending resources in the community.

Within the action phase of arrangements, the role of the family support social worker continued to be important. The management role during the placement contributed to the success of the intervention.

There were some difficulties in fulfilling requirements in relation to reviews because of the short-term nature of the placement. Some reviews were missed because they were to occur just before the end of arrangements. There was a missed opportunity here to evaluate with families the usefulness of the intervention.

Endings were poorly managed with parents, carers and children feeling the absence of a formal and symbolic ending to be unsatisfactory.

Overall both the service and social workers were highly rated by parents. Social workers were seen as significant catalysts in effecting change.

8 *Carers, continuity and consideration*

The last chapter showed the contribution of social workers to the outcome of the short-term accommodation service. This chapter looks at the contribution of carers to the outcome for children and families and factors which helped to shape their contribution.

Much has been written about the role of foster parents in general, but with one or two recent exceptions (Berridge and Cleaver 1987; Sellick 1994; Stone 1995), there has been little detailed study of the role of short-term foster carers offering full-time accommodation or care and even less on the role of carers offering short-term accommodation for children who are not disabled.

It is known that foster carers in general are in short supply (Triseliotis et al. 1995b). Therefore to identify the characteristics of carers which are helpful to parents and children is useful for those trying to target sources of recruitment. Understanding what attracts good carers to offer their services is equally significant in ensuring that sufficient carers are recruited to meet the needs of children from a diversity of families.

This chapter first examines parents' perceptions of carers. This is followed by an exploration of factors that contributed to carers' input, such as influences shaping the partnership between parents and carers; carers' motivation and perceptions of their role; and finally the social work influences on carers in relation to recruitment, training and support.

Parents' views on carers

To allow parents to have time to experience and evaluate the service offered by carers, parents' views on carers were solicited at the end of the placement only. At this point, parents were asked to rate carers on the same five-point scale on which they had rated social workers. This was then collapsed to give parents' rating of carers as good or excellent against the rest.

Carers were rated exceptionally highly by parents on each dimension (n=59).

Approachability

In approachability, 86% (51) of carers were rated highly:

> I was shivering with nerves. She said 'Come in and get warm'. She made us tea and biscuits and had some Smarties for Sharon. She asked if Sharon had any of the usual problems like wetting the bed. I'd been dreading raising this because she is 6. My other kids were all dry at 3. But Sandra [carer] made it easy for me to tell her. She said she'd known lots of kids who wet the bed, especially if they were away from home.

The remaining families found carers difficult to talk to:

> She thought she was something in her posh house. We never wanted the kids there really. She kept asking me questions about the kids. I didn't want to know.

Honesty

Parents had no doubt that 95% (56) of carers were completely honest:

> I could have trusted them with anything – well, to leave your kid with someone – it's a big thing.

> They said they'd tell me if they had any trouble with the kids. They didn't pull any punches – told us how naughty they had been and how they had handled them. I respected that.

Three parents felt carers had on occasions been rather economical with the truth about children being allowed to do things they would not normally do at home:

> She said that Amy would always have her own room. But I know the last weekend all her sister's children were there and they had to sleep in the same room.

Understanding

Eighty-three per cent (49) carers were also seen as very understanding:

> They were so understanding, told me all about the time they had been in difficulties. That made me feel not so bad, you know as if they knew what it was like.

I was so relieved someone was going to help me, I cried. I kept apologising.
They said they would cry too if they had coped with what I'd coped with.

She seemed to know what it was like to be feeling depressed, no energy. She
didn't expect too much of me and just seemed to know it would help if they
collected Martin from my house. I couldn't face the bus journey.

However there were ten parents who believed carers did not appreciate their
problems. For example parents thought they had a hostile reception when
unforeseen circumstances meant they arrived late to pick up the children:

I missed the bus, the phone box was broken . . . how did she expect me
to get there by 3 p.m. but she made me feel really guilty.

Helpfulness

Ninety-five per cent of parents rated carers as helpful:

What can I say? They helped me so much when I needed it.

I felt she was a mum to me. I took my washing round sometimes
and she didn't seem to mind.

I could tell her all my troubles. She helped me sort out my life.

Three parents thought carers could have been more helpful. This was generally to do with incidents at the end of the break. Parents felt carers were not
sensitive to their needs at this time:

Whenever I arrive to pick him up he's not ready. I wish she would be more
organised, she has no idea how difficult it is to get John to stay with the
children on a Sunday evening.

Reliability

Most importantly the reliability of carers was valued by 93% (55) of parents:

They always collected Ben when they said and brought him back on time.

I knew I could rely on them to sort out any trouble – say if Tracy was sick.
You just knew it would be alright.

Four parents did not share this positive view:

Sometimes they've been late picking him up. I get really agitated because
it's the only time I have to myself.

Reasons for parents' positive attitude to carers

There were several reasons for the good press which carers received from parents. By the end of the placement in many cases, except for those where there were very serious problems, carers had taken over the counselling role from social workers. They were also given the responsibility of ending the placement. Most importantly, carers were seen in the role as the direct providers of the accommodation service. By opening their homes to the children, they had made it possible for the idea of some respite to be translated into reality. Consequently, parents' gratitude for the short-term accommodation service was immense and, as shown in Chapter 4, they had been motivated to use the time away from their children constructively.

What is unusual, in contrast to many earlier studies of foster care, is that the majority of carers in this study were not seen by parents as rivals but as working partners who were professional, supportive and sometimes educative. How carers achieved this role will now be explored.

There are several important strands of evidence from research and practice wisdom which have identified factors likely to facilitate or hinder the relationship between foster carers, parents and children. These include child-based factors such as the ages of foster children and children in the household and the motivation to foster, attitudes towards parents, contact with parents and children's behaviour. But the overarching concept likely to impact upon any placement, and emphasised in the Children Act 1989, is a child's need for continuity.

Continuity

The *Guidance and Regulations* for Family Placements specifically urges social workers to recognise a child's need for continuity in placements:

> A child's need for continuity in life and care should be a constant factor in choice of placement. In most cases, this suggests a need for placement with a family of the same race, religion and culture in a neighbourhood within reach of family, school or day nursery, church, friends and leisure activities.
>
> Continuity also requires placement in a foster home which a child can find familiar and sympathetic and not remote from his own experience in social background, attitudes and expectations, a foster home in which he is most likely to settle down and as far as possible feel 'at home' and free from anxieties. This is equally if not more necessary where it is not possible to place a child near home or where there are special reasons for choosing a placement at a distance. (DoH 1991a, p. 33)

Placing children in a suitable home to effect continuity may also call for points of identification between carers and parents. Studies have recounted the humiliation felt by parents whose children were placed with families whom they consider to be materially and culturally more affluent than themselves (Millham et al. 1986; Aldgate 1989). Yet parents also have recorded that they do not wish their children to be placed with families that appear to be chaotic and unreliable (Aldgate 1980), while parents of children in residential care have complained bitterly about a culture which allowed children to do things they would not do at home (Fisher et al. 1986).

In short-term accommodation, where the preservation of satisfactory attachments between parents and children is all important to the task of preventing family breakdown, continuity between families is clearly significant. Further, given the expectation that placements may be able to operate with minimal input from social workers (see DoH 1991a, p. 39), considerable onus is placed on parents and carers to ensure there is a viable working relationship. Anything that can facilitate this is therefore important.

The social workers in this study were acutely aware of the value of placing children with carers whose lifestyle was not too distant from that of their families. As one scheme leader put it:

> It seems to work well if carers are fairly similar to the users in their way of life – only without the difficulties, at least, without them now.

To explore the extent to which there was continuity for the children between their own and the carers' household, several factors were considered.

In evaluating family factors, as with the study parents, one individual was identified in each carer family as the main carer. Only one main carer was male. This was a retired residential social worker, living alone.

Family composition

When comparisons were made between the families of carers and parents, there were several points of significant difference. Nearly twice as many carers were living in a two-parent family compared with parents (41 compared with 22).

Carer families, although slightly larger than the national average (see Utting 1995) with almost one-third having three or more children, were none the less rather smaller than families using the service, of whom over half had three or more children.

Employment

All carer families had at least one member in full-time employment by contrast with families using accommodation of whom only eleven had one adult member employed full-time. Additionally, half the families using the service were unemployed (see Chapter 3). Sources of employment were also different with wage earners in almost three quarters of carer families being employed in skilled non-professional work compared with 6% of parents who were in work. By contrast, only 14% of carers in work were in semi-skilled or manual jobs, compared with 90% of parents in work. There were eight carers in professional posts compared with one parent.

For 18 carer households, classed within the skilled, non-professional group, the main income derived from the task of looking after children.

Income

There were two important points here. As Table 8.1 shows, carers were more affluent than the majority of families but, in comparison to the general population, two-thirds were living on the relatively low income of under £200 per week (see Utting 1995). This was important because it did provide a point of connection between carers and families. The less affluent carers remembered hard times and consequently could empathise with families. In return, the lifestyle of the carer families was not so different in some cases from that of the study parents. Indeed, for the parents it represented the lifestyle to which they would like to and could realistically aspire. As shown in Chapter 4, comparing themselves with carers, far from being threatening, spurred some parents on to improve their lifestyle.

Table 8.1 *Net weekly income of carers and families (n=60)*

Weekly net income	Carers		Families	
	Number	Percentage	Number	Percentage
Over £200	23	38	5	9
£150–£199	37	62	6	10
Under £150	0	0	49	81

Accommodation

Study and carer families lived in different types of accommodation. Forty-eight (80%) carers lived in owner-occupied housing compared with five families. By contrast, 50 (82%) study families lived in local authority housing compared with 12 (20%) carers. Nevertheless, in about a quarter of cases, families were living in very similar housing stock. What was particularly striking was that over half the carers and families lived within the same neighbourhoods, used the same shops and their children went to the same schools. This shared locality was a point of significant continuity between the two families.

Proximity: connections within neighbourhoods

A further point of continuity related to locality was the proximity of homes to each other. Distance between homes has been identified as one of the barriers to contact between parents and full-time foster placements (Aldgate 1980; DoH 1991b). By contrast, the placements in this study were characterised by their proximity to families' homes. Half the arrangements (31) were made between families who lived within two miles of each other, with 17 placements being within one mile. A further 18 (30%) lived within five miles of each other. The remaining families (ten) lived more than six miles apart. Although all but two of these children were over five, the greater distance did not appear to introduce difficulties in relation to school or out-of-school activities because most of the care was at the weekends. Further, carers collected and returned children in eight of these ten placements.

Transport

Proximity to a placement geographically has to be seen in tandem with the accessibility of the carers' home to families. Only six families owned cars. This contrasted with carers of whom all but four owned cars. However, transport was not a problem for the majority of parents who did not possess cars for several reasons.

Ten placements were within walking distance of each other. In 19, the carer collected and returned children. In ten cases social services provided transport. In the remaining fifteen, parents used public transport which, though time consuming was relatively easy. In this respect the study areas represented a more favourable picture of inner-city transport. Had families been living in villages the picture might have been rather different. As it was, almost three-quarters of families could get to the carer home in less than half an hour. Those on very low incomes living further away were offered some compensation through payment of bus fares by the social services departments.

Ages of carers and parents

Previous research on foster care has suggested that carers over 40 may be more effective and less threatening to parents than younger ones (see Berridge and Cleaver 1987; Berridge 1996).

Table 8.2 *Age ranges of carers and parents (n=60)*

Age of main carer/parent	Carers		Parents	
	Number	Percentage	Number	Percentage
Under 25 years	3	5	13	22
25–34 years	26	43	38	63
35–40 years	20	33	6	10
Over 40 years	11	19	3	5

As Table 8.2 shows, the age profile of carers shows a greater proportion (52%) were 35 years and older compared with only 15% of parents in this age group. However, although carers were older than parents, in this study a significant proportion were younger than those involved in full-time foster care (Berridge 1996). It may well be that in short-term accommodation, other factors such as proximity of households to each other and similar lifestyles are given more weight in recruitment strategies.

Race, religion and culture

Although some of the areas in which the study populations were located had sizeable minority ethnic populations, these were only represented in nine (15%) carer families. There were three black families, four Asian families (one Urdu-speaking and three Gujerati-speaking) and two families in which one parent was black and one white.

The placements were reasonably well able to offer the ideal family in terms of race and religion. The four Asian children fared best being placed with carers from the same racial and cultural background. Of the four black children in the study, three were placed with black carers and the other with a white carer. Two of the three dual heritage children were placed with dual heritage carers and the third with white carers. Social workers were aware of the dearth of choice for families because black carers were a scarce resource and in two of the study authorities were actively seeking to recruit more carers from a wider range of racial origins.

Seden (1995) had drawn attention to the importance of attending to the spiritual needs of looked-after children and to the need to link religious and cultural issues. In this study, with the exception of one Muslim child, there was little attention given to placing children in families from the same religious persuasion. While it may be less important to consider this issue in short-term accommodation, because children retain continuing links with home, nevertheless, the fact that religion and lifestyles are connected suggests that more attention should be given to this issue.

The symmetry of nuclear families

While many children in reconstituted families live in asymmetrical family groupings, research has suggested that the relative ages of children in a foster household can influence the outcome of the placement. Parker (1966) and Berridge and Cleaver (1987) both found the placing of children with families whose children are close in chronological age to the foster child was an indicator of breakdown.

In this study, social workers said they deliberately discounted this factor although it was well known to affect placements by social workers in all four authorities. In fact, there were 16 placements where children were placed with carer children within two years of their own age (see Berridge and Cleaver 1987) and a further ten where children had less than five years between them (see Parker 1966).

Overall, as Table 8.3 shows, children in carers' families tended to be older than accommodated children. Almost two-thirds of the carer children were over 10 years old (58%), while just under a third were between 5 and 9 years old. By contrast 37% of accommodated children were under 5 compared with only 13% of carer children. This reflected the fact that carers had reached a more mature point in their life cycle.

Table 8.3 *Age ranges of carer's own and accommodated children*

Ages of children	Own children		Accommodated children	
	Number	Percentage	Number	Percentage
Under 5 years	14	13	22	37
5–9 years	32	29	31	52
10–15 years	44	40	7	11
16 years and over	20	18	0	0
	(n=110)		(n=60)	

Partnership between carers and parents

Links in lifestyles can be an important indicator of continuity for a child but the nearness of houses and similarities in day-to-day living count for little if foster carers cannot work in partnership with parents to promote children's welfare. As shown earlier, from the point of view of the parents, partnership with carers was in evidence and effective. Many previous studies have suggested that foster carers, both short- and long-term may be motivated by their concern for the children (George 1970; Aldgate 1977; Berridge and Cleaver 1987; Sellick 1994; Stone 1995). This positive motivation has been shown to be tempered by negative attitudes towards parents and contact with them (Aldgate 1980; Millham et al. 1986) and any initial enthusiasm to have been dampened by dealing with children's difficult behaviour (Aldgate and Hawley 1986). This study explored whether the same problems were in evidence in relation to short-term accommodation.

Why foster?

In common with many other foster carers (see Aldgate and Hawley 1986; Berridge and Cleaver 1987; Sellick 1994; Stone 1995), all the short-term carers said they were motivated by a desire to help children under stress. All carers had a strong interest in caring for children, often borne out of considerable experience of working with children in a community-based setting. Nearly three quarters (43) had worked with children in play groups, family centres or nurseries, and almost as many, 41 (69%), had extensive experience as child-minders. In addition, over half (31) had experience of other areas of fostering, and three had experience of residential care of children. But their motivation extended beyond their child care skills.

Almost half the carers were also motivated by a desire to help parents under stress. For 17 families, this motivation had been fuelled by their own life experiences of loss and disruption, including divorce and separation, the death of a partner or a child. They talked of their gratitude for support, including respite care, from family or friends during their difficult times. They were individuals who felt a strong desire to express their gratitude for their good fortunes by offering help to similar families in difficulties. One or two liked looking after children to compensate for their own childlessness:

> If it wasn't for Sandy [her friend of many years standing], after Mick and I split up, I think I'd have gone barmy. She gave me just enough of a thread of normality while I got myself together. That's what I hope this does for Graham's mum.

One couple had lost a child of their own when they were younger:

> The experience shattered us – I didn't know what day it was – endless, I
> thought it was endless, grey, awful. Our other children suffered too. When
> something blows your mum or dad apart . . . it's terrifying. It was our family
> who helped us through it . . . by nudging us back into everyday life. I hope
> our little bit of support helps her, I think it does.

Other carers understood the isolation and distress that families lived with:

> When you just don't know where to turn to . . . it's hard to keep a hold
> on anything . . . harder than we can sometimes imagine. If the visits just
> give something sure, it's a start, some certainty, isn't it?

Some were motivated by a desire to look after children:

> I have time now that my children are more or less grown-up. I've always
> wanted to be with children, and this seems something very . . . constructive.
> I wouldn't want to foster . . . I really like the idea that I'm helping the family.

> I always wanted children – but it wasn't to be. I've always been single though
> I come from a big family myself. I love my work, but now I find I have a bit of
> time, and energy . . . and I get such a lot from them coming. It really suits me!

Most of the carers recognised that their altruism was combined with the need
to use fostering as a source of income. One-third (21) said short-term accommodation conveniently fitted in with other earning patterns and family
commitments. Two-fifths (24) of carers had full-time foster children as well as
the short-term children, mostly with one or two foster children and, as already
reported, caring for children was the main source of household income for 18
of these 24. Additionally, 35 families childminded at least one child.

This pattern of fostering undoubtedly enhanced their professional identity.
Those who had come to short-term accommodation through child-minding
held a particularly strong vision of a needs-led service. They took for granted
that short-term accommodation was an extension of the child-minding
services which parents had a right to need and to use. This attitude provided
a natural base for a businesslike partnership between parents and carers. As
shown in Chapter 4, it also helped facilitate the re-integration of parents into
the community.

Those who had experience of both part-time and full-time care of children
commented on the constant comings and goings which presented an entirely

different rhythm from full-time foster care. Different demands were made on carer families. There was no escape from recognising that looking after the children was very much part of a service to the whole family. On the one hand this allowed for a more natural relationship with parents but it also brought more demands by way of working with them:

> Because it's quite short, and intensive really, there's more time with parents. I think this is really important but it can be very hard. To begin with there are such strong feelings – you're both sort of sniffing round each other, quite nervous . . . and wanting it to go well. It can be a bit prickly, especially at the start.

> We hope we're in the background . . . for both of them. Not propping them up, waiting for the next disaster, but being there day-by-day while they get things steadier.

> I think it's quite a lot different from fostering . . . it's really important to get a decent contact with parents . . . it's the parent and their child you're doing something for.

> The comings and goings can be very hard . . . when you think about it, that is what is so difficult. Yes, we do get into a routine but it always takes something out of you.

> I hate the end. Sometimes you get very close. I keep in touch cards and so on – but it's sad sometimes. You get to know them and then you don't see them anymore.

However, there was compensation for supporting parents as well as children because there was a space between breaks which allowed the carer family some respite from the task. Those who child-minded were particularly aware of this difference:

> It is very satisfying . . . and very hard. There's a lot to do in that time. I'm really glad of the time in between, because quite honestly, I need to recharge.

Testing the Children Act principles

Principle 6 of *Principles and Practice in Regulations and Guidance* says:

> Just as some young people are more vulnerable than others, so are some mothers and fathers. Their parenting capacity may be limited temporarily or permanently by poverty, racism, poor housing or unemployment or by

personal or marital problems, sensory or physical disability, mental illness or past life experiences. Lack of ability to provide adequate care should not be equated with lack of affection or with irresponsibility. (DoH 1990, p. 8)

The majority of carers (85%) shared the view that families may need help from the state from time to time:

How can you say where it starts? Some people have a harder job than others – they have a bad start, and so it goes on. You can't often say 'this is the reason, this is the cause'.

It's partly about things that are very hard to change . . . how you're brought up yourself, for a start. Then there are things you can change, with a bit of help. I hope we're part of that.

Well, there are good times and bad times for all families. That we know. And so much of it is luck. If I had her lot, where would I be?

You know, you can't help what happens to you, often. You can help what you do about it, with a bit of the right kind of help.

Carers were asked to list at least three factors which they thought contributed to adversity for the families with whom they were working. A typology of factors was constructed from carers' replies which is shown in Table 8.4 and revealed some ambivalence lurking beneath the surface of altruism.

Table 8.4 *Factors contributing to adversity in study families*

Adverse factors	Number	Percentage
Low income/poverty	51	85
Poor housing	43	72
Poor physical health	43	72
Poor mental health	42	70
Long-standing family problems	51	85
Too many children	41	68
Generally irresponsible	23	38
Ought to be able to manage	7	12
Should not be parents	7	12

(n=60 for each variable)

As Table 8.4 shows, while over 70% carers perceived families to be significantly affected by a chain of social adversity, such as low income, poor mental and physical health, and social isolation, at the same time some carers felt that there were aspects of the parents' approach to life which contributed to their difficulties.

Two-thirds of carers took a more moralistic attitude in believing that parents had too many children, were irresponsible, or ought to be able to manage. Their ambivalent attitude is summarised by one carer:

> Of course families get into difficulties and they need all the help they can get. Take Susan, for example, she really struggles. But she is her own worst enemy. Why did she have this latest baby? She can barely feed herself and the other two. It's not fair to kids to bring them up on social security.

It was, however, significant that whatever views some carers held privately about parents, they were able to separate personal attitudes from carrying out their professional task. Carers behaved with integrity and generosity towards parents, helping them often at the expense of their own families.

The professionalism of carers was demonstrated in several ways:

- ♦ clarity about their task;
- ♦ preparing for the task;
- ♦ handling contact with parents; and
- ♦ responding to children's needs.

Clarity about their task

Carers clearly saw a tripartite task:

- ♦ meeting children's needs;
- ♦ giving parents time to themselves; and
- ♦ working with some parents to enhance their parenting skills.

Two-thirds of carers (39) regarded their main responsibility as responding to children's need for a break from stressful circumstances at home and for some individual attention. Thirteen saw their principal responsibility as enabling parents to have time for themselves to sort out their lives. Among these were carers whose task included working with parents to improve their parenting skills.

Eight carers saw their task as extended child-minding and emphasised that they were offering a service which parents had a right to use.

In summary, providing children with a break from stressful circumstances at home and giving individual attention and time with a family who could offer experiences that were not available in their own homes was an important part of their role. However, these factors were only part of the overarching aim of carers to make a contribution to children in need and their families, by helping to prevent family breakdown.

Preparing for the task

The complex task of being a carer involves being part of the professional team. To work in partnership with parents, carers in their turn need to work in partnership with social workers.

The majority of carers, 51 (85%), felt they had been fully and appropriately consulted throughout the period when the negotiations were taking place about children's placements. In most of these cases, arrangements had been negotiated and agreed between themselves, the family and the agency before the visits began. Nine thought they could have been consulted more and that children were placed with them without adequate information. In spite of this, 70% (42) of the carers felt they had made a significant contribution to the formal arrangements.

Carers had been given the opportunity of preparing the children and their parents for the breaks in most cases. Only three carers (5%) did not meet the child and parent before the first visit, and 18 (30%) were able to meet parent and child more than once. Carers were satisfied with the quality and extent of their work in this respect, and found it invaluable in setting the scene for visits which were, in the majority of cases, effective and pleasurable for the children.

Handling contact with parents

Contact between carers and families has long been held as one of the most contentious areas for children looked after full-time. This study is different in looking at contact in the context of short-term accommodation. As in previous studies, the relationship with parents undoubtedly provided the strongest test of carers' professionalism (Millham et al. 1986; Berridge and Cleaver 1987).

The most frequent point of contact between carer and parent was at the times when the children arrived and left the carer home. For the majority (54) this gave the opportunity to provide feedback on what has happened during the break. This was also the time when carers offered support to families.

Almost two-thirds of the carers (38) rated their contact with parents as highly satisfactory. Sixteen had some reservations and six carers stated that contact was not at all satisfactory.

Most difficulties concerned the day-to-day relationship between carers and parents. Some carers thought parents took them for granted and expected too much. Alongside the child care, these parents behaved towards carers as might adolescents towards their parents, dumping their washing on them, arriving late to collect children. For these parents, this was the first opportunity they had experienced in their lives to take a care-taking person for granted. Thus, it was appropriate from parents' point of view to exploit the generosity of carers, knowing that carers in return would respond like caring parents and not exact reprisals.

Other carers felt that parents were initially ambivalent about handing over their children. While carers understood the complexities of parental feelings, they found it difficult to cope with hostile parents in practice.

Difficulties could also arise when carers held different attitudes from parents about what were appropriate methods for controlling children. They also found it distressing to listen to parents' accounts of their loneliness and isolation and deprived living circumstances. Their hearts went out to these families, sometimes they admired their fortitude; they were overwhelmed by a desire to help them in their adversity.

Three-quarters of the carers (46) felt strongly that, in spite of any problems, they could forgive all because they believed that they had an important and direct part to play in preventing family breakdown by enabling parents to develop and strengthen their capacities. Supporting parents to carry on in difficult circumstances was rewarding.

Responding to children's needs

The behaviour of foster children has been established as a factor influencing breakdown (Aldgate and Hawley 1986; Berridge and Cleaver 1987). In this study, although the breakdown rate for placements was very low, none the less, in 18 cases carers found children's behaviour problems difficult to cope with. For example, carers cited incidents when children acted out their aggression violently or retreated into sulking or silence. They managed these situations well. Few called on social workers for help and saw it as their role to respond appropriately. Like social workers, a minority of carers did feel that, in spite of their responsible attitude, children might have been better placed elsewhere. Unlike social workers, they did not see the solution in better training but rather in placing the child in a residential, therapeutic facility.

Other problems related to the issue of continuity and the management of the comings and goings associated with short-term accommodation. The problems experienced were similar to those reported in studies on contact where children are living between two households (Mitchell 1985). The feelings and behaviour associated with changing from living in one home to another, were also much more evident in the early stages. Carers felt that both arriving at the carer's home and the return to their own home were stressful times for both the children and the adults. They felt they had an important role with both parents and children to smooth these points of transition.

In spite of any problems, there was no doubt that carers found their work with children satisfying. They enjoyed the challenge of getting to know children and making them feel at home. They were pleased to provide some children with genuine respite from a stressful home life. As will be shown in the next chapter, the skills of carers did not go unnoticed by the children themselves.

Finding and keeping short-term carers

The success of carers, whether they are for short-term accommodation or full-time family placements depends very much on how they are recruited, trained and supported. The carers in this study felt they had been offering a good service to families, a factor that was validated by parents' ratings of their capabilities. Finding and keeping good carers is notoriously difficult (Triseliotis et al. 1995b). The final part of this chapter therefore addresses factors which have been held to contribute to the success of the carer role – recruitment, training and support from social workers.

Recruitment

Attention has been drawn by several commentators to the shortage of foster carers nationally (see Triseliotis et al. 1995b). Parker's 1978 analysis of the reasons for this still has relevance two decades later. The reasons are linked to the increase of women in the work place, a shorter period of child-bearing and changes in patterns of divorce and reconstitution in families.

All four agencies recruited their carers from a range of sources. Some had been found among 'mainstream foster carers' with a particular interest in short-term and part-time caring. Some had 'evolved' from child-minding and others had been specially recruited for the task.

The fact that many carers had similar lifestyles to the study families, and had in the past experienced adversity in their own lives led them to doubt their eligibility to look after other people's children. The social workers had grasped the Children Act principle that 'there is no one, perfect way to bring up children and care must be taken to avoid value judgements and stereo-typing' when recruiting carers (DoH 1990, p. 7). In addition, the social workers had the breadth of vision to see that these families could offer children continuity and stability.

An important aspect of recruitment was the assessment of carers. At the time the study began the Children Act Regulations on the registration of short-term carers had just been implemented (DoH 1991a). The change in regula-tions was welcomed by the majority of the study carers because they gave carers more status, had clarified their roles and tasks, and made them feel part of the professional team. However there remained a few who resented 'all the new red tape'. Most of these carers had been offering 'respite care' to families informally prior to the Act under Section 1 of the 1980 Child Care Act. Under the old legislation parents had been able to recruit their own carers paid for by 'Section 1 money' on the grounds that the informal care service was 'likely to diminish the need to receive children into care'.

Training

The preparation and support which carers receive is vital to the way in which they are able to carry out their complex and demanding task, and to their capacity to continue in their work over time. Sellick (1994) described this particularly well in relation to short-term carers. He pointed out how much the task of foster carers has changed from the days when foster placement meant the 'rescue and removal' of children from their families of origin, with no hope of restoration.

Carers were asked to evaluate how well their training prepared them for the role as short-term carer. The majority (82%) felt they had been well or ade-quately prepared for their task. Five received no training but all were experienced child-minders and saw their task as an extension of what they were already doing. None the less there were six carers who felt they were inadequately prepared to cope both with the children's disruptive behaviour and the demands that parents placed upon them.

Training programmes covered a number of issues including:

♦ normal child development;

♦ racial and cultural needs of children and families;

♦ the effects of child abuse;

♦ an understanding of the impact of disadvantage on families;

♦ children's behaviour problems; and

♦ health and safety, and first aid.

Carers also received training on working in partnership with social workers. Training was led by family placement social workers, short-term accommodation social workers, specialist outside speakers, and other carers.

Carers were asked to identify the most important elements of their training, and the gaps in their preparation (see Table 8.5).

Table 8.5 *Carers' perceptions of most important aspect of their training (n=60)*

Most important aspect of training	Number	Percentage
Learning about caring for and coping with children	24	41
Learning about families	16	27
Learning from the experience of other carers	4	7
Experiential aspects – role-play, etc.	2	3
Self-examination	1	2
Learning about the agency	2	3
Training useful overall	11	17

Eleven carers (17%) found the training helpful in its entirety. However, two-fifths (24) found learning about the children for whom they would be caring the most important aspect of their training. A quarter found it most helpful to learn about the circumstances of the families with whom they would be working, and to have the opportunity of thinking about the kind of difficulties the children may be experiencing in their everyday lives.

A quarter (15) of carers felt the training had fallen short of their needs. They had not learned enough about families, their circumstances and how to manage children's behaviour. They particularly felt ill-prepared in relation to matters relating to health and safety.

There were two models of training. In one model the training programme was specifically designed to meet the needs of short-term carers. In the second model preparation for accommodating children short term was an additional module to the basic training offered to all foster carers. The type of model was not associated with carers perception of satisfaction with training and preparation.

Support

Sellick (1994) has argued cogently that support for foster carers should come from a variety of sources and should include social support, specialist support and financial support as well as membership of local associations. Overall, carers in this study felt well supported in their role and drew on a variety of sources. In three of the four areas, training and general support for carers was organised through the family placement social workers. Children's social workers also offered support and advice over the problems of children and parents. In the fourth authority, Midcity, it was significant that the scheme leader both trained and supported carers and acted as the family support social worker for parents and children. This arrangement gave the social worker an understanding of the needs of all concerned. It also helped communication between carers and families and gave all parties the impression of a coherent service.

Although support was good throughout the placement, carers shared parents' criticisms about the ending of the placement. *Guidance and Regulations* suggests that, in short-term accommodation, once the placement is established carers and parents may be able to manage arrangements without social work support (DoH 1991a, p. 39). However, carers, parents and children felt that ending the placement should have had more formality. For carers, there were several problems.

Over half the carers felt guilty about ending the placement if children wanted to continue to stay with them:

> I felt I was letting them down . . . she cried when it was the last visit.

Another concern was anxiety about children's welfare after the placement ended. In most instances this was because referrals were initially related to problems between children and their families:

> I found it hard to bear sometimes . . . she would be so sharp with Becky
> and I worried that she might lose control when the breaks stopped.

A third problem was having to be tough with parents who had come to rely on carers for emotional support. Carers felt an undue burden had been placed on them by parents during the placement but equally felt they were abandoning parents if all links were terminated at the end of the placement. Some were anxious about parents' welfare and thought the placement was not long enough to meet families' needs. In a minority of cases carers took it upon themselves to continue contact with the family even though the placement had formally ended:

> During the placement we sometimes felt she wanted to stay . . . she was having such a difficult time because she really envied the children. We got really close as the placement went on and she talked to us about her problems. We helped her as best we could but I don't think it was really enough. At the end of the breaks I suggested she kept in touch. We actually see her most weeks.

Given the consistency of views of parents and carers over the inadequacy of ending an arrangement, more attention needs to be given to formalising endings. In contrast to *Guidance and Regulations* relating to full-time accommodation, which are helpful in specifying the preparation needed to return a child home (DoH 1991a, p. 40), the findings of this study suggest that there is a need for a formal structure to end short-term arrangements. Many carers resented managing the endings without social work support.

Carers' attitudes to social workers

In spite of the problems over the ending of the placement, it was clear that the relationship between social workers and carers was very good. When asked to rate the social workers who had main responsibility for their support and development, the majority believed social workers offered them a good service.

Figure 8.1 shows the carers' assessment of social workers rated as good or excellent. The five dimensions are the same as those used to rate parent's perceptions of carers and social workers.

Figure 8.1 shows that carers were more sceptical about social workers than were parents. For example, although 70–73% found social workers approachable and understanding, over a third had concerns about their honesty, helpfulness and reliability. A frequent concern was that social workers had not always been entirely truthful about the children's behaviour problems. Another common criticism was that the demands parents would make on them had not been clearly spelt out. The greatest dissatisfaction was about social workers' unreliability, for example cancelling appointments at the last

Figure 8.1 *Carers' opinions of social workers' qualities (n=60*)*

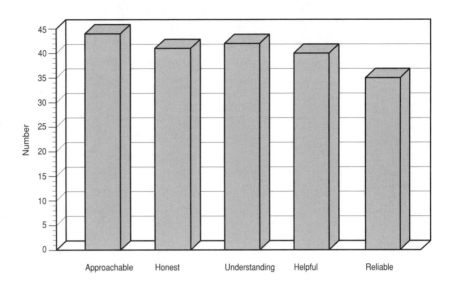

*Categories are not mutually exclusive

minute, and not upholding promises to sort out practical problems such as foster placement payments.

Summary

Parents held carers in high regard. They were extremely grateful to carers for providing them with time away from their children and valued their kindness and consideration towards themselves and their children.

Although carers differed from parents in terms of income, employment, and owning cars and houses, there were many points of continuity for children and parents.

Carers tended to live near parents and were easily accessed by public transport. Families and carers lived in the same neighbourhoods, in similar housing stock and shared shops and schools.

Factors such as proximity of ages of foster and own children did not seem as important in short-term accommodation as differences in lifestyles.

Carers were motivated by a desire to help children and families under stress borne out of their own experiences in the past. They saw their role in terms of family support rather than child rescue.

Fostering provided an important source of income for carers. For almost one-third, looking after children was their sole source of income.

While carers believed in the Children Act principle that families under stress should be able to seek help from time to time, they held some reservations about the lifestyles of families with whom they were working.

Whatever views carers held privately were well masked. They offered families a professional service which was well received by parents.

Carers had been carefully recruited and reasonably well trained and were generally well supported by social workers. They felt least well prepared and supported to work with demanding parents and children whose behaviour was aggressive.

Problems in the placement related to parents exploiting carers' generosity, to the comings and goings of children, children's demanding or aggressive behaviour and to ending the placement. Carers felt too much was demanded of them by workers in some cases.

Implementation of Children Act Regulations relating to the recruitment and supervision of carers had been well received. Carers felt the Regulations gave them a much clearer role and enhanced their status as members of the care team.

9 *The children's story*

Children's experiences of short-term accommodation

Short-term accommodation was clearly a positive experience for parents, who appreciated the social work processes that carried it through, and who used the time away from their children to good effect to help address their problems. The findings of this study echo those of earlier work by Robinson (1987) on families of children with disabilities, which found respite care was helpful to the parents. Robinson also suggested that relief for parents could be at the expense of children's wishes and well-being. In any placement of children away from home, there is potential for conflict between the needs and wishes of the children and those of their parents due to the impact on children of being placed away from home. Consequently, any discussion of children's perspectives of placements needs to be rooted in attachment theory.

Attachment theory has changed its cultural context since the writings of Bowlby in the 1950s but the principle of recognising the impact on children of separation from significant adults and siblings is no less important today than it was four decades ago (see Fahlberg 1981a; Jewett 1984; Aldgate 1992). There are dangers in assuming that short-term accommodation does not hold the same fears for children as full-term accommodation, graphically described by Fahlberg (1981a), but the fear of the unknown and the temporary loss of attachment figures are likely to engender in all children a range of emotions, which may be tempered by certain factors:

> Their experience of attachment will have a primary influence on their reactions to separation but there are other factors which may determine the way they respond, including cultural expectations, age, temperament, gender, cognitive appraisal and 'set', and social circumstances before and after separation.
> (Aldgate 1992, p. 46)

Over the decade or so prior to the Children Act 1989, there was a growing recognition in law of children's position in the care system as independent individuals who have a right to have their wishes and feelings taken into account in any decision affecting their lives. Research prior to the Act (DHSS 1985b) had discovered how children felt they were pawns in the lives of adults, moved between placements in the care system at the will of an ever-changing army of social workers, a fate summed up by one young person: 'I swopped and changed my social worker like I do my socks – I had that many' (Stein and Carey 1986, p. 44).

Consequently, the Children Act places an emphasis on three processes likely to influence a child's cognitive appraisal (or perception) of being accommodated:

- consultation between social workers and children;

- involvement of children in decision-making (partnership); and

- preparation for the placement.

Handled well, it could be argued, these processes are likely to ensure a positive cognitive 'set', that is, the 'sense of self-esteem and self-efficacy that makes successful coping more likely' (Rutter 1985, p. 603), which is an essential part of children's welfare.

If children's wishes are to be taken seriously, apart from looking at these specific processes, it is also important for adults to grasp that children may ascribe to events and individuals very different priorities than adults do. It is necessary to grasp what things are important to children. One child protection study, for example, found that children bitterly resented being hauled out of class early to meet social workers and police. A wait of a few minutes might have preserved children's dignity (Sharland et al. 1996). So in this study, attention has been given to children's views of what factors are important in creating a positive or negative experience for them. Information was gained directly from the children, who were interviewed at the start of the intervention and again after six to nine months, depending on the length of individual arrangements. Age and cognitive ability limited who was interviewed, none the less over two-thirds (41) of the children were able to participate fully. When children were re-interviewed, two children had been accommodated full-time during the study period; as a result findings on outcome are based on interviews with 39 children.

A starting point for the children's story was to explore their anxieties about being accommodated.

Children's anxieties about being accommodated

As parents revealed in Chapter 4, the taint and stigma of the care system lingered longer than the rhetoric of the Children Act would wish. Interviewed at the same point, when accommodation had been agreed but had not yet started, children also had anxieties, some echoing those of their parents and others relating to their own world view. What was striking was the rational nature of children' s anxieties, faced, as they were, with a rather unusual situation. Some children spoke clearly about how they felt. Others said they were worried but could not articulate why. Overall, 17 of the 41 older children (41%) were worried about being accommodated. Nine were unsure whether they were worried or not and 15 (37%) were looking forward to going away without anxieties.

Those who could articulate their views said a major anxiety was about going somewhere strange:

> I was nervous a bit. You see, I'd not stayed with strangers before and
> I was worried. But they seemed nice . . . and friendly. (Mark, aged 8)

The strangeness from children's point of view included anxieties about missing important TV programmes and worrying about strange food:

> What I worry about most is not seeing *Gladiators*. I always watch that
> on Saturday nights. My teacher doesn't like it – says its too aggressive.
> I think it's great. They have to let me watch it. (John, aged 12)

> I hope my mum tells them I don't like onions and eggs. I really worry
> about that. They won't like me if I don't eat their food. My gran says that
> sort of thing upsets people. I don't know why, if my friends say they are
> 'veggie' I don't have any problems with that. (Sue, aged 10)

For others, there was the fear of a hidden agenda of rejection by parents:

> I was afraid that I wouldn't go home again. I don't know why I was . . .
> I was afraid. (Robin, aged 6)

> I kept wondering where my mum would be. Maybe she'd forget about me.
> Or maybe she'd be worried. (Katie, aged 7)

Attachment is a two-way process and children were worried about the effect of their absence on siblings and parents, although some views also thinly disguised anxiety about their own separation:

See, my mum, I look after her since my dad went. She needs me to feed the cat and go to the shops. I will miss Fluffy [cat]. I like playing with her. I hope she won't forget me. (Pam, aged 9)

A further source of anxiety was whether the carer family would treat them well:

My friend – he was in a children's home. He hated it. The other kids beat him up. Do you think the children will do that to me? (John, aged 12)

Will they be kind – not hit me or anything. I worry about that. (Neil, aged 9)

It was perhaps significant that eight of the 15 who felt positive knew the carers as child-minders before they were placed:

I know Alice. She looks after me sometimes when my mum is working. I like going there. I will like staying longer. (Rosie, aged 12)

Consultation and involvement in decision-making

One way in which children's anxieties can be lessened is if they understand why the placement is necessary and have an opportunity to put forward their views about the arrangements. The Children Act 1989 requires that all children accommodated are consulted. This is a two-part process, outlined in *Guidance and Regulations* Volume 3. First:

The child's views should be sought in discussion with the child, subject to the child's understanding.

But before a child can respond:

The implications and options in the plan should be explained, discussed and, if necessary, reassessed in the light of the child's views.

The emphasis is on giving children the opportunity to make an informed choice:

All children need to be given information and appropriate explanations so that they are in a position to develop views and make choices.

The potential tension here between conflicting views of child and parents is also acknowledged:

> The social worker should be aware and acknowledge that there may be good reasons why the child's views are different from those of his parents or the responsible authority.

In such cases it is hoped that through participating in discussion any potential conflicts can be resolved. But there remains the let-out clause for the adults that the responsible authority should:

> take account of the wishes and feelings of the child. Further, while children should feel they have been properly consulted, that their wishes have been properly considered and that they have participated as partners in the decision-making process, the adults should take final responsibility. They should not be made to feel that the burden of decision-making has fallen totally upon them, nor should they be forced to attend meetings if they choose not to do so. (DoH 1991a, pp. 12–13)

For parents and social workers to achieve the balance between asking children about their thoughts and feelings and retaining the interests and responsibilities of the adults is a highly complicated matter. One issue which the Act fails to address in its guidance is the need to ensure that, by attending to the child, parents are not threatened. The value of considering children's thoughts and feelings to inform decisions needs to be explained to parents in a way which endorses their concern and responsibility for the child rather than undermines it.

Moreover, the consultation of children can raise dilemmas for social workers. What is consultation? Does it need to be 'formal'? Does it require special skills? How can one be sure that the child understands? Who are the best people to carry out the consultation? Should this be delegated to parents, undertaken jointly with parents or, in order to ensure the requirement for recording is fulfilled, should a social worker always be present?

Children in the study were asked about consultation in terms of the information they had received and the opportunity they had been given to express their views about being accommodated. It was encouraging to find that the majority of older children (38 of 41) recalled being informed by someone about what was happening. Mostly, this was the parent but in a minority of cases children recalled talking to social workers.

But information-giving is only one aspect of consultation. When it came to having the opportunity to talk about how they felt and having an input into the decision-making, just over half the children (22) thought that this had happened, eight said it definitely had never happened while the remaining 11 (27%) were uncertain:

> She [the social worker] came and talked to me . . . just went over what was being talked about, and asked me what I thought about it. My mum had told me, like, but I was glad that she [social worker] did too. (Tom, aged 13)

> I was scared but no one asked me. My mum said I had to go for her sake or else she would be ill. I didn't like it but I couldn't say. (Mark, aged 8)

> The lady told me I was going to stay with Mrs Timothy. She took me and my mum to see her I was scared – she was nice but I didn't want to leave my mum. (Pam, aged 9)

> My dad said I had to go – so I did. (Dan, aged 11)

> I don't think I was asked what I thought. I just knew I had to go. (Rosie, aged 12)

There was a distinct feeling from children's comments that there had been little opportunity to protest or change plans. Consultation was very much on the side of information-giving. By contrast, when children's views were compared with those of parents and social workers, it was clear that the adults thought children had been given the opportunity to air their views in rather more cases. Although differences between the views of the children and the adults were not statistically significant, it seemed likely from children's comments that they had felt more intimidated and coerced by any consultation than adults realised.

Involvement in planning meetings was more fruitful in terms of children's impact on the process. According to the adults, a minority of children (13 of the 41 children) had attended planning meetings. It was difficult to establish what constituted a meeting in children's minds. Some meetings had taken place at the child's home but these were registered by children as 'chats'. In children's minds, a meeting was only recognised as such when it took place outside the home. But in the nine cases where this did occur, both children and parents believed the meeting allowed the children to influence the shape of arrangements:

> I didn't want to go every weekend. I said this to the social worker and my dad. They said OK – we'll make it every other weekend. (Dan, aged 11)

> I wanted to go on Saturday not Friday night because I go to basketball with my friends. My mum was surprised I came on so strong – but she said she didn't mind. (John, aged 12)

The findings do suggest that there needs to be clarification of the meaning of consultation with children. To separate out the component parts into information-giving, talking over anxieties and giving children the opportunity to influence plans is important. Each element needs a slightly different approach. To conflate the components into one session may not be helpful. Additionally, account needs to be taken of the natural power parents may wield over their children in any circumstances to get them to conform to the parents' agenda. Independent sessions with children either with social workers or, in some cases, if they are known, carers, may be more objective.

Although no child in this study complained about the abuse of power by adults, it is all too easy to see how consultation could degenerate into tokenism. If short-term accommodation is targeted at parents in the interests of preventing family breakdown, this needs to be made explicit to the children. Not being accommodated may not be an option. It is as much an abuse of power to set children up to make spurious choices as it is not to ask them for their views. The conclusion from this tentative exploration into new territory of practice can only be to think more honestly about the true nature of the balancing act which will necessarily need to be performed between the short-term needs of adults and children and the long-term interests of the family as a whole.

Whatever the shortcomings of the consultation process, it was clear that children did have views on the purpose of the short-term accommodation.

Figure 9.1 *Children's views on the purpose of arrangements (n=41)*

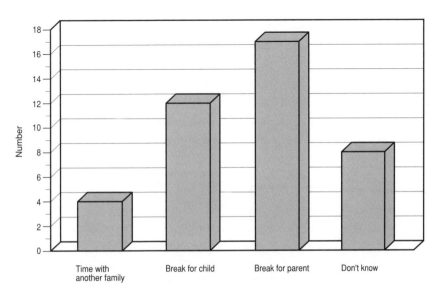

Children most frequently (41%) thought that the breaks were arranged to allow their parents some respite from the ongoing rigour of bringing them up. Indeed many children had some awareness that respite from them would help parents continue to look after the family, and that this was therefore a good thing:

> I think my mum needs a break and then she feels a lot better. It's quite nice for me, I like them [carers] and I know she's at home. (Mary, aged 14)

> She needs us out of her hair sometimes. Well, can't say I blame her. (Pam, aged 9)

> My dad has been very ill. He goes to hospital a lot. He will get rest if me and Jason [brother] aren't there. (John, aged 12)

> I go because I drive my dad nuts. I get up in the middle of the night, and I sit on top of the chest . . . when I can't sleep. I'm always in trouble. (Neil, aged 9)

Where children thought that the arrangements were made primarily for their sake, very few viewed this as an indication that there was anything amiss with them. Much more frequently, children showed a 'down-to-earth' understanding of what the arrangements were about:

> There are a lot of us at home. It gets very busy. It will be nice to have someone to play with me. (Lisa, aged 10)

> I don't like my new dad. I think we both need to go away from each other. (Ryan, aged 13)

Some children simply accepted parents' views of the benefits of being with another family and wished to leave the matter there:

> Well I think my mum thought we could do with a break. They [carers)] would be sort of like a friend, an aunty. Our family lives quite far off. Mum said it would be a bit of fun.

Eight children were not at all sure why they were going to be accommodated. All but one of these children were under 8 years:

> No, I don't know. My mum knows, why not ask her? She'll tell you. (Katie, aged 7)

Younger children were even more muddled. For example, a 6-year-old-girl struggled in her understanding of why she was going to the carer family:

> Well, I don't know . . . When I'm invited, I think.

What children expected from the service

As well as exploring children's understanding of the purpose of the intervention, at the beginning of the accommodation, children were asked to say whether or not the arrangements would be helpful and to elaborate on who might be helped.

Nearly two-thirds (27) of the children definitely thought the breaks would be helpful to their parents and occasionally also to them, a finding which supported their view of the purpose of accommodation:

> Definitely it will help me and my mum and Chris. Oh, for sure.
> (Charlie, aged 11)

> I think it will help us because I will enjoy going . . . I think. (Katie, aged 7)

> When we go there, then mam can have a rest and go out. Both
> enjoy it, I suppose. Having a rest is good, isn't it? (Don, aged 7)

A further quarter (ten) were not sure whether the breaks would help, and four felt they would not. It seemed hard for them to envisage how the breaks would help anyone:

> What? What do you mean? Will it help to make life better for me or my mum?
> Why should it? I think it'll be nice there, but . . . what else. (Alan, aged 10)

The preparation stage

As suggested in Chapter 6, preparing children and families for a placement has been an integral part of good child care practice for several decades. In the 1950s Charnley claimed: 'Children are least harmed when they are least surprised' (Charnley 1955). In the 1970s, studies of children in hospital suggested that preparation was a factor influencing children's attitude to treatment (Stacey et al. 1970), while Thoburn (1988) emphasises this as an integral part of child placement.

Preparing the children for stays away from home was a key element of all four agencies. To some extent, there is overlap between the information-giving and dialogue stages of consultation *before* decisions have been made, and what can be properly called 'preparation', that is, the dialogue and events *after* the decision for accommodation has been made and the placement chosen.

For the purposes of this study, preparation was confined to information-giving about the carers and preparatory visits to the carers' homes. In fact the two events were conflated in children's minds. Two-fifths of children (16) had the advantage of knowing the carer as a child-minder and therefore did not make a special visit before their first overnight stay. Nineteen children (46%) did visit specifically to prepare for their stay. Only three children did not have the opportunity to visit, because there was no time before the placement started. An additional three younger children were confused about whether or not they had visited the carers' home, although visits had been reported by parents. It may have been that these children thought the pre-placement visit was part of the accommodation arrangements.

During the preparation stage, practically two-thirds of the children (27) reported some feelings of apprehension. Despite their worries, the study children went on their visits to the carers' homes partly because they hoped it would be enjoyable and partly because they thought it would be helpful for their parents. In fact, their bravery was vindicated. Visits to the carer family's home were often recounted as the point when children began to feel more confident about having breaks away, and less anxious about what was going to befall them there. For those unfamiliar with the carers, the introductory visit enabled children to view the physical layout of the house and learn a little of what life would be like there. The importance of the introductory visit cannot be overestimated. It seemed to allow them to judge for themselves what kind of care they would receive. Each experience and expectation was unique. For one child, for example, knowing she was seen as an individual made all the difference:

> We went for tea . . . and there were egg sandwiches. I didn't like to say, but I hate egg. She noticed . . . and just said . . . how about some cheese? Like no fuss, or anything. I thought she was OK, and she is. (Charlie, aged 11)

Others commented on the sense of reassurance they found in observing the ordinariness of carer family life:

> After a bit, we went with Jonathan, and he let us play on his computer. They [parent and carer] just talked, I suppose. Then we played with Fred [the dog] . . . it was a good laugh! (Dan, aged 11)

Preparatory visits undoubtedly did a great deal to reassure the children, but the anticipation of the changes involved remained unsettling for the children at the start of the short-term accommodation period. The anxiety over separation increased when children were worried about things at home, or uncertain about what was happening and why. Part of the preparation process is to help children talk about their worries and provide them with strategies for managing the transition to the new home. Several writers, including Fahlberg (1981b), Jewett (1984), and Aldgate (1992) have commented on the significant part adults can play over this period. Accordingly, children were asked who might provide that support in terms of someone to talk to about the impending experience.

Figure 9.2 *Who children talked to about short-term accommodation (n=41)*

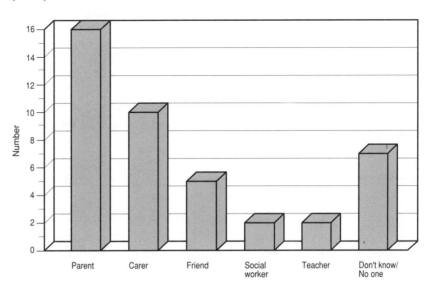

When children were worried about anything to do with the short-term breaks at this early stage, nearly two-fifths (16) said they would turn to their parents for help and reassurance but, as Figure 9.2 shows, children were also likely to see their carer as someone to turn to if they had concerns about the breaks. In most of these cases, carers were already known to the children as child-minders. Social workers are rarely seen as someone children would talk to, which might be expected because they are strangers. Though more familiar, few children talked to their teachers, but this might have related in part to social workers' guidance.

Given the emphasis on the service being to support the family, it is disappointing that not more children felt they could talk the matter over with their parents. Of some concern are the seven children who reported that they did not know to whom they could turn if worried. We were left with questions about the communication patterns in the families of these children and were reminded of Howe's views of secure and insecure attachments:

> Secure attachments are associated with free-flowing conversation; feelings are expressed and fully acknowledged. Insecure attachments are characterised by restricted and disjointed communication; some signals are read while others are ignored or misinterpreted; there is less talk about feelings; and there is less conversation and dialogue. (Howe 1995, p. 76)

The findings suggest that there is room for emphasising the role of parents in supporting their children at this time. Parental desires for respite for themselves should not override parental responsibility. It was clear that the children who were able to speak to their parents gained considerable reassurance from so doing. Especially important to children was knowing that there was no hidden agenda of rejection:

> My mum explained to me it was like going to Gran's only Gran couldn't have us because she's been ill. We used to go there a lot. My mum told me I'd go on Friday and come back on Sunday morning. Auntie Janet [carer] would fetch me in her car. When I knew that, it was OK. (Lisa, aged 10)

Of considerable interest was the relationship between the accommodated children and their peer group. Earlier studies of children looked after have suggested that children may feel stigmatised by 'being sent away from home' or they may fear the envy of their friends for having a treat. Either way, children may be reluctant to tell their peers about the placement. At the early stage in the arrangements, only 20% of children anticipated talking to friends about any worries about the visits. Two-thirds (68%) said they would not want their friends to know and certainly would not talk to them about their fears. The children illustrated their feelings in their remarks:

> I thought I'd rather not say anything just yet. They think you're the dregs if you get help from social workers, sometimes. (Sue, aged 10)

> I did not want anyone to laugh at us. To know that I was going away . . . they think there's something wrong with you. (Dave, aged 10)

In discussion with some of the study social workers about these early findings, two social workers said that they were aware that children could encounter stigma from peers and had discussed the pros and contras of talking to friends in the preparation period. These workers thought it important for children to know how to deal with questions from friends and teachers at school – and that children needed to be helped to find a 'good cover story'. Such a view, while realistic, is sad in that it demonstrates that the Children's Act intention to eradicate the stigma of accommodation is far from being achieved on this front.

Comings and goings: how children managed

Much has been written about the transition from home for children being looked after full-time (see Aldgate 1992). The *Guidance and Regulations* are geared to advise social workers on the importance of this event. With the exception of work on children with disabilities (Robinson 1987), little has been written about the effects on non-disabled children of the multiple comings and goings. Short-term accommodation is characterised by these changes, with children negotiating a series of transitions as they leave home, enter the carers' household and return home. This pattern is repeated for each accommodation episode. How children coped with the process was explored during the early stage in the arrangements.

Settling into the carers' home

First, children were asked about the initial transition. Would the knowledge of the finite length of the placement alter the way they reacted to separation. To explore this area, albeit rather tentatively, children were asked about how they felt about the initial stay. More specifically, how children settled in to the carer's home was seen as a possible indicator of how they had coped with the initial transition (see Table 9.1).

Table 9.1 *Children's experiences of settling into carer's home (n=41)*

Settling into carer's home	Number of cases	Percentage
No difficulty	12	29
Some difficulty	24	59
Great difficulty	5	12

Twelve children (29%), all of whom had previously known the carer as a child-minder, had no difficulty in settling on the first stay. Practically three-fifths of the children experienced some difficulty in settling into the carer's home and five children said they had great difficulty. A girl of 8 describes her early experience:

> Just getting used to it took a while . . . just different, you know. I missed my mum, and Becky, and Nick . . . but . . . it's alright now.

Figure 9.3 *Children's experiences of settling into carer's home (n=41)*

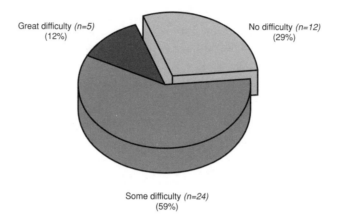

Great difficulty *(n=5)*
(12%)

No difficulty *(n=12)*
(29%)

Some difficulty *(n=24)*
(59%)

And a boy of 9 found:

> Well, it was strange. I didn't feel quite at home. Had to be really good, too. When I got used to it, they were just normal – d'you know what I mean?

The prevalence of homesickness

The other side of the coin to settling away from home is the degree of homesickness felt by the children. In fact, there was no relationship between the two factors. Irrespective of how easily children settled in, the majority (85%) missed their family and home. In short, they felt homesick. Nor was there any change in the strength of feelings of homesickness according to age.

A child of 5 recalled:

> I wished I could go home . . . but I couldn't. And I just wanted to hide.

and another of 12 years commented:

> I missed my mum and Jenny [best friend] and my bed and my CDs. It was all a bit funny. My mum said I had to behave well. It was a strain.

Homesickness is a normal part of separation feelings for both adults and children. The attachment to absent people and places is not uncommon but there has been hitherto little exploration of how children manage their feelings. Children in this study displayed a diversity of techniques (Figure 9.4).

Figure 9.4 *Ways children coped with feelings of homesickness (n=41)*

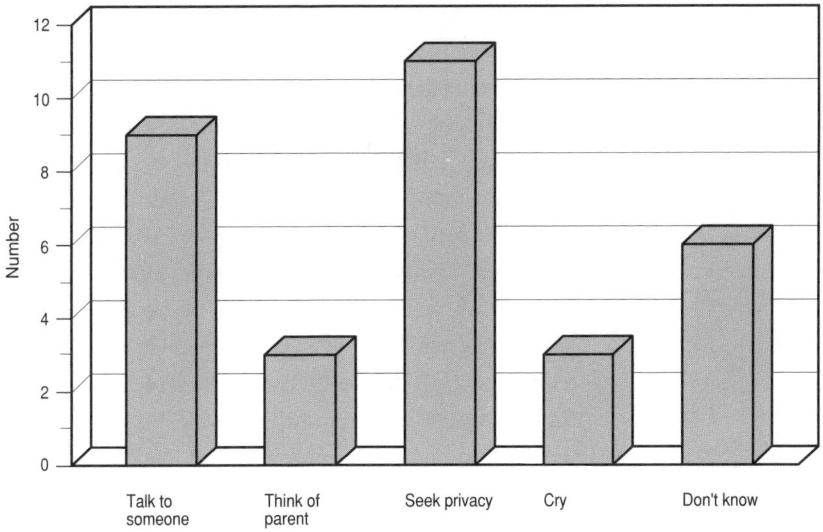

Nine children talked to someone about their distress, usually the carer mother:

> I used to go and talk to her (carer) . . . in the kitchen for a while . . . no, not
> about anything special really. She seemed to know how it was. (Neil, aged 8)

Three said they would think about home and family:

> I think about Mum and Dave and Henry and Teresa and then I feel alright.
> If I see them in my mind I know they are there. (Rosie, aged 12)

> I did feel bad at the start . . . I don't know why . . .. I just missed being home,
> but when it seemed real bad, I'd just think about being home for a while.
> (Charlie, aged 11)

Three cried with the main carer:

> She gives me a cuddle – she says it's OK to cry. (Mark, aged 8)

But by far the largest group (21), just over half the children, dealt with their
emotions privately:

> I missed everyone . . . Mum, and Dee and Sue and I miss Fluffy [the cat]
> and . . . Well, I used to go off for a while . . . to my room and think a bit,
> by myself. I always knew I could go home if I wanted. (Pam, aged 9)

> She knows when I need to be alone – says why don't you go and give
> that Care Bear a hug and I'll bring you a drink and a chocolate biscuit.
> (Lisa, aged 10)

The fact that children of primary school age sought to cope with their feelings in private is of considerable interest and is rarely referred to in child care textbooks. It is an area which warrants further exploration and one which may need more highlighting in the training of carers.

Settling in and being homesick is only one aspect of the 'comings and goings', returning home is the other. The study by the Dartington Social Research Unit (Millham et al. 1986) explored this area in some detail but their sample referred mainly to children who had been looked after for longer periods of time. However, in part of their work, they refer to the position of Navy families and the problems posed by the weekly comings and goings of fathers.

For the children in this study, going home after their first stay away brought relief and happiness for well over half the children (25):

> It was good to see my room and my mum. (Hannah, aged 9)

> I could watch the TV in peace and go to bed when I wanted. (Tom, aged 13)

> You can just eat crisps when you want to at home – you don't have to ask.
> (Neil, aged 9)

A further 19 (46%) expressed no strong feelings either way:

> It was OK – didn't affect me much either way. I soon got used to it.
> (Don, aged 11)

Of concern were the eight children who recounted feelings of anxiety and uncertainty on returning home:

> My mum and dad fight all the time – it is different at Paul and Elaine's house.
> (Sue, aged 10)

Four worried that things had changed:

> When I hadn't been there . . . I expect it would be different. (Dave, aged 10)

Familiarity with a system generally brings with it a decrease in anxiety. For the study children, however, the difficulties in returning home continued. At the end of the series of short stays away, there was very little change in the children's views. Those who had felt at the start that going home after a visit could be a difficult time continued to feel this.

The findings are useful in highlighting salient aspects of preparing children for being looked after away from home. It is important to recognise that children feel homesick even if the stay away is a short and temporary one, and that good as well as painful experiences while away can contribute to difficulties or awkwardness between parent and child at the moment when they come together again. Because short-term accommodation does not remove children entirely from their homes, it is tempting to think that the effects of brief separations will be of a slighter intensity than those where separation is longer or the length is uncertain. The findings of this study suggest that adults need to be sensitive to individual children's reactions to any separation, however brief. At the same time, it must be stressed that generally, with appropriate support and sensitivity from adults, children managed their feelings and the comings and goings well.

Contact with family while away

In response to earlier research findings about the impact on children of loss of contact while they are being looked after (DHSS 1985b) the Children Act 1989 highlights the importance of children retaining links with their families while they are away from home (see DoH 1991a). Little is known about the relative merits of contact for children accommodated short-term. Consequently, this area was explored in this study.

Although there was a general understanding that parents would not actually visit during the breaks, except in special circumstances, there were no restrictions on indirect contact, for example by phone. However, given that only seven of the 60 (12%) families involved in the study had easy access to a telephone, it is not surprising that few children expected any contact between the carer home and their own home. As it turned out this expectation was realistic. During the short-term accommodation period contact, always by phone, between the child's home and that of the carer occurred in only 12 of all 60 (20%) cases – equally divided between the under- and over-fives. No child (or parent) complained of feeling unable to be in contact during the visits. Three older children said they knew they could walk home if they wanted. Several of the under-eights remarked that their parents knew where they were. The specificity of the arrangements, and the knowledge that communication was possible between the two homes, seemed to be enough to make children feel secure. Contact may not be so much of an issue in short-term cases.

Staying at the carer's home

As shown in Chapter 8, there were many links in lifestyle and proximity of homes which, in theory, provided continuity for the study children. From the children's point of view, to live with another family still places demands on them because, however similar are the homes, each family will be unique in its values, customs and rules. To explore how children adapted to the carer's regime, they were asked, at both the start and the end of the period of short-term accommodation, about changes relating to tangible everyday events such as bedtime, meals, seeing friends, pocket money and watching television. Overall, children experienced relatively few problems:

> I watched less telly. Didn't miss it much. because we were playing.
> (Tommy, aged 9)

> Of course playing was different . . . bound to be, isn't it? What I did like was that Joe [carer father] played and wrestled and took us out or swimming.
> (Dan, aged 11)

However, changes at the start of the placement in some routines held more significance than others. Just over half of the children (23) experienced a different bedtime regime. On the whole, this meant going to bed slightly earlier. For one or two, it meant not watching TV in bed. But for a handful (six) it meant not being able to seek comfort from parents in the night. Most children quickly adapted to this change as 9-year-old Mandy explained:

> A bit different. Comfy and all that, but sometimes if I get frightened or I wake up . . . then I go through to my mum. I missed it . . . but anyway, I didn't get frightened or anything, so it wasn't bad . . . just different. (Lisa, aged 10)

Food also presented differences for 19 (46%) of the children. This was occasionally (in five cases) to do with what was on offer, but more often to do with the normal constraints of being a guest in someone's house:

> Oh, yes it was nice food . . . what I missed was that I couldn't just go to the cupboard and get something . . . biscuits, or crisps. Well, she'd say yes mostly. But I had to ask. (John, aged 12)

One disadvantage of the majority of the placements for the older children was that they disrupted normal weekend routines. This included going shopping locally and seeing relatives and friends:

I missed going to the shop . . . like I usually do on a Saturday for my mum.
(Rosie, aged 12)

I missed my Aunty . . . but I do see her after school. (Hannah, aged 9)

Seven children did see their friends during the weekend but the majority did not expect to do so and accepted that being away from home brought a different routine. Their views suggested that, for many, the excitement of the placement outweighed any real disadvantage. Some of the over-tens also had faith that the relationships of home and peers would endure beyond the placement:

I did different things, the people were different . . . good fun mostly.
My own friends are there still. (Matthew, aged 14)

The children did not mention this as a disadvantage and none suggested that their regular friendships were affected by their periodic absences.

The information gathered from children at the end of the stays showed that familiarity had brought some changes in perception. For all areas except one, the differences were minor and were not found to be significant.

One issue held considerable significance for children – watching television. There were two areas of contention: missing favourite programmes because of alternative activities and not being allowed to stay up to watch particular programmes. This issue became more marked as the placement progressed. At the second interview stage there was a statistically significant increase in the numbers who felt customs over watching television were different from those at home ($p = <0.05$, df=1, Chi square). It is difficult to tell whether the direction of difference was positive or negative, indeed children's comments suggested a variety of reactions:

Telly? I watched less, 'cause we were mostly outside or playing. Didn't miss it much. (Kevin, aged 8)

The one thing I didn't like was not being able to see *Miami Vice*. They said it was too late. I was glad when I was at home some Saturdays because I could see it then. (Julie, aged 9)

No-one liked to watch football. At home we have Sky TV. Me and my Dad we watch football and sport all the time. I missed that a lot. (Mark, aged 12)

None of the differences perceived by the children was unsettling enough to affect the arrangements drastically, and nearly all were things with which the children quickly felt reasonably happy.

Relations with members of the carer family

The majority of children got on well with all members of their carer family.

Figure 9.5 *Children's perceptions of their relationship with individual members of carer family*

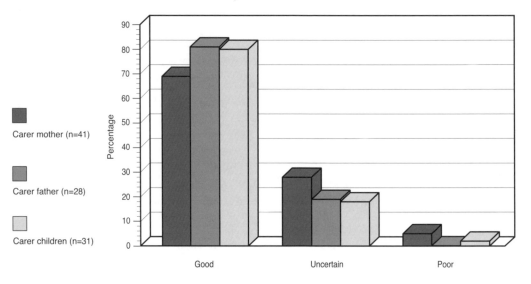

Figure 9.5 however suggests that children had a greater degree of uncertainty with relation to the carer mother. Although practically 70% of the children said they got on well with the mother, a further 27% were uncertain and 5% were not happy with the relationship. Ambivalence seemed mainly to relate to the fact the carer mother would generally be responsible for setting and upholding family norms and rules:

> Well, not sure about Mrs Harris. She was very strict. (Sophie, aged 9)

In addition, some children hinted that to develop a good relationship with the carer mother would have been disloyal to their own mother:

> I liked being there but it wasn't like being with Mum. She said I could call her Mum. I didn't. I thought my mum wouldn't like it. (Dave, aged 10)

Good relationships with fathers seemed to relate to individual personalities rather than any comparison with children's relationship with their own fathers. There was no association between liking fathers and whether children came from a one- or two-parent family.

Good or poor relationships with the children in the household were characterised by the attitudes and attention of children to each other.

What children liked and disliked about carer family members

Children were asked to give their views on why they liked or disliked members of the carer family. These views fell into five categories as shown in Figure 9.6. Children highlighted different characteristics when they talked about what they liked in different members of the carer family. There was a tendency to divide characteristics of mothers and fathers by gender.

Figure 9.6 *'Liked' characteristics of carer mothers, fathers and children as identified by short-term accommodation children*

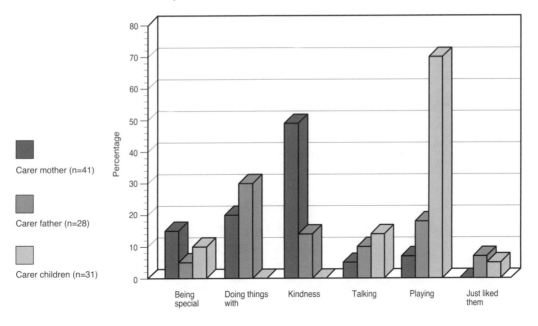

Carer mother (n=41)

Carer father (n=28)

Carer children (n=31)

Carer mothers were valued more for their attitudes than for any shared activities. For example, kindness was high on the agenda for practically half (48%) of the children, with also an emphasis on nurturing:

> She was kind . . . treated me special, made me sandwiches and gave me Coca-Cola. (Don, aged 10)

Six children stressed being treated as 'special' by their carer mother. All came from families where there was a good deal of tension:

> What I liked was that she was kind . . . treated me special. (Sue, aged 10)

The attitude and attention of carer fathers was also valued but was more focused through shared activities:

> I liked it that he was there . . . and could play, and talk and that. (Fiona, aged 8)

> I helped him mend the car . . . learnt a lot. (Richard, aged 12)

> He took Helen and me swimming . . . we had a good time. (Pam, aged 9)

Several children from households where fathers were unemployed commented that they did not like it when the carer father went to work and one 6-year-old boy felt quite put out:

> Well, he did keep going off . . . I think he was going to work . . . every day, like!

Where there were other children in the home, playing together was the thing that children enjoyed most. Appreciation of other qualities, such as 'talking to' and being 'treated as special', when referring to carer children was associated only with the presence of older carer children.

Throughout the exploration of the children's perceptions of their relationships with the carer family, the question of comparisons between their own home and that of the carers rarely arose. Although children appreciated small treats like popcorn at the cinema there was no sense of envy of carer households. Children were much more preoccupied by the attitudes of adults towards them. Although it can only be speculation, this may relate to the fact that cultural and economic differences between families were kept to a minimum and the fact that children did care about and value their own families.

The children found it far more difficult to identify features about their carer family which they did not like. Practically two-thirds could not identify any characteristic they disliked about their carer mother (65%), carer father (62%) or carer children (58%). It was impossible to develop any typology of dislikes because of the small numbers involved and the diversity of reasons given by individual children. Descriptions of what was disliked showed that criticisms of both carer mothers and fathers tended to the ordinary and largely represented part of the normal negotiations of boundaries between adults and children in many families. Children felt put out when they were in trouble or their wishes were thwarted:

> She was grumpy if we made a mess . . . well, sometimes. (Kevin, aged 8)

> Yeah! . . . when she told you off – you knew she meant it! (Hannah, aged 9)

> Bossy! like if it was bedtime you just had to go. Yes . . . he said we must.
> (Dave, aged 10)

There was a minority of children who did not like their carer families, did not settle and wished continually that they were at home. Some dislikes seemed to relate to the fact that there was simply no rapport between child and carer.

Five-year-old Nick continually felt uncomfortable with his carer mother:

> Just felt . . . funny. Funny.

The few children who felt uncomfortable about their carer father tended to locate reasons in unfamiliarity. Seven-year-old Katie reported:

> I wasn't too sure . . . not used to him, I suppose.

Difficulties between the study children and the carer's children tended to be associated with favouritism shown towards own children or more commonly (in 11 cases) with specific instances of disagreement or clashes of personality reminiscent of normal peer group alliances and dislikes:

> A real creep . . . thought she was 'it' alright . . . sometimes she was alright.
> (Diane, aged 9)

> Awful! Thinks he knows it all, he does. But he doesn't. (Mick, aged 13)

> She's just lazy . . . does nothing all the time. (Barbara, aged 14)

Summing up the experience

What children enjoyed most about being at the carers

Summing up the things that they had most enjoyed about being accommodated, at the end of the intervention, children again located their views within their relationships with the carer family. Figure 9.7, based on the 40 children who were followed up (excluding one whose family had moved away), shows children's perceptions of their experience at the end of the accommodation period.

Sixteen children described their pleasure at finding that they were responded to as individuals – that time was put aside for them:

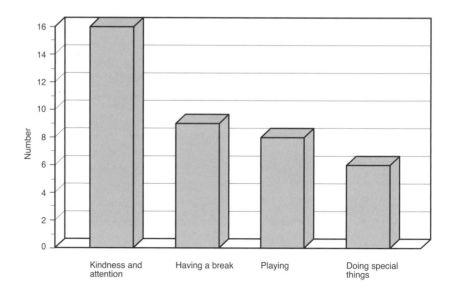

Figure 9.7 *Things children most enjoyed about being at the carer's home (n=41)*

Just how they were interested . . . what I did and what I liked . . . just talking, not too much . . . but I knew I could. (Alex, aged 8)

Relaxing and having a break was mentioned by 11 children:

I think it was nice knowing I'd be coming, that I was expected. Especially once I was sort of used to it. (Pam, aged 9)

The special things children enjoyed included walks, visits to the park or the countryside, visits to the cinema, having treats to eat – like a curry or a take-away. These would be fairly ordinary pleasures to many children in the community. They were especially valued by some of the study children for being new experiences and 'special' occasions:

We did go to the pictures and had popcorn and drinks, as a special treat . . . all of us went . . . the whole family. (Tessa, aged 5)

What children least liked

Children were also asked what they had least liked. Half the children questioned could not think of anything they had particularly disliked. For those who did identify negative aspects of the stay, seven mentioned being away from home as the worst aspect of accommodation. The rest related their negative views to the behaviour or attitudes of members of the carer family. Being told off, being prevented from doing what they did at home and quarrelling with the carer children were the main problems. Two children had clearly been very unhappy, did not get on with the carer family at all and resented being away from home:

> I just didn't like it – it wasn't like home. (Robin, aged 6)

> I was so lonely – I just went to bed and cried. I am glad I don't have to go there again. (Sally, aged 9)

> She [teenage daughter] was really bitchy. She hated my guts and I hated hers. (Grace, aged 11)

> They always told me off – I couldn't do anything right. (Peter, aged 10)

> I hated them – they were so strict. I was always in trouble. I never want to go there again. (Tom, aged 13)

Perceptions of the value of the intervention

By the second interview, 78% of the children (31 of 40) believed the breaks had helped them personally while all but three thought that the breaks had been helpful to their parents. Children's answers about how the experience had helped them fell into four categories, defined by themselves:

1   They had had a good time (35%).

2   They felt happier (29%).

3   They had had a break from worries at home (20%).

4   The breaks had made things easier at home (16%).

> I liked going there. I wish I could still go. We had some good times. (Samantha, aged 7)

> I don't know really. I think I feel happier, sort of less worried. I don't get so tired now. My dad says I'm easier to deal with. I don't climb on the chest of drawers. I just play with my Nintendo pocket game that George [carer father] gave me. (Neil, aged 9)

I can cope with my sister now. I just tell her to get lost. And I don't mind the rows so much. I just go off to my room. I wish I could go some more. (Elizabeth, aged 12)

It did seem to help my mum . . . I suppose she could relax a bit. Things got much more sorted out . . . she just got a lot more relaxed. (Dave, aged 10)

What children would have changed

Two-thirds (26) of the children either did not suggest any changes to the arrangements they had experienced, or could not think of anything they would have liked to be different.

For those who did want things changed, this was usually in terms of the overall period of breaks. Nine out of the thirteen who wanted to change arrangements would have liked a longer series of breaks, while the remaining four wanted the opposite. These four children had not wanted to be accommodated in the first place and remained resentful about being sent away from home. All were from families defined as in chronic need. Their lives were unsettled and unpredictable, often farmed out to other relatives or having to cope with yet another new 'father' and all were children about whom social workers had more than a passing concern. They were children who were anxious about being away from home, because they feared they might not be allowed to return. Two also had some fairly severe behaviour problems, such as temper tantrums or aggression to other children. In short, they were very unhappy children who did not seem confident enough in themselves to cope with any more disruption in their lives.

The group who would have liked a longer series of placements were more mixed and came from a wide range of circumstances. Some wanted a longer arrangement because of the stresses at home; others had enjoyed themselves a great deal and did not want to give up their new family and friends. It was difficult for these children to grasp why the placement had ended and there was some resentment because such a good experience had been terminated.

Summary

Children were anxious about going away from home. Their anxiety did not diminish because of the short-term nature of arrangements.

Children worried about strangeness: going to stay with strangers, but as importantly, what this would imply in relation to missing TV programmes or being faced with strange food.

There was confusion in children's minds about the consultation process, which tended to be slanted towards information-giving rather than a dialogue about children's views. The tensions between children's immediate needs and the long-term interests of the family were not always addressed.

There needs to be greater clarification in Guidance of the meaning of consultation with children. To separate out the component parts into information-giving, talking over anxieties and giving children the opportunity to influence plans is important.

Children's views on the purpose of short-term accommodation were mixed. As might be expected, older children could grasp that the arrangements were not simply to give respite to parents but also for their personal benefit.

In spite of the fact that most children met the carers before the placement the transition to the carers' home was unsettling and continued to be so throughout the placement. Children learnt to manage the comings and goings.

Children found it difficult to talk over their anxieties. Less than half felt they could turn to their parents for solace but of most concern was the minority of children who had no one they felt able to turn to for reassurance.

Children also found it difficult to tell friends about their breaks either through fear of stigma or envy. Social workers thought it important to help children develop 'cover stories'.

The majority of children had some difficulties settling with the carers. Most were homesick and in some cases this did not diminish with familiarity.

How children managed their homesickness was an important finding. Many chose to cope with their feelings in solitude rather than talk to parents or carers.

In spite of some similarities in lifestyle between carers and families, children found some differences. Most diminished with time and none of the differences was unsettling enough to affect the arrangements drastically.

There was little contact between families and children but children felt that they could easily access their parents through the carers if they wanted to. This was an important finding and indicated that children felt a measure of control over their lives.

Children valued members of the carer family for different qualities: mothers for kindness, fathers for activities and children for play and talking. Overall children got on well with the carers.

The majority of children liked their carers and increasingly enjoyed the time they spent there.

Being told off, being prevented from doing what they did at home and quarrelling with the carer children were the main problems about the placement. Two children had clearly been very unhappy, did not get on with the carer family at all and resented being away from home.

Children most liked being at the carers for the attention they were given and the new activities they experienced with the family. They least liked discipline, 'being told off' and not being allowed to do what they would at home.

Endings were difficult, made more so by the absence of social workers to explain why 'a good thing' had to come to an end.

Most children had enjoyed themselves and would have liked more. There was a minority who hated being away from home and heaved a sigh of relief when they did not have to go any more.

There is an important place for the family support social worker to keep in contact with children to ensure children can, if they wish, talk about the stress of the placement.

10 Family support and the future of short-term accommodation

The Children Act 1989 intended that there should be a broad range of services to support children in need and their families. The service described in this study does not, and cannot, claim to represent a panacea for all children in need. It can do no more than show the extent to which one service in four localities helped 60 children in need and their families. To say those children are representative of all children in need would be, at best, presumptive and, at worst, unscientific. The contribution of this study to the debate about the implementation of the Act is to show one example of the application of family support services to a particular group of children and their families and to attempt to identify the components of this service which contributed to both its success and its shortcomings.

But what the study does show is that the majority of the 60 parents felt the service had helped them and were able to identify how it had met their needs. What reservations children may have had at the outset also lessened over time and many found the experience acceptable and, in some cases, pleasurable. It also shows the social work processes and input from carers that contributed to parents' and children's perceptions of outcome.

Finally, the study has explored the way in which the *Guidance and Regulations* governing short-term accommodation and family placements were used in four social services departments in the early stages of implementing the Children Act 1989. This provides valuable feedback to policy makers on the use of these documents.

The study families

The families in this study shared characteristics with families of 'looked-after' children reported in other studies. They were characterised by their low income, health problems, and social isolation. About half had long-standing connections with social services. Black families were under-represented. What set the majority apart from some other studies of families in the community was their cognitive appraisal of social services, which was not seen as a child rescue agency but as an organisation which could, and did, offer family support. By the end of the study, the majority were confirmed in this view.

In spite of similarities in socio-economic characteristics, the 60 families showed considerable diversity in the types and severity of social problems that had brought them to social services. They were, however, characterised by lack of social support from kin and community. One-third could be described as families who, though struggling, generally managed their lives independently and who had turned to social services at a point of acute need. Some had a crisis of ill health, others were struggling with the management of their children, and there were those who had problems in managing the dynamics of establishing a new partnership alongside meeting the needs of children.

There was, however, a sizeable number whose problems were more entrenched. They had been known to social services for some time and were characterised by the ongoing chronicity of their problems. Within these were families where social workers had serious concerns about parenting skills and the welfare of children. Social workers judged a minority of children to be on the borderline of being at risk of neglect or emotional abuse, and several children had been the subject of child protection enquiries in the past. Two children were on at risk registers, both in relation to neglect, but no children in the study were deemed to be at risk of significant harm as defined in the Children Act 1989 with respect to ill-treatment in the form of either physical or sexual abuse.

Outcomes for parents

The parents' expectations of the services were mostly met. They were extremely grateful for the help they were given and made good use of it. What was striking was the normality of their expectations: for time off from their children, to manage their children's behaviour, to have a good relationship with spouses or partners and to improve their health and employment prospects. What was also noticeable was the extent to which, at the beginning of the study, families were socially isolated and were unable to draw on their own social networks for help. Neither did they have the wherewithal to purchase relief child care to give them space to address their problems, a solution which many more affluent families estranged from their kin would take for granted. Thus they turned to social services for help.

An important finding from the study was how social isolation could be improved, first, through the intervention enabling parents to rebuild links with extended family and second, through the development of links into the community via the carers.

Balancing parents and children's needs

Another important finding was that, with one or two significant exceptions, children's needs were not sacrificed to meet those of their parents. The exceptions were children who were unhappy at home and who felt even more insecure away from home.

Children's views of the service

While being sceptical initially, the majority of children found the experience of short-term accommodation to be positive. They enjoyed the attention they were given by the carers and playing with carer children. There was a distinct division by gender in children's perceptions of carers. Mothers were valued for their kindness, fathers for their attention and shared activities. Talking between children and adults was less important to the children than adults' attitude and shared activity.

An extremely significant finding was the degree of homesickness experienced by the majority of children over 5 years old. Although this appeared to be a normal reaction to their temporary loss of important attachment figures, it is an area that warrants attention. The fact that the accommodation lasted days rather than weeks did not diminish the strength of children's feelings. What was new in this study was information on the way children chose to manage their homesickness. Although some turned to carers for comfort, the majority chose to come to terms with their feelings in solitude. It is important to recognise children's choice here, to ensure that the need for solitude is not misinterpreted as indifference towards the carer family and to ensure that the adults adopt a sensitive, child-centred approach.

The importance of social work

The social work input in this study was crucial in effecting a positive outcome for parents and children.

This was not an open-door service. Considerable gatekeeping was exercised at the point of entry. At this point, the service was very much resource led. It was outside the scope of the study to find out how many families had been turned down. The negative effect of the gatekeeping was that, because of tight resourcing, some families might well have been deprived of the service. The positive outcome was that those assessed eligible for the service made good use of the scarce resources available.

Once families had been accepted for the service, there was evidence of services being adapted to meet the needs of individual families as far as resources would allow. There was also evidence of social workers working in partnership with parents at the planning stage and throughout the placement.

It would be dangerous to assume that others could not have used the services just as well. However, given the inevitability of finite resources there was no doubt that skilled social work assessment proved cost-effective in the particular schemes in the study. Although it was not possible to attribute outcome to intervention in any experimental way, failure to prevent family breakdown occurred in only two of the 60 cases. What is more important in this study is that parents' perceptions of the service and its outcome were positive.

The short-term accommodation service was arranged and directed by social workers. The input of social workers was germane to the quality and the outcome of the service as perceived by parents and children. This was a study in which social work was highly valued by clients. There are several aspects worthy of note.

Interagency working

The study did not look at interagency collaboration at the service planning level. However, there was evidence of innovative working together between social workers and health visitors at the point of referral in one social services department. A shared view of need and a high trust relationship existed between these two professionals, which enabled health visitors to refer families to the short-term accommodation scheme, and decide jointly with social workers about eligibility and access to the service. This system was cost-effective in terms of time and expertise. It also helped to make the service more easily accessible to families.

The importance of social casework

What emerged during the study was the complex role of the family support social workers as complete care managers, integrating the activities of social care planning and social casework. Not only did social workers organise the service but they undertook direct work with parents, identifying problems and together seeking strategies to ameliorate them. Carers were co-opted into these strategies when appropriate, for example, to advise parents on improving their parenting skills or to make children feel special. Throughout the placement, the family support social worker kept in touch with parents by letter or phone to monitor the progress of the placement. In short, they engaged in the classic social work processes of assessment and intervention which are best described as social casework. This professional relationship was valued and used by clients to good effect.

Alongside the direct work, social workers arranged packages of intervention to address the needs of the more serious problems of some families. Where intense direct intervention was needed, either with parents or children, this was generally offered appropriately by other social work specialists. Similarly, there was liaison with health professionals where parents or children needed medical or psychiatric treatment. In a minority of cases, the services of other professionals such as educational psychologists were used.

The support of carers

Social workers were equally skilled in training and supporting carers so that carers were able to provide a service which empowered parents rather than undermined them. *Guidance and Regulations* had confirmed and improved standards of practice in relation to carers.

Working with children

Social workers were rather less expert at supporting children, and their interpretation of the statutory role of consulting children was unclear and unfocused. There was evidence of some good specialist direct work with a minority of children during the placement, usually undertaken by social workers with special skills in this area within social services or within child and family guidance.

Ending the placement

Ending contact between client and social worker is an important generic task in all social work intervention. One major omission in this study was the lack of attention paid to the ending of the short-term accommodation service. Where parents did not need any other service, the ending of the placement was handed over to carers who felt uncomfortable in their role, especially when parents and children did not want the placement to end.

Neither was there any attempt to help parents and children make sense of the service. An 'ending meeting' along the lines of the planning meeting would have helped clarify what had been achieved and identify any residual needs. Carers, too, would have welcomed the opportunity to review their part in the process and outcome of the placement, although many were given some opportunity for reviewing their role through their ongoing support systems which were a feature for all foster carers in three of the four local authorities. In the fourth, the scheme leader provided a support role for the carers.

Implementing the *Guidance and Regulations*

A major aim of the study was to explore how the *Guidance and Regulations* in relation to family placements were being implemented. The findings on this were mixed. Although planning meetings had been arranged in 100% of cases, elaborate care plans as envisaged by the Guidance rarely existed. Neither were written agreements much in evidence. Social workers had taken the initiative to adapt the Regulations to fit their own perceptions of the nature of the short-term accommodation service.

Parents felt that services had been offered in partnership. The majority felt they had been properly consulted and involved in decision-making. The service was needs led, in spite of strong rationing of the resource by workers and there being a limited choice of carers. Many parents would have liked a longer period of accommodation.

Preparation of children was reasonably well handled, although some children were confused at the outset about whether or not they had been consulted. Consultation centred more on information-giving. There was little evidence of children being given choices about whether they wished to be accommodated or not but some older children had felt able to influence the detail of arrangements. This process revealed the potential for tension in family support arrangements where the needs of parents have to be balanced against those of the children.

Most children had met their carers before they were placed. Older children were also fairly clear about the purpose of their stay and there was evidence of thoughtful help being given to children so they might have cover stories to explain to friends and teachers why they were away from home.

Creating continuity for children between home and placement, as suggested in *Guidance and Regulations,* was achieved on some dimensions but not on others. Carers and families had many points of similarity in lifestyle and the majority lived in the same community, sharing shops and schools. There was a dearth of placements for black and dual-heritage children.

Finally, the Regulations relating to carers had just been fully implemented when the study began. These had been well received. Experienced carers told the research team that the Regulations had strengthened their sense of being professionals and had given them very clear boundaries and expectations of their work. *Guidance and Regulations* confirmed practice in relation to the training and support of carers rather than effecting any changes of substance.

The role of carers

The recruitment of carers from a diversity of sources was of considerable interest. The findings suggested that carers who had been recruited via the traditional family placement route could be as effective in offering 'inclusive' placements as those recruited via a child-minding route. However, recruitment of child-minders offered parents the chance to work with carers who lived in proximity to them and shared similar lifestyles. Child-minder carers also had a natural sense of the offering of a contractual service to families which had to be learned by the others.

Some traditional indicators of placement breakdown, such as the age of the foster mother or the relative ages of foster and own children did not seem to apply in this study. The most important factors within the placement effecting a successful outcome, as perceived by parents and children, were the attitudes of carers towards parents and children, and similarity in lifestyles. Children valued carers for their kindness, shared time and activities rather than for any material factors.

The professionalism of the carers was impressive. Some credit for this must go to the social workers who selected and trained them. Any private misgivings carers might have had about the capabilities and lives of parents were kept firmly to themselves. Parents saw carers as their champions, their substitute family and as friends. In return, carers extended their generosity to parents well beyond any duty. They were remarkable people whose commitment and kindness to the families they served were fully recognised and appreciated by both parents and children.

Messages from the research for policy and practice

The policy context

This study was one of several commissioned to look at the implementation of the Children Act 1989. Its value lies in the fact that, like the study by Packman and Hall (1995) on full-term accommodation, it attempted to investigate a newly defined provision which was grounded in the Children Act philosophy to provide a continuum of services for children in need. Breaking down the barriers between community-based support and out-of-home placements was a major part of this philosophy. It involved moving from a narrow definition of prevention to 'diminish the need to receive children into care' to a broader definition of family support.

As early commentaries on the Act pointed out, however (Aldgate and Tunstill 1995), the success of this broad and positive definition would depend heavily on how local authorities categorised children in need, and further, within the overarching categories of children identified in need in their area, how they might set priorities for service provision. As Aldgate and Tunstill (1995) found in their study of the first 18 months' implementation, there was a tendency for authorities to err towards a narrow definition of need, centred around children for whom authorities already had some statutory responsibility. But as Packman and Hall (1995) showed, authorities were also attempting to get to grips with the new concept of accommodation. This study fell between the other two in its task of investigating a service located ideologically in family support but offering what had previously been classified as an 'in care' service.

What was heartening, and proved to be unusual nationally, was that, in three of the four authorities studied, the service was seen as a necessary part of a portfolio of services to support families, although in the fourth authority, the service was suspended soon after the study began and the resources diverted to other services, including child protection enquiries. During the course of the study, the results of the Department of Health's research programme on child protection was published (DoH 1995a). This concluded:

> The research studies suggest that too much of the work undertaken comes under the banner of child protection . . . A more balanced service for vulnerable children would encourage professionals to take a wider view. There would be efforts to work alongside families rather than disempower them, to raise their self-esteem rather than reproach families, to promote

family relationships where children have their needs met, rather than leave untreated families with an unsatisfactory parenting style. The focus would be on the overall needs of children rather than a narrow concentration on the alleged incident. (DoH 1995a, pp. 54–5)

To this conclusion was added evidence from the Audit Commission (1994) on the attitude of social workers to family support, which concluded:

Many social workers have not yet made the intellectual shift away from categorising children according to services . . . Health visitors were concerned that children referred to them by social services were not getting any support. (p. 58)

Finally, the first inspection of children in need affirmed the state of practice. Commenting on social services' implementation of the key Children Act principles of welfare of the child, the child's wishes and feelings, partnership with parents and others and equal opportunities, the inspectors concluded:

All authorities acknowledged these key principles of the Children Act, and claimed that the principles guided the way they approached their work with children and families. However, because services for children in need were so underdeveloped in most of them, cases other than those in crisis did not routinely receive the priority which their circumstances merited. Consequently, the welfare of children concerned was not always well addressed. It is arguable that if cases received help earlier, the need for crisis responses later would be lessened. (Social Services Inspectorate 1996, p. 15)

As a response to these messages, the Association of Directors of Social Services and National Children's Homes (1996) produced a monograph giving examples of some effective community-based services for children in need.

The Department of Health has now implemented Children's Services Plans, emphasising the need for a holistic and co-ordinated approach to planning for children to maximise the resources of social services, health, education and other local authority services to work together for the promotion of children's welfare. The implementation of these plans should provide a much firmer plank on which to stand family support services.

These outputs provide an appropriate context for the messages from this study on short-term accommodation.

Implementing the *Guidance and Regulations*

1   The study suggests that overall, the *Guidance and Regulations* in relation to short-term accommodation is being implemented but with some modifications.

2   Carers are undoubtedly benefiting from being regulated in terms of status and increased expertise.

3   There are some problems in applying the very detailed arrangements for planning to short-term accommodation arrangements. Without undermining the spirit of the legislation, a shorter process may be more appropriate in some cases which allows consultation with parents and simplifies the making of plans and agreements.

4   Social workers need help in understanding their role in relation to consultation with children and guidance on how to balance the needs of children and parents.

5   The guidance on ending short-term arrangements is ambiguous and needs clarification. While carers and parents may manage the course of the placement alone, social workers need to return to effect proper endings to the arrangements with all concerned.

Locating short-term accommodation in family support services

Family support in this study was seen as being helpful by parents. They believed the service offered them the opportunity to address problem at several levels. The findings suggest that there is a place for supportive services within the direct provision of social services. To provide a framework for locating short-term accommodation within a range of services, it is useful to draw on the work of Hardiker et al. (1996), which has helped a number of local authorities assess need, prioritise services and plan and develop new services (see ADSS/NCH 1996). The levels of response to family problems outlined in the framework help to identify where different types of family support may be located:

First Level

For social services departments, this level addresses vulnerable groups and communities. The aims at this level are to prevent the need for children and families becoming drawn into welfare services at subsequent levels and entering a 'client status'; this is because services may be stigmatising and families' autonomy may be reduced. Interventions aim to enable families in difficulties to use community and universalist services wherever possible. Advice, guidance and signposting services in health centres, libraries, schools, churches and community centres often successfully achieve this. The aims are to empower families and to strengthen their own support networks.

Second Level [early stresses]

This level of prevention addresses families in temporary crisis or early difficulties. It certainly targets 'children in need'.

Approaches at this level may include short-term, task-centred and crisis-intervention methods. The aim is to restore personal and social functioning so that *direct* interventions by social services departments are no longer required and families can be helped by first level, that is, universal community-based, prevention services. In the meantime, families may be enabled to use day care and family centres, respite care, befriending networks and brief counselling services.

Third Level [serious stresses]

These risks may include significant harm, family breakdown or entry into the care system. Families may have severe and well-established difficulties or face serious crises such as homicide, sexual abuse, cruelty, grievous bodily harm and wilful neglect. Third level prevention services aim to mitigate the effects of these problems and to restore family functioning and links between parents and children. Helping interventions aim to facilitate 'good enough' parenting and to enable families to use a range of therapeutic and community facilities. (Adapted from Hardiker, Exton and Barker 1996, pp. 14–15)

The short-term accommodation service was primarily used as a second-level service to prevent a deterioration in families when early risks or stresses had been identified. This level was most applicable to the families defined as being in acute or chronic need although some of the chronic need families strayed over into the serious risks category. These were families whose children had identifiable behaviour problems or where parenting problems were giving cause for serious concern.

The framework proposed by Hardiker et al. suggests there is value in inter-agency collaboration within the *'enabling authority'*. It also helps define the social work processes through which family support necessitating a social work presence, such as short-term accommodation, may be provided. The service inputs that helped families in this study correspond to the three activities of casework and social care planning, therapeutic interventions and community development within the Hardiker et al. framework.

The enabling authority

The evidence from the study supported the aim of Children's Services Plans to create a co-ordinated family support service between different agencies in the local authority. Although there was little evidence of interagency collaboration at a strategic level, at the ground level, active co-operation between health visitors and social workers in one of the study authorities helped to create a streamlined process of assessment that made the service more easily accessed by families. The presence of health visitors also did much to allay families fears about any hidden agenda of child rescue in social services. There is considerable potential for developing interagency collaboration to improve access to family support services.

In another area, the accessing of short-term accommodation occurred through a children's centre which incorporated a family centre. This helped to de-stigmatise access and to enable smooth referral to the family placement team which arranged short-term accommodation and would suggest that the development of a locally based 'one-stop shop' for social services and other services is a viable way forward.

Casework and social care planning

The role of the family support social worker as a complete care manager was central to the social work input in the study. The centrality of this role in combining social care planning role, that is, arranging the service, and packages of care for some families and the social casework role (of joint assessment with families, identifying problems and agreeing the strategy to ameliorate them, consultation with parents, making care plans, preparation for the accommodation service, and casework with parents during the placement) contributed to its success.

Casework with children is equally important to allay their fears and prepare them for the experience. The study showed that social workers may have the necessary but uncomfortable duty to balance the immediate needs of children and parents in order to achieve the goal of preventing family breakdown. At no time should children's developmental needs be sacrificed but it may be necessary to override children's initial ambivalence in some cases in the interests of family preservation. This is a fact that has to be faced. Special care will always need to be taken in making judgements about the suitability of the service for individual children. Where decisions are made to go ahead but concern about the child's needs remain, more focused support should be given to children during the placement from social workers and carers to reassure them they are not rejected and to preserve attachments with their families. This points to the need for the development of expertise in child care social workers at the post-qualifying level. Any accreditation scheme should include skills in working directly with children.

The application of social care planning and casework skills to the recruitment, training and support of carers underpinned the complex role of carers as direct providers to children, and in many cases, to parents. For this service to be both cost-effective and successful, it has to be resourced adequately so that carers will feel well supported and thus will be retained.

Therapeutic interventions

Planned carefully with each family, the short-term accommodation service may be a therapeutic intervention for parents and children in its own right. But in cases of more serious risks, there is a role for combining short-term accommodation with more specific and targeted therapeutic interventions from a range of agencies. To offer the service alone in these cases may not be enough to meet the needs of either children or parents. Careful social work assessment and consultation with the parents and children is needed here to identify the cases of serious risks and the services that may help lower them. Again, a multidisciplinary approach may be the most effective.

Community development

There are two important strands to the short-term accommodation service which relate to the discussion of community development.

The first relevant finding was that this was a community-based service, located in the neighbourhood in which families lived. This was especially important where carers were recruited from child-minders. The similarities of location and lifestyle helped reinforce parents' self-esteem and provide continuities for children. This was indeed called a 'neighbourhood care service' by one of the authorities. Any short-term accommodation service needs to account for the neighbourhood factor especially in relation to the recruitment of suitable carers.

Carers provided for parents access to other community resources and helped them strengthen links with their extended kin. The development of short-term accommodation as a neighbourhood-based service undoubtedly has a role in helping to integrate some families into the community.

More than this, the service helped to address the important problem of social isolation. The respite from the children gave the parents energy and confidence to improve specific aspects of their lives, of which one important area was the combating of social isolation. In this respect, short-term accommodation offers a source of family support with some similar aims to befriending schemes such as Homestart or the Department of Health's Child Care Circles initiative. Parents in this study agreed with Ball (1996) that 'the positive effects of respite are often easiest to appreciate when it stops' (p. 25).

It could be argued that the development of a more supportive environment within neighbourhoods, especially where families are living on low incomes, may obviate the need for short-term accommodation. This is too simplistic a view and takes no account of the diversity of families in need.

The families in the study had needs over and above those that could have been helped by community support alone. What short-term accommodation offered was a more complete response that reached beyond short bursts of respite or group support. It helped families address problems that had become more entrenched or out of control by combining respite with social work and other therapeutic interventions. The needs of children in this study had been assessed as sufficiently serious to access priority services under Section 17. This is an important point because it emphasises that children and families would have been struggling without services. Some families would have benefited from the availability of support such as drop-in family centres or befriending schemes at an earlier stage. Indeed, had these supports been available, they might have prevented the deterioration of some families to the point where early risks had brought them to seek help from social workers. There were other families where a self-help response would not have been enough to divert serious or even some early risks. In these cases, there continues to be an important part for the social work response. Short-term accommodation, therefore, needs to be available as one of a broad range of services for families under stress. Only by offering a large menu of family support services can there be more choice for families. Creating choice is in itself the foundation of community-based social services to promote the welfare of children in need.

References

Aldgate, J. (1976) 'The child in care and his parents', *Adoption and Fostering*, **84**(2), pp. 29–40

Aldgate, J. (1977) *Identification of Factors Influencing Children's Length of Stay in Care*, unpublished PhD thesis, University of Edinburgh

Aldgate, J. (1980) 'Identification of factors influencing children's length of stay in care', in Triseliotis, J. (ed.) *New Developments in Foster Care and Adoption*, London: Routledge & Kegan Paul, pp. 22–40

Aldgate, J. (1989) 'Foster and residential care – some interpersonal dynamics', *Children and Society*, **3**(1), pp. 19–36

Aldgate, J. (1991) 'Partnership with parents – fantasy or reality', *Adoption and Fostering*, **15**(2), pp. 5–17

Aldgate, J. (1992) *Work with Children Experiencing Separation and Loss*, in Aldgate, J. and Simmonds, J. (eds) *Direct Work With Children: A Guide for Social Work Practitioners*, 2nd edn, London: Batsford pp. 36–48

Aldgate, J. and Hawley, D. (1986) *Recollections of Disruption*, London: National Foster Care Association

Aldgate, J. and Heath, A.F. (1992) *The Educational Progress of Children in Long-Term Foster Care*, Final Report to the E.S.R.C.

Aldgate, J. and Simmonds, J. (eds) (1992) *Direct Work With Children: A Guide for Social Work Practitioners*, 2nd edn, London: Batsford

Aldgate, J. and Tunstill, J. (1995) *Making Sense of Section 17: Implementing Services for Children in Need within the Children Act, 1989*, London: HMSO

Aldgate, J., Pratt, R. and Duggan, M. (1989) 'Using care away from home to prevent family breakdown', *Adoption and Fostering*, **13**(2), pp. 32–37

Ambrose, P., Harper, J. and Pemberton, R. (1983) *Surviving Divorce: Men Beyond Marriage*, London: Wheatley Books

Amin, K. and Oppenheim, C. (1992) *Poverty in Black and White: Deprivation in Ethnic Minorities*, London: Child Poverty Action Group

Argyle, M. (1992) 'Benefits produced by supportive social relationships', in Veiel, H.O.F. and Baumann, U. (eds) *The Meaning and Measurement of Social Support*, NewYork: Hemisphere Publishing Corporation

Association of Directors of Social Services and National Children's Homes (1996) *Children Still in Need – Refocusing Child Protection in the Context of Children in Need*, London: NCH Action for Children

Astrachan, M. and Harris, D.M. (1983) 'Weekend only: an alternative model in residential treatment centers', *Child Welfare*, **LXII**(3), pp. 253–61

Audit Commission (1994) *Seen but Not Heard*, London: HMSO

Ball, M. (1996) *Round and Round the Circle: Support for Isolated Families through the Department of Health's Childcare Circles Initiative*, London: Department of Health

Barrerra, M. (1986) 'Distinctions between social support concepts, measures and models', *American Journal of Community Psychology*, 4(4), pp. 413–45

Bayley, M. (1987) *Mental Handicap and Community Care*, London: Routledge & Kegan Paul

Bebbington, A. and Miles J. (1989) 'The background of children who enter local authority care', *British Journal of Social Work*, **19**, pp. 349–68

Belsky, J. and Vondra, J. (1989) 'Lessons from child abuse: the determinants of parenting', in Cicchetti, D. and Carlson, V. (eds) *Child Maltreatment*, Cambridge: Cambridge University Press

Beresford, B. ((1994) *Positively Parents: Caring for a Severely Disabled Child*, London: HMSO

Berridge, D. (1996) *Foster Care – The Research Reviewed*, Report to the Department of Health

Berridge, D. and Cleaver, H. (1987) *Foster Home Breakdown*, Oxford: Blackwell

Bradshaw, J. (1990) *Child Poverty and Deprivation in the UK*, London: National Children's Bureau

Bullock, R., Little, M. and Millham, S. (1993) *Going Home: The Return of Children Separated from Families*, Aldershot: Dartmouth

Caplan, G. (1974) 'Organization of support sysytems for civilization', in Caplan, G., (ed.) *Support Systems and Mutual Help: Multidisciplinary Explorations*, New York: Grune and Stratton

Challis, D. (1986) *Case Management in Community Care*, Aldershot: Gower

Charnley, J. (1955) *The Art of Child Placement*, Minneapolis: University of Minneapolis Press

Cleaver, H. and Freeman, P. (1995) *Parental Perspectives in Cases of Suspected Child Abuse*, London: HMSO

Cleaver, H., Wattam, C. and Cawson, P. (1996) *Assessing Risk in Child Protection*, Report to the Department of Health

Compton, B.R. and Galloway, B. (1989) *Social Work Processes*, Belmont, CA: Wandsworth

Dartington Social Research Unit (in conjunction with the Support Force for Residential Care) (1996) *Matching Needs and Services, The Audit and Planning of Provision for Children Looked After by Local Authorities*, Dartington: Dartington Social Research Unit

Department of Health and Social Security (1984) *Report of the House of Commons Social Services Committee (*The Short Report), London: HMSO

Department of Health and Social Security (1985a) *Review of Child Care Law*, London: HMSO

Department of Health and Social Security (1985b) *Social Work Decisions in Child Care*, London: HMSO

Department of Health and Social Security (1987) *The Law on Child Care and Family Services*, London: HMSO

Department of Health (1988) *Protecting Children: A Guide for Social Workers Undertaking a Comprehensive Assessment* (The Orange Book), London: HMSO

Department of Health (1989) *An Introduction to the Children Act 1989*, London: HMSO

Department of Health (1990) *The Care of Children, Principles and Practice in Regulations and Guidance*, London: HMSO

Department of Health (1991a) *The Children Act 1989, Guidance and Regulations*, vol. 3, *Family Placements*, London: HMSO

Department of Health (1991b) *The Children Act 1989, Guidance and Regulations*, vol. 2, *Family Support, Day Care and Educational Provision for Young Children*, London: HMSO

Department of Health (1991c) *Patterns and Outcomes in Child Placement*, London: HMSO

Department of Health (1995a) *Child Protection, Messages from Research*, London: HMSO

Department of Health (1995b) *Children Looked After by Local Authorities, Year ending 31 March 1995*, London: HMSO, Government Statistical Services

Everitt, A. and Hardiker, P. (1996) *Evaluating for Good Practice*, London: BASW/Macmillan

Fahlberg, V. (1981a) *Attachment and Separation*, London: British Agencies for Adoption and Fostering

Fahlberg, V. (1981b) *Helping Children When They Must Move*, London: British Agencies for Adoption and Fostering

Family Rights Group (1982) *Fostering Parental Contact*, London: Family Rights Group

Farmer, E. and Owen, M. (1995) *Child Protection Practice: Private Risks and Public Remedies*, London: HMSO

Fisher, D., Marsh, P., Phillips, D. and Sainsbury, E. (1986) *Children In and Out of Care*, London: Batsford

Fundudis, T., Kolvin, I. and Garside, R.F. (1979) *Speech Retarded and Deaf Children: Their Psychological Development*, London: Academic Press

George, V. (1970) *Foster Care, Theory and Practice*, London: Routledge & Kegan Paul

Gibbons, J. (1992) 'Provision of support through family projects', in Gibbons, J. (ed.) *The Children Act 1989 and Family Support: Principles into Practice*, London: HMSO pp. 23–36

Gibbons J., Thorpe, S. and Wilkinson, P. (1990) *Family Support and Prevention – Studies in Local Areas*, London: HMSO

Glaser, B.G. and Strauss, A.L. (1967) *The Discovery of Grounded Theory*, Chicago: Aldine

Gray, P.G. and Parr, E.A. (1957) *Children in Care and the Recruitment of Foster Parents*, Social Survey Paper 249, London: HMSO

Hammersley, M. and Atkinson, P. (1983) *Ethnography: Principles in Practice*, London: Tavistock

Hardiker, P., Exton, K. and Barker, M. (1996) 'A framework for analysing services, in national commision of inquiry into the prevention of child abuse', *Childhood Matters: vol 2: Background Papers*, London: HMSO

Holman, B. (1980) *'Exclusive and inclusive concepts in fostering'*, in Triseliotis, J. (ed.) *New Developments in Foster Care and Adoption*, London: Routledge & Kegan Paul, pp. 69–84

Holman, B. (1988) *Putting Families First*, Basingstoke: Macmillan

Howe, D. (1995) *Attachment Theory for Social Work Practice*, Basingstoke: Macmillan

Jenkins, S. and Norman, E. (1972) *Filial Deprivation and Foster Care*, New York: Columbia University Press

Jewett, C. (1984) *Helping Children Cope with Separation and Loss,* London: BAAF

Kumar, V. (1993) *Poverty and Inequality in the UK: The Effects on Children,* London: National Children's Bureau

Loftland, J. (1971) *Analyzing Social Settings: A Guide to Qualitative Observations and Analysis*, San Francisco: Wadsworth

Mahon, A., Glendinning, C., Clarke, K. and Craig, G. (1996) 'Researching children: methods and ethics', *Children and Society,* **10**(2) pp. 145–54

Maluccio, A.N. (1981) *Promoting Competence in Clients – A New/Old Approach to Social Work Practice*, New York: Free Press

Maluccio, A.N., Fein, E. and Olmstead, K. (1986) *Permanency Planning for Children – Concepts and Methods,* London: Tavistock

Marsh, P. (1993) 'Family reunification and presevation – the need for partnership between users and professionals', in Marsh, P. and Triseliotis, J. (eds) *Prevention and Reunification in Child Care*, London: Batsford,1993, pp. 39–53

Millham, S., Bullock, R., Hosie, K. and Haak, M. (1986) *Lost in Care,* Aldershot: Gower

Mitchell, A. (1985) *Children in the Middle: Living Through Divorce,* London: Tavistock

Morrow, V. and Richards, M. (1996) 'The ethics of social research with children – an overview, *Children and Society,* **10**(2), pp. 90–105

Oswin, M. (1984) *They Keep Going Away*, London: King Edwards Hospital Fund for London

Packman J. (1968) *Child Care Needs and Numbers,* London: Allen & Unwin

Packman, J. and Hall, C. (1995) *Draft Report on the Implementation of the Children Act 1989,* Dartington: Dartington Social Research Unit

Packman, J., Randall, J. and Jacques, N. (1986) *Who Needs Care? Social Work Decisions about Children*, Oxford: Blackwell

Parker, R. (1966) *Decisions in Child Care*, London: Allen & Unwin

Parker, R.A. (1978) 'Foster care in context', *Adoption and Fostering*, **93**(3)

Parker, R.A. (ed.) (1980) *Caring for Separated Children*, Basingstoke: Macmillan

Parker, R.A., Ward, H., Jackson, S., Aldgate, J. and Wedge, P. (eds) (1991) *Looking After Children – Assessing Outcomes in Child Care*, London: HMSO

Perlman, H.H. (1963) *Social Casework: A Problem-Solving Process,* Chicago: University of Chicago Press

Perry, M. (1995) *The Policy and Practice Context of Children Looked After*, unpublished paper for the MPhil, University of Leicester

Platt, S. et al. (1989) 'Damp housing, mould growth symptomatic state', *British Medical Journal*, **298**, pp. 197–200

Pugh, E. (1968) *Social Work in Child Care*, London: Longman

Quinton, D. and Rutter, M. (1988) *Parenting Breakdown: Making and Breaking of Intergenerational Links*, Aldershot: Gower

Robinson, C. (1987) 'Key issues for social workers placing children for family-based respite care, *British Journal of Social Work*, **17** pp. 257–84

Rowe, J. and Lambert, L. (1973) *Children Who Wait*, London: ABAFA

Rowe J., Cain, H., Hundleby, M. and Keane, A. (1984) *Long-term Foster Care*, London: Batsford

Rutter, M. (1985) 'Resilience in the face of adversity', *British Journal of Psychiatry*, **147**, pp. 598–611

Ryan, M. (1991) 'The legal framework for family support services', in Family Rights Group, *The Children Act 1989, Working in Partnership with Families*, London: HMSO, pp. 7–13

Seden, J. (1995) 'Religious persuasion and the Children Act', *Adoption and Fostering*, **19**(2), pp. 7–15

Sellick, C. (1994) *Supporting Short-term Foster Carers*, Aldershot: Avebury

Sharland E., Seal, H., Croucher, M., Aldgate, J. and Jones, D. (1996) *Early Investigation in Child Sexual Abuse*, London: HMSO

Smith, T. (1992) 'Family centres, children in need and the Children Act 1989', in Gibbons, J. (ed.) op.cit., 9–22

Social Services Inspectorate (1995) *The Challenge of Partnership in Child Protection: Practice Guide*, London: HMSO

Social Services Inspectorate (1996) *Children in Need – Report of an SSI National Inspection of SSD Family Support Services 1993/1995*, London: Department of Health

Stacey, M., Deardon, R., Pil, R. and Robinson, D. (1970) *Hospitals, Children and Their Families*, London: Routledge & Kegan Paul

Stalker, K. (1989) *Share the Care: an Evaluation of a Family-Based Respite Care Service*, London: Jessica Kingsley

Stein, M. and Carey, K. (1986) *Leaving Care*, Oxford: Blackwell.

Stone, J. (1995) *Making Positive Moves: Developing Short-term Fostering Services*, London: Batsford

Subramanian, K. (1985) 'Reducing child abuse through respite center intervention', *Child Welfare*, **LXIV** (5), pp. 445–49

Swanson, M. (1988) 'Preventing reception into care: monitoring a short stay refuge for older children', in Freeman, I. and Montgomery, S. (eds) *Child Care: Monitoring Practice*, London: Jessica Kingsley, pp. 46–60

Thoburn, J. (1988) *Child Placement, Principles and Practice*, London: Wildwood

Thoburn, J., Lewis, A. and Shemmings, D. (1995) *Paternalism or Partnership? Family Involvement in the Child Protection Process*, London: HMSO

Thoburn, J., Murdoch, A. and O'Brien, A. (1986) *Permanence in Child Care*, Oxford: Blackwell

Timms, N. (1962) *Casework in the Child Care Service*, London: Butterworths

Triseliotis, J. (1980) 'Growing up in foster care and after', in Triseliotis J. (ed.) *New Developments in Foster Care and Adoption*, London: Routledge & Kegan Paul, pp. 131–61

Triseliotis, J. (1989) 'Foster care outcomes, a review of key research findings', *Adoption and Fostering*, **13**(3), pp. 5–13

Triseliotis, J. and Russell, J. (1984) *Hard to Place: The Outcome of Adoption and Residential Care*, London: Heinemann

Triseliotis, J., Borland, M. and Hill, M. (1995a) *Teenagers and Social Work Services*, London: HMSO

Triseliotis, J., Sellick, C. and Short, R. (1995b) *Foster Care Theory and Practice*, London: Batsford

Tunnard, J. (1991) 'Setting the scene for partnership' in Family Rights Group, *The Children Act 1989, Working in Partnership with Families*, London: HMSO

University of Bristol (1983) *The Child Health and Education Study*, Bristol: University of Bristol, Department of Child Health

Utting, D. (1995) *Family and Parenthood: Supporting Families, Preventing Breakdown*, York: Joseph Rowntree Foundation

Ward, H. (ed.) (1995) *Looking after Children: Research into Practice*, London: HMSO

Webb, S. (1990) 'Preventing reception into care: a literature review', *Adoption and Fostering*, **14**(2), pp. 21–25

Webb, S. and Aldgate, J. (1990) 'Adapting existing services to develop respite care in one local authority – a positive response to the Children Act 1989', *Adoption and Fostering*, **15**(1), pp. 6–13

Wilcox, B.L. and Vernberg, E.M. (1985) 'Conceptual and theoretical dilemmas facing social support research', in Sarason, I. G. and Sarason, B. R. (eds) *Social Support: Theory, Research and Applications*, The Hague: Nijhoff

Woodroffe, C., Slickman, M., Barker, M. and Power, C. (1993) *Children, Teenagers and Health: The Key Debate*, Buckingham: Open University Press

Woods, P. (1986) *Inside Schools: Ethnography in Educational Research*, London: Routledge & Kegan Paul

Index

Page numbers in italic refer to figures and tables

Dartington Social Research Unit 52, 66, 190
decision-making 117–18, 178–82
developmental assessment 34–5
disabilities, children with 2–3, 140, 175, 187

ecological model 88–9
education-related services 148
eligibility criteria 95–9
emergency arrangements 97
emotional support
    definition 48
    parents' reliance on carers 171–2
    sources in community 51–2
        perceived improvements 71, *72*
employment 45–6, 64, 79
    carer families 157
empowerment of parents 87
    see also participation; partnership
enabling authority 214
ending of placements 139–40
    evaluations 141, 171–2, 207–8
ethnicity
    carer families 159–60
    family types 42
    interpreters 30
    study locations 23
evaluation of service *see* outcomes
everyday life 62, 63–4, 77, 78
expectations
    children's 183
    parents 60–5, 75–9
extended families 49–51
    consultation with 116

families
    and accommodation service
        contra-indications 97–8
        perceived purpose 10
        responding to chronic needs 133, 143
    child care arrangement within 49
    patterns of using social work/services 146–9
    in study 27–8, 203–5, 216
        assessments 33–5
        feedback 35
        interviews 29–33
        payments 35
    see also children; parents

family breakdown, prevention of 39–40, 129–30
family centres 50, 81–2
    referral system 93, *94*, 214
family problems 57–9
    amelioration of 68–73
    and levels of support 212–13
    partnership approach to assessment 109–13
Family Rights Group 5
family support social workers 105, 139, 206–7
    interventions 106–21, 135–9
family support systems 48–53
family types 41–3
    carers 156, 160
    income according to 45
fears *see* anxieties
finances *see* funding; income, family
fiscally-driven model 9
food 192
full-time accommodation 128–9
funding 11
    study schemes 24–5

gatekeeping 92–5, 205–6
    exaggeration of problems 11
    parents' access strategies 99
gender and age of children 43–4
gender roles, parents 49
general practitioners (GPs) 52, 81, 91–2, 117, 148
Gibbons, J. 40, 41, 47, 48, 50, 51, 131
    et al. 42, 48
Guidance and Regulations
    accessibility of service 89
    consultation 113–14, 116
    continuity 155
    definition of need 18
    implementation 208–9, 212
    parenting capacity 163–4
    partnership with parents 22, 85, 105
    planning placements 7, 103, 108
    significant others 112
    written care plans 127–8

Hardiker, P., et al. 52, 96, 133, 212–14
    Everitt, A. and 95
health 47–8
    parental needs 81, 134–5, 144, 148

Index by Elizabeth Ball